Gorbachev's Struggle for Economic Reform

STUDIES IN SOVIET HISTORY AND SOCIETY

edited by Joseph S. Berliner, Seweryn Bialer, *and* Sheila Fitzpatrick

Gorbachev's Struggle for Economic Reform

The Soviet Reform Process, 1985–88

Anders Åslund

Cornell University Press
Ithaca, New York

First published 1989 by Cornell University Press.

Library of Congress Cataloging-in-Publication Data

Aslund Ånders, 1952–
    Gorbachev's struggle for economic reform : the Soviet reform process. 1985–1988 / Anders Åslund.
      p.   cm. — (Studies in Soviet history and society)
    Bibliography: p.
    Includes index.
    ISBN 0-8014-2339-2 (alk. paper). — ISBN 0-8014-9590-3 (pbk. : alk. paper)
      1. Soviet Union—Economic policy—1986– 2. Soviet Union—Commercial policy.   I. Title.   II. Series.
    HC336.26.A84   1989   89–966
                                                CIP

Printed in Great Britain.

Contents

Tables

Abbreviations

CC	Central Committee (of the CPSU)
CMEA	Council for Mutual Economic Assistance (Comecon)
CPSU	Communist Party of the Soviet Union
Ek. gaz.	*Ekonomicheskaya gazeta*
FBIS	Foreign Broadcast Information Service (Daily Report: Soviet Union)
GDR	German Democratic Republic
GKES	State Committee for Foreign Economic Relations
GKNT	State Committee for Science and Technology
Gosagroprom	State Agro-Industrial Committee
Goskomtrud	State Committee for Labour and Social Problems
Goskomtsen	State Price Committee
Gosplan	State Planning Committee
Gospriemka	State Acceptance (quality control)
Gossnab	State Committee for Material and Technical Supplies
Gosstandart	State Committee for Standards
Gosstroi	State Construction Committee
KGB	Committee for State Security
Lit. gaz.	*Literaturnaya gazeta*
NEP	New Economic Policy
NPO	Scientific-production association
PO	Production association
RAPO	*Raion* agro-industrial association
RSFSR	Russian Federal Republic
Sots. ind.	*Sotsialisticheskaya industriya*
SP	*Sobranie Postanovleni SSSR*
TsEMI	Central Economic-Mathematical Institute
Vneshekonombank	Bank for Foreign Economic Relations
VE	*Voprosy ekonomiki*
VPK	Military-Industrial Commission
VVS	*Vedomsti Verkhovogo Soveta SSSR*

Acknowledgements

This book was prepared under a grant from the Kennan Institute for Advanced Russian Studies of the Woodrow Wilson International Center for Scholars, Washington, DC, during the academic years 1987–8. Additional funding has kindly been provided by the American-Scandinavian Foundation, New York. The statements and views expressed herein are mine.

I would like to thank those who have provided me with the opportunities to develop my ideas at seminars and conferences. Chapter 2 has been presented at the Russian Research Center of Harvard University and the Rand Corporation; Chapter 6 at the University of Pennsylvania; and various steps towards Chapter 7 at the University of Texas at Austin, Georgetown University, East-West Roundtable in New York, a conference organised by the *Financial Times* and the National Bank of Hungary in Budapest, and at the Wilson Center. The participants at these occasions offered a multitude of useful comments.

I have greatly benefited from comments on various parts of the draft by Wlodzimierz Brus, Alec Nove, Peter Rutland, Myron Hedlin, Werner Hahn, Ivan Major, Kalman Mizsei and Maria Los. Sarah Klaus and Toby Goodwin have worked as my research assistants, facilitating my bibliographical work. In addition, Sarah Klaus has improved and clarified my language.

From November 1984 to August 1987, I had the advantage of living in Moscow, and had the opportunity to consult with more than one hundred Soviet economists, a large number of Soviet officials, and numerous Soviet citizens of various professions. Since I do not know whom I can thank by name, I prefer to thank them all anonymously. In the same manner, I would like to express my gratitude to the many western diplomats and journalists in Moscow who shared their information and analysis with me.

During my year in Washington, Peter Reddaway, Ed Hewett, John Hardt, Richard Ericson, Igor Birman, Henry Rowen, Harry Gelman, Patrick Cockburn, Celestine Bohlen and Vladimir Kontorovich have offered me particular stimulation and encouragement. The Kennan Institute and the Soviet Forum at Brookings have been excellent fora for intellectual exchange and informative events.

John Spiers has encouraged me and expediently facilitated the publication of this book and finally, I would like to thank Wlodzimierz Brus, Michael Kaser, Alec Nove, Mario Nuti and Torsten Örn for their unfailing support.

Anders Åslund
Stockholm, October 1988

Introduction

More than half a century ago the Soviet economic system was established. After World War II, it was implanted in East and Central Europe. Repeatedly, modifications or transformations of Soviet-type economic systems have been attempted, but so far only Yugoslavia and Hungary have managed to break away from the original Stalinist model. The recurring endeavours at economic reform as well as the persistent reversals attract our attention.

The Soviet development has been characterised by a vacillation between periods of centralisation (war communism, the first five-year plan, the war, the late 1950s and the 1970s) and periods of decentralisation (the New Economic Policy 1921–8, the mid-1930s, the immediate post-Stalin period, the second half of the 1960s and the last few years). These swings, or reform cycles, appear to be inherent features of the Soviet economic system, though the depth of each wave has varied greatly.

The purpose of this book is limited in time and space to an investigation of the process of economic reform in the Soviet Union from 1985 to 1988. Our prime concerns are what shape the reform has assumed and how the reform strategy has evolved. In a first chapter, we shall briefly discuss the causes and the setting of the reform. Lenin's words about the primacy of politics over economics remain valid. Therefore, we shall identify the actual economic programmes preferred by the leading politicians in Chapter 2. Their alternative programmes of economic revitalisation interact. Some measures are broadly accepted, but their effectiveness might be another matter, while far-reaching changes are mostly controversial. Our intention is to proceed from measures not involving systemic changes to reforms going outside the present system of allocation and ownership. We shall distinguish between four qualitatively different groups of measures in Chapters 3 to 6: changes within the traditional framework, reform only at enterprise level, economic reform of the central functions, and a new policy towards cooperatives and private enterprise. Our aim is to provide a deep and comprehensive analysis of the development of the economic reform so far. In order to concentrate on the present reform process, we shall assume that the reader is acquainted with the Soviet political and economic system, as well as Soviet economic history.[1] Background information and analysis will be limited to the most necessary.

The essence of the economic system is the *model*, which as defined by

Wlodzimierz Brus, 'denotes the economic institutions, the principles by which they function and the nature of the relationships which are established between them within the economic system' (Asselain, 1984, p.6; Brus, 1961).

An economic reform comprises changes in the model, while virtually any economic change may be referred to as an economic reform in journalistic language. Our interest is restricted to reform in a socialist economy, and we understand it, as defined by Janos Kornai (1986, p. 1691), as a 'change in a socialist economic system, provided that it diminishes the role of bureaucratic coordination and increases the role of the market'. By this criterion, the USSR experienced economic reform in the mid-1950s and the second half of the 1960s, but not after the organisational changes of April 1973 and the 'perfection' of the economic mechanism of July 1979. The present Soviet system will interchangeably be called 'communism', 'real socialism', 'socialism', 'command economy', and 'Soviet-type' without any particular connotations.

Soviet writings, however, are patently ideological, rendering ideological nuances important. General Secretary Mikhail Gorbachev seems to try to elude traditional Marxist-Leninist categories. His favourite terms *perestroika, glasnost* and democratisation have no firmly established meanings in Soviet political vocabulary. When Gorbachev started speaking of perestroika in December 1984, it seemed to imply little more than 'perfection'. The translation into English became 'restructuring'. Academician Abel Aganbeg-yan (1987a, p.12) has reported how the conservative leadership of the State Price Committee declared that a perestroika of the prices did not mean a price reform, so they intended only to *perfect* the price system. In vain, reformist economists advocated that this ambiguous term meant reform. At the 27th Party Congress of the CPSU in February 1987, Gorbachev suggested another interpretation by calling for 'radical reform'.

In July 1986, he transformed the concept in his speech in Khabarovsk: 'I would equate the word perestroika with revolution' (*Pravda*, 2 August 1986). Gorbachev seems to have chosen the term perestroika as a suitable vehicle for his overt radicalisation. Instead of changing terminology, he redefines it, allowing him both to advance and retreat when convenient. The same is true of glasnost and democratisation. The western discussion about whether glasnost means publicity or openness appears beside the point. The issue is not purely linguistic. Meanings vary between political situations and persons. It would be foolhardy to try to establish firm definitions of these intentionally elastic concepts. We have to check their meaning in each context, and we shall refrain from translating perestroika and glasnost, while the reader should be aware of the ambiguous connotation of 'democratisation'.

Throughout this process, sensitive terminology has become thoroughly confused because of alternating political pressures. Reformers try to introduce new terms and radicalise their meaning, while their adversaries resist the introduction of reformist concepts, and start redefining them after the party has approved of them. Words such as economic accounting (*khozraschet*), self-financing, self-management, brigade contract, *semeiny podryad* (family contract or leasehold) are patently equivocal. Depending on the apparent meaning, *khozraschet* will be translated 'accounting' or 'accountability', and exceptionally 'self-financing'.

We are now witnessing the third postwar wave of economic reforms in the Soviet Union. The Plenum of the Central Committee (CC) of the CPSU in April 1985 is officially perceived as its start, as signified by the expression 'post-April'. The reform had a prelude. The oldest party decision with implications for economic reform that is currently referred to is the Food Programme, adopted at the CC Plenum in May 1982. The CC Plenum in November 1982, when Yuri Andropov had just become General Secretary, initiated the pre-reform debate. Boris Kurashvili's article in June 1982 was the first harbinger of what was to come (Kurashvili, 1982). From 1984, centrally-initiated economic experiments started proliferating. However, the authorities had not yet declared that they desired major changes. The debate remained stifled. Only with the election of Mikhail Gorbachev as General Secretary of the CPSU on 11 March 1985 did the inquiry start in earnest.

This was the real pre-reform debate aimed at designing the reform. The adoption of the 'Law on State Enterprises' and the 'Basic Provisions for the Fundamental Restructuring of Economic Management' at the end of June 1987, as well as a large number of subordinate decrees, marked an end of the first stage of the reform process. A second transitionary stage of concrete preparations for the implementation of the economic reform is supposed to last for three years from 1988 to 1990, to be followed by a third stage of implementation of comprehensive reform.

This study will concentrate on the first stage of perestroika, but the prelude will also be scrutinised, and developments during the second stage will be followed till October 1988.

SOURCES

The nature of Soviet sources makes it vital to assess their biases and employ elaborate methods for neutralising them. The main sources for this study are Soviet publications. In addition, I made numerous personal observations while I lived and worked in Moscow from November 1984 until August 1987 and travelled extensively in the country. My long stay in the Soviet Union has enabled me to interview a large number of knowledgeable Soviets from all walks of life both officially and unofficially. For my perceptions, I draw extensively on conversations with more than one hundred Soviet economists, a large number of officials in all relevant bodies, and a variety of personal encounters, but I shall try to use published evidence as far as possible.[2]

Although the Soviet Union claimed to have 113,000 economic researchers in 1985, it is relatively easy to survey the economic debate. As in many other countries, most 'researchers' do not pursue research. Their productivity is very low; many are political economists who merely repeat Marxist-Leninist dogmas; another large group do applied research akin to administrative work in institutes attached to branch ministries. The interesting economic research is concentrated in half a dozen large institutes belonging to the USSR Academy of Sciences. Each institute is hierarchical, with its own political line, determined by its director and a few of his confidants. A director of an academic economic institute is in fact appointed by the Politburo and tends to sit for a long time. The Economic Department of the Academy of Sciences is headed by one Academician-Secretary, elected out of about ten Academicians in economics. Below them are almost a score of corresponding members of the Academy of Sciences. These titles carry a great deal of prestige. A director of an institute is usually an Academician.

In the 1960s, Soviet economists divided themselves politically into two large camps, '*tovarniki*' and '*antitovarniki*'. The former word means literally 'commoditeers', implying supporters of money-commodity relations or simply market relations, while *antitovarniki* are Marxist-Leninist dogmatists opposed to the market in principle. Alternative labels have been 'marketeers' (*rynochniki*) and 'conservatives', but all these words are colloquial. We shall use the words reformers and conservatives which are more in line with western language. The conservatives have been much more numerous, because of all the dogmatic professors in political economy around the country, but the reformers have dominated the Economic Department of the Academy of Sciences and included the best minds.

Traditionally, four academic economic institutes have dominated the field. Three of them have been reformist and one conservative. The progressive Institute of Economics and Organisation of Industrial Production in Novosibirsk was headed by Academician Abel Aganbegyan from 1966 until 1985. The leading Soviet sociologist Academician Tatyana Zaslavskaya was a prominent head of department of his institute. The other important academic institutes were located in Moscow. The biggest, and leading reformist, institute was the Central Economic-Mathematical Institute (TsEMI), headed for more than two decades by Academician Nikolai Fedorenko, but he was sacked in the spring of 1985 for having failed to achieve concrete results and having wrong personal connections. His pet was a 'System of the Optimally Functioning Socialist Economy'—an ideal of optimal planning that foundered. Fedorenko was ousted as Academician-Secretary in March 1985, and later replaced on that post by Aganbegyan.

TsEMI has brought up technically competent, rather theoretical economists on a large scale. After Fedorenko's departure it was divided into two institutes. The larger part retained the name TsEMI. Its strong man in the reform discussion is its Deputy Director Nikolai Petrakov, corresponding member of the Academy of Sciences, who is the leading academic expert on finances and pricing. Almost one third of TsEMI became the Institute of the Economics of Forecasting and Scientific-Technical Progress, whose most prominent spokesman is Deputy Director and Academician Stanislav Shatalin, another of Fedorenko's former protégés.

TsEMI's old enemy was the conservative Institute of Economics. In the spring of 1986, a leading reformer and political economist Leonid Abalkin (soon to become Academician) was appointed its new director and many old conservatives were swiftly replaced by reformers. The academic castle of the conservatives had fallen, and the Institute of Economics has become a centre for general reform issues as it was in the 1960s.

The thoroughly reformist Institute of the Economy of the World Socialist System has been directed by Academician Oleg Bogomolov since the end of the 1960s. It possesses outstanding expertise on the economics and politics of other socialist countries. Therefore, it has made important contributions to the discussion on Soviet reform, while its unique knowledge has shielded it politically. It has been consulted particularly on foreign trade, political economy and agriculture. Bogomolov himself pushes for a reform with many Chinese and Hungarian elements (Bogomolov, 1987).

The Institute of State and Law, which is the academic legal institute, has been a centre for influential and radical reformist thinking of high academic quality. Boris Kurashvili is one of its researchers. Members of these five institutes have elaborated most of the economic reform programme presented by General Secretary Gorbachev.

With the retirement of the conservatives at the Institute of Economics, few conservatives remained among the leading economists. Only one of the Academicians was regarded as conservative, Tigran Khachaturov (born in 1906), but he is no dogmatist. Gosplan's Economic Research Institute, which is widely considered the best institute outside the Academy of Sciences, may be labelled middle of the road, but that is hardly an accurate presentation of its new director from June 1987, Vladimir Kostakov, who has brought the issue of unemployment into the open (Kostakov, 1987). Instead, the central economic organs, especially the State Price Committee and Gosplan, have to take on the academic reformers themselves. Really conservative voices appear in the popular debate in letters from professors of political economy in the provinces and in Russophile literary journals, notably *Nash Sovremmenik*.

As General Secretary Gorbachev has pointed out, perestroika started from above. Therefore, it is easy to distinguish the various steps. Gorbachev's major speeches mark breakthroughs and are the main sources on official policies. As perestroika gained momentum, its front became broader and initiative lower down has become important. However, really radical articles by people of a lesser political standing only achieved prominence as late as 1987. The most notable economic articles were published in the literary journal *Novy mir* in 1987.[3] Each daring article has expanded the boundaries of permitted debate.

Journalists and publicists have played an important role in radicalising perestroika. Radical pace-setters are Vasili Selyunin, a retired senior economic observer at *Sotsialisticheskaya industriya*, Professor Nikolai Shmelev at the USA and Canada Institute, the economic editor of

Literaturnaya gazeta Aleksandr Levikov, Professor Gennadi Lisichkin at Bogomolov's Institute and the publicist Andrei Nuikin.[4]

A large number of editors-in-chief have been appointed since 1985. They have assumed new powers in the present conditions of glasnost and political strife. The spectrum of published organs has broadened, and Soviet newspapers have turned into organs of different political opinions. The replacement of an editor-in-chief is usually enough to transform a newspaper or journal completely, though a large number of prominent journalists and commentators have their own political profiles. We must consider what each editor and writer stands for. While the Soviet press provides us with a great deal of information, we have to remember that the declared main function of the Soviet press is not to inform but to spread propaganda.

Pravda remains the central party organ, but its editor-in-chief Viktor Afanasiev, appointed as early as 1976, is clearly more conservative than Gorbachev. Its deputy editor-in-chief, Dmitri Valovoi, has become a conservative standard-bearer (in spite of having criticised gross output targets consistently for more than a decade). Yet, one of its economic editors, Vitali Parfenov, is a prominent reformer. The editorial line of *Pravda* is basically conservative, but it varies in a not very comprehensible manner. Signed articles in *Pravda* represent a broad spectrum of party opinions. Reformist newspapers more or less identified with Gorbachev are *Izvestiya, Sotsialisticheskaya industriya, Komsomolskaya pravda, Sovetskaya kultura, Ogonek*, and *Moscow News*. The last two weeklies are the most reformist. As the main government newspaper, *Isvestiya* is more cautious but offers extensive economic coverage and investigative journalism of very high quality.

Sovetskaya Rossiya, the RSFSR party organ, has a rather mixed profile; essentially conservative, it has published radical liberal articles as well. The economic daily *Sotsialisticheskaya industriya* and the economic weekly *Ekonomicheskaya gazeta* became reformist on the turn of 1985, when both got new editors-in-chief. The former is a reformist muck-raker with sensational details on mismanagement and economic crimes. The trade union daily, *Trud*, is preoccupied with wages, pensions, prices and social benefits. Its role is to voice social concern. The national literary weekly, *Literaturnaya gazeta*, is a curious newspaper publishing many of the most sensational and radical economic articles.

The dailies, weeklies and literary monthlies are of great importance to the Soviet political and economic debate. Within the boundaries of censorship and political pressures, Soviet newspaper articles tend to be well-researched. The style verges on the academic. Print errors are rare. For many purposes, Soviet newspapers are far more useful for a researcher than western newspapers, not least because they publish large amounts of unedited official material, including laws. Opinions are not published by chance but enjoy some amount of political approval and are often handed down.[5]

Soviet academic journals are all the more disappointing, reflecting all the weaknesses of Soviet social sciences. The most important reformist articles have appeared in literary journals. The highly authoritative theoretical party journal *Kommunist* was transformed from one of the pillars of communist orthodoxy to a vanguard of reformist ideas, when Gorbachev's later aide Ivan Frolov became its editor-in-chief in the autumn of 1986, and the CC issued a detailed decree urging a reformist course. Now each of its issues contains something of significance to the economic debate, and the candid reformer Dr Otto Lacis, formerly of Bogomolov's Institute, is its new deputy editor-in-chief.

The old editors-in-chief of academic journals have managed to hold on for a long time. The traditionally most important economic journal, *Voprosy ekonomiki*, remained conservative until the spring on 1986, when the conservative Academician Tigran Khachaturov was replaced as editor-in-chief by the outspoken reformer Professor Gavriil Popov. Half the members of its editorial board were replaced at the same time. Still, *Voprosy ekonomiki* had also published reformist articles by senior economists. Gosplan's journal, *Planovoe khoziaistvo* is relentlessly conservative under its orthodox editor P.A. Ignatovski (1988). It is mainly of interest as it publishes new official statistics and material. The main economic journal in Novosibirsk, *EKO*, was edited by Academician Abel Aganbegyan until the summer of 1988. It used to function as a loyal opposition and be the most interesting economic journal before Gorbachev's rise to power, but it has hardly become more exciting than it used to be. There are many more economic journals, but they offer little of significance. The legal journal *Sovetskoe gosudarstvo i pravo* is more useful.

Usually, it takes almost a year for an academic article to be accepted and published. Therefore, academic journals are slow to reflect new trends. Soviet academic writing is sloppy. Few references are given, apart from Lenin, Marx and the General Secretary. Polemics are often veiled and indirect, leaving an outsider guessing. The accuracy and sources of statistics are often unspecified. In fact, literary journals and newspapers are barely less academic. The publication of academic books is naturally even slower. In addition, few scholars anticipated perestroika and it will take some time for a serious academic Soviet literature on perestroika to develop.

Soviet publicists and economists do not necessarily write what they think. The vanguard might express their personal views, but people in higher position must take into account what their institutions stand for. Also leading economists have political responsibilities. It is plain that the two top economists, Aganbegyan and Abalkin, go much further in interviews than in articles and books.[6] After many years of prominence combined with caution, Bogomolov suddenly came out as a staunch radical in 1987, while Zaslavskaya has been saying approximately the same for years. It is difficult to establish what is determined by restrictions imposed from outside, self-censorship and personal rethinking. For state officials there are clearer rules. If the institutional title of the official appears in print, it is to be seen as a statement by the institution, but officials often publish articles with no institutional title, implying that they speak for themselves, though they can hardly contradict their superiors.

Soviet statistics remain in a sad state. From the early 1970s until 1985, ever fewer statistics were published. The reversal has been slow. Certain suppressed statistics, notably infant mortality, life expectancy, alcohol consumption and the number of private cars, have been published. A far bigger problem remains, namely to improve the quality of patently flawed statistics. Virtually everywhere, upward biases are incorporated since all economic organisations are anxious to reach their gross output targets. One Soviet expert, Aleksei Sergeev of the Institute of Economics of the Academy of Sciences, estimates that as much as 5–25 per cent of the alleged production of raw materials consists of fraudulent reports (*Sovetskaya Rossiya*, 18 March 1987). Thus, there is no ground for the usual assumption of western Sovietologists, that Soviet physical data are more or less reliable. It has even been argued that the falsification of agricultural data has intensified since 1985 (Leonid Ivanov in *Lit. gaz.*, 11 May 1988). As it is easier to falsify other more complex statistics, they are likely to be all the more exaggerated, but no one knows how significant the biases are. In recent years numerous Soviet articles have offered alternative assessments. The most thorough recalculations have been undertaken by Grigori Khanin, who estimates the hidden inflation in official national income statistics at slightly over 3 percentage units a year (Selyunin and Khanin, 1987, pp. 194–5). We are left with little choice but to use Soviet statistics, though the reader should remember our objections. Unfortunately, alternative estimates cannot be made with satisfactory precision.[7]

Regardless of all alternative sources of information, many essential facts are kept tightly under wraps by the authorities, and campaigns of disinformation remain in constant use. It is not uncommon for different spokesmen to change their views in a coordinated manner. With these general reservations about Soviet sources, we shall use them, trying to discern reality.

Information on individuals has been traced from a wide range of materials. The basic sources are *Deputaty* (1984), notices in the Soviet press, and the valuable compilations done by Radio Liberty. In addition, people's own publications say a great deal, but oral information is a vital complement

NOTES

1.   The literature on the Soviet economic system is immense. Views that have influenced me particularly are represented by Brus (1961, 1975), Kornai (1980), Bauer (1976, 1984), Berliner (1957, 1983), Nove (1977, 1980) and Wiles (1977).
2.   Since my conversations have been off the record, I shall avoid referring directly to them, but my interviewees have frequently indicated articles reflecting their insights which I have used instead; see also Åslund (1987).

3. In the article 'Cunning Figures' in February 1987, Vasili Selyunin and Grigori Khanin debunked Soviet economic statistics, and in 'Advances and Debts' in June 1987 Nikolai Shmelev attacked most of Soviet economic development since 1928 in a vociferous manner.

4. Outstanding examples are Selyunin (1985, 1988), Selyunin and Khanin (1987), Shmelev (1987, 1988), Levikov (1986), Lisichkin (1985) and Nuikin (1988ab).

5. To save space and offer many sources, I indicate references with only newspaper and date. As Soviet newspapers are so thin (4-6 pages), in any case, it is easy to find a reference. The bibliography is limited to works actually cited plus a small number of general references. Another restriction is that the bibliography does not contain articles in dailies or weeklies. Until August 1987, I refer to the Moscow evening edition of *Izvestiya*, which is—as a rule—dated one day before the morning edition used in the rest of the world, but from September 1987 I refer to the morning edition. I have used the FBIS for seeking articles from the autumn of 1987, and sometimes for controlling my own translations. However, I have tried to check the original source in Russian on each instance. If I have not managed to find it, the FBIS is given as the source. With such exceptions, the translation from Russian is my own.

6. A comparison between Aganbegyan's interview in *Ogonek*, Nos. 29 and 30, 1987, and his book published in the West in 1988 makes this point evident. Nobody who had read Abalkin (1987ac) would have expected him to go as far as he did at the 19th Party Conference.

7. As I have developed elsewhere, I consider the Soviet statistics reconstructed by the CIA not sufficiently deflated (Åslund, 1989). The CIA calculations are based on 'conservative' assumptions, implying that numerous upward biases are disregarded, though CIA estimates of Soviet growth-rates appear less exaggerated than their estimates of the relative size of the economy. With few exceptions, the CIA does not deflate Soviet physical data; it does not acknowledge the deterioration of quality; and it appears to underestimate the technical wastage in the economy, while it probably uncovers hidden price increases well. Besides, the CIA has been compelled to make an excessive number of assumptions because of scant Soviet data.

1. Origins of the economic reform

LESSONS FROM PREVIOUS SOVIET ATTEMPTS AT ECONOMIC REFORM

The economic reform of 1965 was both the latest and the most comprehensive of previous reforms. It is the self-evident point of reference. By establishing the causes of its reversal and comparing them with the situation in 1985, we can get some idea of whether the present attempt at reform is more or less likely to succeed.[1] There were many reasons why the reform was reversed at the end of the 1960s.[2]

1. The outstanding shortcoming of the reform was that it lacked support at the highest political level. It was a Kosygin reform rather than a Brezhnev reform, since it was primarily promoted by Prime Minister Aleksei Kosygin and not General Secretary Leonid Brezhnev. When Brezhnev reinforced his political power at the expense of Kosygin in 1968, Kosygin's programme was downgraded (cf Breslauer, 1983). Today, the most important condition is fulfilled, since General Secretary Mikhail Gorbachev pushes for reform, but the problem has been that the commitment from the majority of the Politburo has been muted.
2. In the 1960s, the economic necessity of reform was not abundantly clear. As an economic reform deprives politicians of some power, they are prone to avoid it if possible. The apparent success of the economic reforms in the second half of the 1960s, with a significant rise in the official growth, contributed to their demise.[3] This time no swift improvement has occurred, because the economic problems have grown much more complex. The present severity of Soviet economic dilemmas makes radical reform a necessity if economic decline is to be avoided.
3. From 1968, the international environment hampered the reforms in numerous ways. The paramount event was the Warsaw Pact invasion of Czechoslovakia. It ended the Czechoslovak economic reform and brought about an intense domestic agitation against revisionists, including Soviet reformists. The Chinese cultural revolution and the new left in the West threatened to outflank Soviet communism on the left. The worldwide euphoria about socialism might also have reinforced the

Soviet leaders' confidence in the superiority of socialism, so why change it? From the early 1970s, the Soviet bloc boosted economic growth through large-scale imports of western machinery financed by cheap western credits. Western imports became a substitute for economic reform. Now, communism experiences a worldwide crisis, and there is no potent leftwing challenge. The growth based on imported machinery proved unsustainable, while large debts remain. The US pipeline embargo has highlighted the dangers of dependence on western imports. For all these reasons, the international situation appears more conducive to reform today.

4. Ideology was not sufficiently broadened in the 1960s. Marxism-Leninism is a very narrow ideological framework, labelling most phenomena pertaining to modern economics 'capitalistic' and thus illegitimate. Major dogmas such as central planning and socialist ownership were not questioned. Meanwhile the extended role of profits and money-commodity relations exposed these phenomena to dogmatic criticism. At present, an unprecedented revision of virtually all dogmas is under way. The reformist leaders call for a 'socialist market' and envisage a large independent cooperative sector. Their goal seems to be a regulated market economy with mixed ownership.[4] Since the ideological revision goes much further, a broader range of options is acceptable and dogmatic criticism loses its edge.

5. Soviet economic theory was, and remains, utterly impoverished after the long dark night of Stalinism (cf Yakovlev, 1987a). Therefore, the theoretical foundation for an economic reform has been weak. The rise of mathematical economics in the 1960s was a mixed blessing. The level of economic discourse rose, but a harmful fallacy was nourished as well, namely the excessive belief in 'optimal' planning through computerisation. Twenty years of failure to accomplish any concrete results have cured leading Soviet economists of such illusions, clearing the way for market-oriented thinking. Soviet economic theory may be weak, but strong enough to find the principal avenues, which was not true in the 1960s.

6. An economic system must be reasonably consistent to be effective. No chain is stronger than its weakest link. The design of the reform of 1965 contained numerous inconsistencies. Several were typical dilemmas of limited reform. Conservative Soviet economists discount the apparent good results of the reform as mounting hidden inflation, caused by the enterprises' greater interest in profits which led to covert price increases (because of surplus demand and far-reaching monopolisation). Another important issue was conspicuous shortages of certain commodities, as enterprise directors manipulated the product mix even more ruthlessly than before to raise profits and gross sales by concentrating on expensive products with large profit margins. Since prices were not influenced by demand, such changes could run counter to demand. Conservatives

favoured a return to detailed physical planning, while reformers, on the contrary, wanted to balance the market and check the inflationary process through the unleashing of market forces. Finances were more decentralised than the allocation of material supplies. Therefore, the imbalance between material supplies and monetary funds was aggravated, and it became impossible to relax the rationing of producer goods. Capital charges were too small to have any effect, and their influence on bonus funds was weak. A basic contradiction was that most legal extensions of enterprise rights were not matched by corresponding reductions of the regulating powers of ministries and central economic bodies. Therefore, these agencies maintained their hold on enterprises regardless of what laws stipulated (Kulagin, 1983, pp. 94–5; Medvedev, 1983, pp. 58–62). The obvious reformist conclusion is that it is necessary to go further towards greater marketisation, involving the whole economic system. The danger of a sincere belief in half-measures is small today.

7.   Moreover, the implementation of a reform must be of a certain consistency. In 1965, each piece of legislation was introduced as soon as it had been elaborated, with little or no coordination. One reason for inconsistency was that the details of the reforms were designed by conservative Gosplan bureaucrats; another that the reforms were being implemented by the very bureaucracy that had opposed all changes from the outset. In practice, the border-line between design and implementation is muddled since the final touches of the design are left to executive bodies and we shall not try to make this distinction. The present situation is similar.

8.   A reform reduces the power of the bureaucracy by definition, and most of the administration will inevitably oppose reform. Therefore, a successful reform must break the power of the anti-reform bureaucracy. In the 1960s, the reform was regarded as exclusively economic and the central economic apparatus was even reinforced. To break the power of the party and state bureaucracy might be seen as the key problem of a reform. It is difficult to perceive any other solution than a far-reaching democratisation with a strong popular pressure and openness balancing the bureaucracy. Moreover, some degree of institutional pluralism is necessary if enterprise directors are to dare to make independent decisions. Any well-functioning economy presupposes flows of reasonably correct information, which are difficult to achieve without a rather open society with independent criticism of incorrect data.

Thus, in most regards the preconditions for economic reform look much better today than in 1965, because the economic situation has deteriorated and communist illusions have faded away. However, the implementation is likely to be as inconsistent now as in the 1960s.

In July 1979, the Soviet leadership adopted a decree on the most comprehensive change of the economic system since 1965, but it was a plethora of ineffective half-measures.[5] The number of changes indicated a sense of crisis in the leadership which was facing a rapidly deteriorating economic performance. On the other hand, the timidness of all the changes showed that the regime was not prepared to confront powerful vested interests. In a very Brezhnevian way, the measures aimed at increasing complexity and coordination, and thus bureaucratisation. Typical examples were the modification and extension of plan indicators as well as the boosting of so-called complex programmes—long-term projects involving several ministries. An increase in the number of material balances administered by Gosplan and more centralised controls of investment implied attempts at recentralisation. Old ideas such as counterplanning, stable plans and more emphasis on the five-year plan, that had repeatedly been rejected by the system, were tried again. The effects of the modifications were hardly noticeable. The best that can be said of them was that they showed that the system could not be further perfected, only replaced.

Gorbachev has soberly described the attempts to change the management system in the 1950s, 1965–9 and at the end of the 1970s as

incomplete and inconsequent. They gave in the best case a brief effect and did not proceed to the necessary breakthrough. However, the stimulating impact of the old economic mechanism became ever weaker, while the braking [impact] grew (*Pravda*, 26 June 1987).

REASONS FOR RENEWED ATTEMPTS AT ECONOMIC REFORM

Why did perestroika start? By its own standards, the Soviet regime did well in domestic politics, and in foreign policy until about 1980. The outstanding weakness was the economy. Economic growth had declined sharply in 1979 and stayed at a low level. Military demands are likely to have dramatised the need for an economic revitalisation. The rapid US arms build-up, characteristic of the Reagan administration, posed a serious challenge to the Soviet Union. In Gorbachev's first programmatic speech in December 1984, one sentence stands out:

Only an intensive, highly-developed economy can safeguard a reinforcement of [our] country's position on the international stage and allow her to enter the new millennium with dignity as a great and flourishing power (Gorbachev, 1987a, p.86).

This was an apparent recognition that the USSR was losing out in the arms race with the USA because of insufficient economic strength. Moreover, Gorbachev judged the economic shortcomings so serious that he set his eyes on the year 2000—fifteen years ahead. In June 1985, Gorbachev (1985, p. 5) developed this theme:

The necessity of an acceleration of the social-economic development is also dictated by serious external circumstances. The country has been forced to devote considerable means to defence ... facing the aggressive policy and threat of imperialism, it is necessary to strengthen the defence power of the Motherland persistently, and not allow military superiority over us.

The Soviet ambition to compete with the USA is deeply rooted. The rise of US economic growth in the 1980s in excess of the official Soviet growth rate was taken as an affront. When Aganbegyan (1985a, p.6) gave three reasons for the importance of economic acceleration, the third (after increased standard of living and technological development) was to 'attain decisive successes in the economic competition with the United States and other developed capitalist countries'.

The Messianic mission of the CPSU should not be forgotten. The outside image of the Soviet Union had become an enormous bureaucracy ruled by gerontocrats. Moscow-oriented communist parties were on the decline in the West. Gorbachev touched upon this issue as early as April 1985: 'The historic fate of the country, the position of socialism in the contemporary world, depends in many ways on how we proceed' (*Pravda*, 24 April 1985).

Thus, a combination of economic problems and strains in foreign policy led to perestroika. Domestic political stability was impressive, with no public pressures worth mentioning. The KGB had firmly repressed dissident movements. The population had been effectively passified, but this gave rise to social problems, such as demoralisation, alienation, apathy and lack of initiative. Most Soviet citizens had abandoned any hope for change. There was a widespread sense of social, cultural and ecological decline, signified by a rapidly expanding alcoholism. A variety of nationalists emerged in defence of the cultural, historical and environmental heritage of their respective nations. The main danger in breaking their apathy lay in domestic political destabilisation, but the stability appeared so great that it might have been seen as a risk worth taking.

The economic 'pre-crisis situation'—as Gorbachev called it in June 1987— had many dimensions. Whatever perspective we choose, problems were ripe, and many of them were discussed in public for the first time in the wake of glasnost. The new picture that emerged contained few recent achievements with stagnation or decline in many spheres of economic and social life. Generally, the situation appears worse—and reform therefore more necessary— than previously perceived in the West. One of the most accurate assessments prior to Gorbachev was made by Richard Pipes (1984, p.49): 'A deeper insight into internal conditions of communist societies, the Soviet Union included, indicates that they are in the throes of a serious systemic crisis which sooner or later will require action of a decisive kind. . . .'

Originally, the overwhelming concern was the decline in economic growth. In April 1985, Gorbachev stated: 'Now, the main question is: how and by what means can the country attain an acceleration of economic development' (*Pravda*, 24 April 1985). The Brezhnev years, from the early 1970s, became called 'stagnation' (*zastoi*). Official Soviet statistics provide a more reassuring picture, but there is a wide agreement among Soviet economists that the official statistics contain a substantial hidden inflation. Recalculations done by the CIA imply an average hidden inflation of about 2 per cent a year. Two Soviet economists, Grigori Khanin and Vasili Selyunin, have done their own recalculations and arrived at an average hidden inflation of approximately 3 per cent a year (see Table 1.1.).

Table 1.1:   Soviet economic growth rate, 1961–85

(average annual growth in NMP produced, comparable prices, per cent)

Years	1961–5	1966–70	1971–5	1976–80	1981–5
Official statistics	6.5	7.8	5.7	4.3	3.6
Selyunin & Khanin	4.4	4.1	3.2	1.0	0.6
CIA (GNP)	5.1	5.0	3.0	2.3	2.0

Sources: Narkhoz 1985, p. 38; Selyunin and Khanin (1987) pp. 194–5; CIA (1982) p. 25; CIA (1986) p. 64.

The most authoritative Soviet economist, Academician Abel Aganbegyan, has stated that there was no growth both from 1978 to 1982 and from 1980 to 1985 (Aganbegyan, 1987b, p.7; 1988, p.2). We might never obtain an accurate assessment of Soviet economic growth , but it appears to have ceased in 1978, as Alec Nove and Michael Ellman suggested as early as 1982 (Nove, 1983; Ellman, 1984, pp. 135–46). If Soviet military expenditure in real terms grew in the early 1980s as is widely accepted (by 2 per cent a year according to the CIA), and there was no economic growth, the military share of the GNP would have been increasing, which would have implied a much greater Soviet internal conflict over allocation of resources than has been perceived in the West.

Similarly, the CIA has successively raised its estimate of the military share of the Soviet GNP to 15–17 per cent in 1987, but it is difficult to find any informed Soviet citizen who believes in earnest that it is less than 30–40 per cent of the net material product, which would correspond to 22–30 per cent of the Soviet GNP. Any assessment must be uncertain because of the poor Soviet statistics, but it is quite possible that the military burden compelled the Soviet leadership to choose between the retention of domestic dictatorship combined with external decline or radical reform.

Gorbachev intertwines three major reasons for the declining economic growth rate: faltering efficiency, technological development and quality:

the economic growth-rates fell to a level which actually approached economic stagnation. We started evidently falling behind in one way after the other. The gap in the efficiency of production, quality of products and scientific-technical progress began to widen in relation to the most developed countries and not to our benefit (*Pravda*, 26 June 1987).

The increasing Soviet technological backwardness was possibly his greatest concern:

the most worrying is that we have started lagging behind in scientific-technical development. At the same time as the Western countries have begun a restructuring of their economies on a broad scale with the emphasis on conservation of resources, exploitation of the newest technologies and other achievements of science and technology, our scientific-technical progress has slowed down (*Pravda*, 26 June 1987).

A telling illustration of Soviet technological backwardness is the slow start of its microcomputerisation. Official data are hard to come by, but by the end of 1987 the Soviet Union probably possessed about 200,000 microcomputers to compare with over 25 million in the United States, and Soviet computers are utterly unsophisticated.

The direct cause of the decline in the growth-rate in the 1970s appears to be a combination of a stagnation in the production of most essential raw materials and a failure to raise efficiency in their utilisation (cf Table 1.2). In Gorbachev's words, 'The present expenditure (*zatratny*) way of developing the economy dooms the country to stagnation' (Gorbachev, 1985, p.6). A Gosplan official, Gennadi Zoteev, has analysed the situation:

The slow-down in economic growth during the years 1976–1982 and a certain acceleration in 1983–1987 is connected with the raw material extracting branches. It evinces an extraordinary dependence of the economy on the natural factor, whose negative influence especially shows in the primary energy sector (*Ek. gaz.*, No. 42, 1987, p. 10).

The Soviet Union prides itself on being the biggest producer in the world of a considerable number of products: crude oil, gas, pig iron, steel, iron ore, mineral fertilisers, tractors, reinforced concrete structures, woollen cloth, shoes, sugar, and animal fats (*Narkhoz 1985*, p. 583). The unfortunate twist is that most of these commodities are not final products but industrial inputs. They are needed in such large quantities because of the excessive material intensity of the Soviet production apparatus (or low quality in the case of tractors and shoes).

Table 1.2:   The dynamics of production inputs, 1971–85

(increase over five years in per cent)

	1971–5	1976–80	1981–5
Total fixed assets	52	43	35
Total investment	43	28	16
Production of fuels and raw materials	25	10	7
Employment in the productive sphere	6	4	2

Source: Aganbegyan (1985b) p. 13.

In the absence of both reliable calculations of national income and input-output relations as well as scarcity prices, it is impossible to establish how much larger the Soviet usage of inputs is than in the West, but about three times more inputs for a similar physical product (of worse quality) appears plausible.[6] For instance, the UN Economic Commission for Europe has calculated that the Soviet energy intensity of production was 3.3 times as high as in Northern and Western Europe in 1984.[7]

The quality of nearly all Soviet products is incredibly poor. According to the candid Professor Nikolai Shmelev (1987, p. 154), only 17–18 per cent of Soviet manufactures are of a quality that corresponds to 'world standards' (exportable to the West) by the most optimistic estimates, and as little as 7–8 per cent according to the most pessimistic. Furthermore, quality is steadily declining: 'with excess demand (a result of low retail prices) the quality of commodities deteriorates' (Bim and Shokhin, 1986, p. 69). In Moscow, there is a rush for virtually all imported commodities including those from Eastern Europe, showing that the quality of Soviet consumer goods is much worse. Aganbegyan has made an eloquent assessment of the situation:

[Quality] is in many cases terrible. From year to year we lose our former advantages and positions. Remember the fifties. Yes, our things were not as beautiful and fashionable as foreign ones, but as a compensation any of ours were more hard-wearing ... And how is it now? It is a horrible situation: more than two thousand times a year colour television sets catch fire in Moscow alone. Together with them the houses burn (*Ogonek,* No. 29,1987, p. 5).

Soviet achievements in space and the military sphere are great, but they are not reflected in the civilian sector. Because of low quality, few Soviet-manufactured goods can be exported to the West. Even in its trade with Eastern Europe, the Soviet commodity structure is typical of a developing country (see Valeri Karavaev in *Lit. gaz.*, 21 October 1987). Moreover, the relative importance of Soviet exports of manufactures is declining. In 1955, 28 per cent of Soviet exports to Western Europe were manufactured goods, but in 1983 this share has fallen to 6 per cent, according to the UN Economic Commission for Europe (ECE, 1985, p. 3–27). The USSR is quickly losing out to newly industrialised countries (NICs). In 1965, it provided the OECD countries with 0.82 per cent of their imports of manufactures, but in 1981 its share had shrunk to 0.51 per cent. Meanwhile, NICs raised their share of western imports of manufactured goods from 2.74 per cent to 6.95 per cent (ECE, 1983, Table 3.7).

As Janos Kornai (1980) has elaborated, shortages are characteristic of socialist economies. In the 1950s, it was widely assumed, both in the Soviet Union and the West, that shortages would diminish over time, but the opposite has happened. There are many contributing factors: the overall financial discipline has deteriorated, aggravating macro-imbalances and boosting hoarding; the complexity of the economy is constantly growing, making it ever more difficult to match supply and demand of particular commodities; after all, consumers are becoming more choosy so that inferior commodities are not easily sold.

The foremost Soviet finance expert, Nikolai Petrakov (1987c, pp. 3–4), has observed that 'the least scarce resource is money ... Consequently, inflationary tendencies are observed in the economy'. These pressures result in open, hidden and repressed inflation (cf Nuti, 1986). Shortages permeate Soviet life to such an extent that the words 'buy' and 'sell' have largely been replaced by 'give' and 'take' in everyday parlance. Until 1986, meat of decent quality could be bought freely in state shops only in Estonia, but even there this is no longer the case. In big cities in the RSFSR, except Moscow and Leningrad, formal rationing of meat, sausages and butter persists,[8] and recently sugar rationing has proliferated. In small towns and in the countryside, there is no rationing, because supplies are too small. In almost the whole country, 'cooperative' sales of meat at prices 2–4 times higher than state prices are taking over.

Besides this, private sales continue. For the nomenklatura, large enterprises and prestigious institutions, there are more or less well-supplied shops charging low state prices.[9] Excess demand is undoubtedly greater in the enterprise sector, as credits to enterprises are far less controlled than wage payments. Surplus funds in the enterprise sphere overflow into the consumer sector. In parallel, 'frozen' surplus stocks are growing as a result of hoarding. The consequences of ever worse market disequilibria are numerous and serious, as elaborated by Petrakov:

'the truncated ruble' in our system has a deforming effect on the social orientation of various groups of workers, impedes the introduction of socialist principles of distribution, lowers the effectiveness of planning decisions and discredits the idea of economic accounting and self-financing (Petrakov, 1987b, p. 219).

Soviet economists discuss the demoralisation of society, with the extension of dishonest economic practices and apathy, as effects of growing shortages. Their language is strong when they approach these problems. Stanislav Shatalin (1986, p. 60) has made a typical assessment:

The lack of balance in the consumer sector of the economy has caused a growth of speculation, corruption, the reinforcement of inflationary processes and the growth of unearned incomes of the population.

Nikolai Shmelev has gone even further:

Apathy and indifference became mass phenomena, theft, disrespect for honest work and a simultaneous aggressive jealousy against those who earn a lot even if they earn honestly; signs appeared of almost physical degradation of a sizeable part of the population on the ground of drinking and idleness (Shmelev, 1987, p. 145).

This sense of demoralisation is spelt out forcefully in contemporary fiction, by for instance Chingiz Aitmatov, Viktor Astafev and Valentin Rasputin (but they do not necessarily connect the decline of ethics with shortages). A social crisis has arisen with elements of both moral and economic nature. The standard complaint is that the social sector has been treated as a residue. 'We have adopted the habit of neglecting social factors, regarding them as second-rank and economising on them' (Aganbegyan, in *Ogonek*, No. 30, 1987, p. 14). Severe shortcomings exist in most social fields.

The Soviet Union claims to be the world leader in numbers of physicians and hospital beds (*Narkhoz 1986*, pp. 697-8), but the utilisation of these inputs has been amazingly inefficient. The ultimate output of the medical sector is the health of the population. With an infant mortality in 1985 of 26 out of 1,000 born, the Soviet Union occupies the fiftieth place in the world, according to the USSR Minister of Health, Yevgeni I. Chazov (*Lit. gaz.*, 15 April, 1987). Life expectancy at birth was 63 years for Soviet men in 1984-5, which is as in upper middle-income countries such as Mexico or Brazil (*Narkhoz 1985*, p. 547; World Bank, 1987, p. 259). The problem is not only inefficient usage of resources, but also that the total resources are small. The Soviet Union devotes a mere 3 per cent of its GNP to the health sector. 'It is the smallest share of the national income of all developed countries in the world' (Aganbegyan in *Ogonek*, No. 30, 1987, pp. 13-14). To a state that has always cherished its social achievements, this is serious news. The alarm has been reinforced by new openness about alcoholism, drug-addiction and prostitution. The ecological crisis should also be mentioned.

The swift industrialisation is one of the great prides of Soviet society, but the economic structure has not caught up with current demands. Employment in agriculture remains comparatively large because of its inefficiency; the industrial sector is bloated, while the service sector remains rudimentary (see Table 1.3). The USSR has failed to transform into a service economy. If we take the relative size of the service sector (in employment or GNP) as a measurement of modernity, the Soviet Union falls behind several Third World countries.

Summing-up, we notice a relative deterioration in public Soviet appreciation of the traditional system on virtually all counts. Economic growth is no longer impressive and barely positive. In particular

Table 1.3:   Employment by sector in 1980

(Share in per cent of labour force)

	Agriculture	Industry	Services
USA	4	31	66
Federal Republic of Germany	6	44	50
Spain	17	37	46
The USSR	20	39	41
Argentina	18	34	53
Brazil	31	27	42

Source: World Bank (1987), p. 265.

minicomputerisation has created a sizeable and growing technological gap favourable to the West. Abundant free resources are finally drying up, while there is little or no improvement in efficiency. As the quality of products declines, the hopes for eventual quality improvements fade away. In foreign trade, the Soviet Union has been outdone on western markets by the NICs, and it has failed to absorb western technology in an efficient manner. The illusions of the 1970s are gone. Market imbalances have aggravated to a point where it should be obvious that a command system cannot steer a modern economy in any meaningful way. Growing market disequilibria breed demoralisation.

In the social sphere, health, education, housing and living standards have turned out to be in a worse state than previously recognised by most foreign observers. Even Soviet prides such as full employment and stable prices are truths with modifications. The former obsession with gigantic plants for the production of raw materials and industrial inputs have turned into liabilities, as the vast production of these goods indicate inefficiency and inability to transform into a service economy with flexibility and innovativeness supported by small and medium-sized firms. An ecological crisis has erupted. As if in conspiracy, all international trends seem to work against the traditional Soviet system at present. The long time since the last reform attempt is in itself an argument for reform.

The one achievement a majority of Soviet citizens seem to appreciate is the high degree of *economic security*. Jobs are easily found and maintained. You are paid approximately the same whether you actually work or not. Flats are extremely difficult to acquire, but once obtained a state flat will stay with the family for generations, and the rent is tiny. Despite hidden inflation and miserable supplies, state prices of food are low. Regardless of unequal access and faltering quality, education and medical care are free. Most reformist economists consider the economic security excessive and want to reduce it in order to enhance work incentives. Conversely, the popular desire to maintain economic security arouses a potent internal pressure against reform.[10]

The only impressive strength the Soviet Union can display today—apart from its rich endowment of natural resources—is its military force. Zbigniew Brzezinski (1983, p.12) observed: 'The Soviet Union is a world power of a new type in that its might is one-dimensional ... the Soviet Union is a global power only in the military dimension'. The militaristic Soviet writer Aleksandr Prokhanov has gone even further: 'One could say that until the Soviet Union achieved military-strategic parity with the West, the USSR had no other national goal than that of survival and defence' (*Detente*, Nos. 9–10, 1987, p. 26).

Our pessimistic assessment of the Soviet economy matches pronouncements of the rising Russian nationalism. The Russian values it praises are little more than goodness, endurance and ability to suffer: 'well, we are kinder and more sympathetic than the inhabitants of other developed countries. Under extreme conditions we can manage' (*Lit. gaz.*, 16 December 1987, p.

11). Such values are typically elevated in a nation with a declining economy and a sense of increasing backwardness. Paradoxically, Aleksandr Prokhanov has made one of the most telling summaries of the causes of perestroika, notwithstanding that it is meant as a criticism of reformers:

There is quite a common view that *perestroika* was sparked off by the strategic lag of the USSR behind the civilisation of the West. Soviet hospitals offer poorer treatment than Western ones, Soviet computers calculate more slowly than Western ones, Soviet cornfields are barer than Western ones. And this lag, ruinous for defence, social development, the whole of national life, has forced us to *perestroika*. The meaning and task of *perestroika* is to catch up with the West. Moving in its wake, to cut down our distance from it (*Lit. Gaz.,* 6 May 1987, transl. in Shenfield, 1987, p. 28).

The Soviet economic system has been counted out many times before, but never has it appeared so devoid of advantages. For a student of the Soviet economy, none of these economic problems is novel. Their causes have been analysed in a rich literature. What is striking is that virtually all problems have deepened and that Soviet leaders have acknowledged them with great candour. Most western assessments of the Soviet economic malaise pale in contrast. Soviet leaders have partly adopted the same vocabulary as western Sovietologists, lamenting the 'command-adminstrative system'. Their complaints are many and not very original, but sensible. The system is considered over-centralised, leading to excessive bureaucratisation and petty tutelage over enterprises. The perseverance of gross output targets and planning from the achieved level causes wastage and restrains production. The growing complexity of the economy, with more than twenty-four million different products, renders central planning and allocation in physical terms ever more inadequate. The system harbours no effective incentives promoting innovations, technical progress or quality. In addition, orders and plans are patently late, and plan targets are frequently adjusted during a year. The consumer is neglected because of the prevalence of the seller's markets, reinforced by far-reaching monopolisation. Departmentalism and localism endure, with autarky within branch ministries and departmental barriers between them. Money is often abundant and remains passive, ensuring soft budget constraints in enterprises. Work incentives are inadequate with little to purchase for money earned and considerable wage-levelling. Workers have little to lose through passivity. The control system has grown lax, not least because of expanding corruption. The situation was perceived as very bad, probably disastrous by several leaders, but it was not at all obvious how the problems were to be solved.

NOTES

1. The reforms of the 1950s are of limited relevance to our topic. The major economic problems were the neglect of consumption and market imbalances, while growth rates remained high. Tamas Bauer (1984, p. 43) sees the changes as

restricted to reorganisation and reallocation of resources, and the Soviet reformist Boris Kurashvili (1987, p. 11) concludes that this reform was 'essentially of an *apparat* character'.

2. The following discussion of the Kosygin reform is primarily based on Schroeder (1968, pp. 1–21; 1969, pp. 462–77; 1972, pp. 97–119); Asselain (1984, pp. 157–74); Ellman (1984, pp. 75–96); Medvedev (1983, pp. 56–63); *Voprosy ekonomiki* (No. 2, 1988, pp. 55–79).

3. This 'acceleration' was probably hidden inflation (Selyunin and Khanin, 1987, pp. 194–5; Kulagin, 1985).

4. At the Politburo level, beside Gorbachev, Yakovlev has set the reformist line on ideology (Yakovlev, 1987a; *Pravda*, 11 August 1988); among the economists, Academician Leonid Abalkin is the authoritative reformist political economist (Abalkin, 1986, 1987abc); Professor Anatoli Butenko (1987) is a more polemic strident reformist in political economy, and Academician Oleg Bogomolov (1987) introduces radical ideas from other socialist countries. However, dogmatic articles are still published in central journals (e.g. Ignatovski, 1988). For an excellent analysis of prior developments in Soviet political economy, see Sutela (1984).

5. The following conclusions are essentially based on a reading of Schroeder (1983), Bornstein (1985) and Hanson (1983).

6. I have elaborated my views on Soviet statistics, growth and national income in Åslund (1989).

7. ECE Energy Data Bank. The ECE defines energy intensity of production as the ratio of primary energy consumption to gross domestic product. Since the ECE conservatively overestimates the GDP of communist countries, the actual energy intensity must be even higher.

8. Moscow and Leningrad are the only cities belonging to the top supply category with preferential food supplies (cf *Pravda*, 26 November 1987). Until 1986, Donetsk was also included in this category (personal information from a competent Soviet official). Even in Moscow informal rationing is common. For instance, a customer is allowed to purchase 400g of one sausage and 1kg of another (observation from the exquisite *Gastronom* shop beside the Soviet Ministry for Foreign Affairs in the winter of 1987).

9. Most of the evidence is personal observations and conversation with ordinary Soviet citizens. Rationing, special shops and discriminatory pricing were taboo in the press until 1985 and are still sensitive topics, though there has been a public reaction against unjust distribution channels (*Pravda*, 13 February 1986; Zaslavskaya, 1986, pp. 71–2; Bim and Shokhin, 1986, pp. 69–70; *Trud*, 2 October 1986.

10. Soviet economic security might appear impressive by American standards, but it is certainly not from a West European perspective. As Peter Wiles and Abram Bergson have pointed out, the distribution of money income is more equal in the Nordic countries than in the USSR, and then no note has been taken of the many administered benefits to the Soviet élite (Bergson, 1984, p. 1092).

2. Alternative programmes for economic revitalisation

Michael Voslensky (1980) has convincingly argued that the principal aspiration of the Soviet regime under Brezhnev was to safeguard the power and well-being of the nomenklatura. Instead, the new Soviet leadership appears to have made economic revitalisation their top priority, though their individual propensity to relinquish ideological and political impediments varies. The Soviet leaders have a choice of alternative strategies, and reform is only one option.

A detailed study of statements and actions of leading politicians evidences that they favour different economic programmes. Open polemics are rare, and factions within the party have been forbidden since 1921. Therefore, we have to classify the approaches of the top politicians ourselves on the basis of their diversions from the orthodox party line.

In practice, politicians need to choose between a limited number of economic models, since an economic model most possess some consistency in order to be feasible (though politicians might not realise this). The real world offers a number of distinct socialist models, notably the Stalinist, Brezhnevian, Hungarian, Chinese, GDR and Yugoslav models. Towards the end of Leonid Brezhnev's life, Joseph Berliner (1983) undertook a perceptive analysis of the most plausible choices of model. He identified four alternatives, which he called the conservative, reactionary, radical and liberal models, respectively. His conservative model is Brezhnevian, aiming at a minimum of change. The reactionary model is neo-Stalinist. Its goals are recentralisation, tighter discipline and isolation from the outside world, making it a suitable option for xenophobic nationalists. The radical model is essentially the Hungarian model, with considerable marketisation, but extensive direct government intervention. Berliner's liberal model 'conserves the traditional planning methods for most of the economy while liberalising the present restrictions on private initiative' (Berliner, 1983, p. 375).[1] With these concepts in our mind, we shall try to establish what the leading politicians actually stand for.

Our main methodological inspiration comes from George Breslauer's (1983) eminent analysis of the Khrushchev and Brezhnev periods. Peter Wiles (1988) has undertaken a similar study of the Andropov and Chernenko spells. Published speeches of the new leaders from the time when the new policy was taking shape (December 1984–June 1987) comprise our main sources,[2] but unlike Breslauer, we shall try to complement with all available evidence—personal background and their connections, also utilising inside information and rumours. The present wealth of alternative sources of information; the author's presence in Moscow, and hence knowledge of the origins and reliability of various information, have made it much easier than before to evaluate soft data.

No senior politician writes his own speeches. External experts—often from the Academy of Sciences—are invited to write different parts of major speeches. Their draft is worked over by the politician's personal staff. A major speech needs to be approved by a few members of the Politburo, and a speech to a CC Plenum by the whole Politburo (though not in detail) as can be seen from Politburo bulletins. Thus, a politician cannot diverge too far from the party line, but the existing diversions are of his own choice and therefore significant. The stronger a politician and the less authoritative the speech, the more can he develop his own views.[3]

Soviet politicians are supposed to concentrate on their own fields of responsibility. Several leading politicians, such as the Chairman of the KGB, the Minister of Defence, the Minister for Foreign Affairs and the CC Secretary for foreign affairs barely mention economic affairs. However, the top politicians have broad responsibilities, providing them with ample opportunities to show their profiles. Even for a junior CC Secretary, it is significant what issues he concentrates on, or avoids, within his sphere of responsibility. The volume of published speeches is so large that a faithful reader becomes acutely aware of divisive issues and favourite ideas of various politicians. Personal variations are surprisingly great and consistent.

It is dangerous to draw definite conclusions about an individual's views on the basis of his background. However, the outlook varies so much with age, profession and regional background in the USSR that these factors need to be pointed out. The generation of war veterans—born before 1928—tend to be irreparable Stalinists, while the middle-aged generation is much more flexible (see Table 6.1). As Alec Nove has pointed out, the Soviet system is designed for engineers, who have long dominated the leadership. A non-engineer is more likely to be critical of the system. Another important difference is based on regional variations in the second economy. In the Caucasus, it is the dominant source of personal income, while it dwindles towards the north and east (Grossman, 1987). In the south, politicians are forced to accommodate the private sector and market forces, while politicians in the Urals and West Siberia can neglect them. This point is substantiated by the policy on *kolkhoz* market prices. The regional party leadership can decide upon the introduction of price ceilings at *kolkhoz* markets. In 1986, such price limits existed in the whole of Siberia, apart from Altai *krai*, and several industrial areas in the RSFSR, the Ukraine and Belorussia, notably in Dnepropetrovsk and Minsk. No price ceilings were maintained in the non-Slav republics, Southern Russia, Moscow, Leningrad, Sverdlovsk and Kiev.[4]

The current positions of present leaders are presented in Appendix 1, and brief biographies of twenty-two of the leaders of particular interest are given in Appendix 2.

GORBACHEV: RADICAL REFORM[5]

The star of this book is Mikhail Sergeevich Gorbachev, who became General Secretary of the CPSU in March 1985. He has been so well studied in western literature,[6] that we shall limit ourselves to the emergence of the salient features of his programme. Born in 1931, Gorbachev belongs to the post-Stalinist generation that call themselves 'the children of the Twentieth Party Congress' (in 1956). Uncharacteristically for a party official, Gorbachev graduated in law. Otherwise, his career path was normal for a provincial politician under Brezhnev—only faster and more successful. From 1955 until 1978, Gorbachev worked his way up in the Komsomol and party apparatus in his native Stavropol *krai* on the northern slopes of the Caucasus.

Stavropol *krai* has fertile farmland and a highly developed private economy. Price ceilings have not been imposed on its *kolkhoz* markets. The development of informal work teams (*shabashniki*) in agriculture and construction has been accentuated in this area (*Izvestiya*, 15 June 1985). Gorbachev was forced to co-exist with private enterprise and market forces, and he did so with reason. One of his legacies from Stavropol was the promotion of 'normless links' (*beznaryadnoe zveno*)—small autonomous work teams in agriculture. Another legacy was his ability to accommodate superior politicians and to adjust his policies accordingly (Weickhardt, 1985). He appears to have been a capable regional manager.

The best that can be said of Gorbachev's tenure as CC Secretary for agriculture (1978–85) is that he probably had little influence, as Leonid Brezhnev and Konstantin Chernenko took great interest in agriculture. It was a period of excessive investment and unsuccessful large-scale farming. The not very substantial Food Programme (adopted in May 1982) must enjoy Gorbachev's support, since he still refers to it. Yet, he has been rather consistent in his support for private agricultural plots and *kolkhoz* markets. When possible, he promoted small independent work units, but he limited himself to improvements in enterprise management.

It is an enigma that a provincial apparachik should turn out to be so reform-minded. One obvious reason is that the state of Soviet society and economy was so bad; another that an intensive review of the country's situation, and a search for solutions, was launched by Andropov, and it was led by Gorbachev. Tatyana Zaslavskaya's (1984) famous 'Novosibirsk Report' is supposed to have been part of this process. Besides, the Gorbachevs had travelled independently in the West in the early 1970s, so unlike most party officials at his level, Mikhail Gorbachev had something to compare with.

The present reform process has not been continuous, but composed of a series of discrete steps. It is Gorbachev who has formulated the agenda. Each step has been initiated by a big speech by Gorbachev, and he has tended to target one broad issue at a time. His choice of topic, degree of radicalism, and timing has been deliberate. To begin with we need to establish when Gorbachev has pushed for a particular major issue. We shall later seek most of the explanations of his manoeuvering in the positions of other Soviet leaders.

Gorbachev introduced his reform agenda on 10 December 1984, three months before his election to General Secretary. He did so at an ideological CC Conference, and his speech involved ideological revision and economic and political reform. Almost the whole spectrum of his reform proposals emerged in that speech. He used most of his later famous catch-words, calling for 'revolutionary decisions', 'acceleration of social-economic progress', 'deep transformations in the economy and the whole system of social relations', 'perestroika of economic management', 'competition' (without the attribute socialist), 'self-management', 'self-government', 'democratisation' and 'glasnost', but he avoided being specific (Gorbachev, 1987a, pp. 75–108). Evidently, Gorbachev had quite a clear idea of the direction of his political and economic strategy already at this time, but he had political reasons for caution.[7]

The essence of this rich speech was ideological revision. Thus, Gorbachev saw a necessity to start with ideology. He took a reformist stand in the debate on the nature of contradictions under socialism: 'they are, of course, not antagonistic. But with a stagnant preservation of obsolete elements of production relations, the economic and social situation may deteriorate.' Hence, he urged a 'perfection of the forms of socialist ownership' and an 'activation and optimisation of the system of interests' (ibid., pp. 80–1).

Gorbachev's point of departure was the need for a stronger economy in order to improve the standard of living and safeguard the country's international status, and he formulated the goals of an economic revitalisation. The main task was to 'achieve an essential acceleration (uskorenie) of social-economic progress', which was a 'titanic job', that 'had to be accomplished with a revolutionary sweep' (Gorbachev, 1987a, pp. 76–7, 86). Gorbachev emphasised the need for qualitative improvements: a breakthrough in the increase in efficiency and quality, an acceleration of the scientific-technical progress, and a better utilisation of the existing potential (ibid., p. 87). The 'role of the human factor in social progress' was growing, and a wide field opened up to 'the initiative of the masses' (ibid., pp. 77, 85). 'Contemporary production is oriented towards the initiative of a thinking worker, highly organised, disciplined, educated and possessing a principally new technological culture' (ibid., p. 89).

To attain these targets Gorbachev urged a 'perestroika of economic management'. Under this heading, he presented a plethora of suggestions pertaining to different economic models. Several belonged to the sphere of market economy. Observing that 'money-commodity relations are inherent under socialism', he suggested a study of its instruments and economic levers, such as prices, prime costs, profits and credits. Competition should be organised so that it was oriented not towards gross production but 'even work rhythm, timely fulfillment of contract obligations, high product quality, introduction of new technology, prudent utilisation' of working time, raw materials and money (*ibid.*, p. 91). Gorbachev complained about the lack of balance between 'supply and demand, which engenders negative economic and moral phenomena' (*ibid.*, p. 98).

But Gorbachev also approved of technocratic streamlining, for instance, 'scientific-production associations' (NPO) with their combination of research and development with production. He advocated an 'essential change in investment policy' to stop the prevailing tendency to conserve the economic structure and promote the introduction of new technologies (*ibid.*, p. 88). He praised the brigade contracts pioneered at a turbine factory in the town of Kaluga and the large-scale economic experiment in industry launched under Andropov at the beginning of 1984. Moreover, Gorbachev also picked up demands from the reactionary agenda, speaking for 'a struggle for a general confirmation of order, organisation, discipline and increased responsibility of cadres' and attacked black, or so-called 'unearned incomes' (*ibid.*, pp. 76, 97). Instead, the socialist principle for distribution of incomes should be introduced, implying a greater differentiation of legal earnings.

Gorbachev did not limit himself to the economic sphere but favoured 'a perfection of the Soviet political system and a further development of socialist democracy' (*ibid.*, p. 93). He advocated a 'democratisation of our social and economic life', and 'glasnost' which he defined as 'broad, timely and open information', and called for a struggle with bureaucratic distortions, departmentalism and localism (*ibid.*, pp. 95, 83). In science, he favoured an 'active competition of ideas' (*ibid.*, pp. 84–5). Important questions in the 'development of the political system' were a transformation to 'workers' self-management' and 'self-government' in the state sphere (*ibid.*, p. 82).

The stage for reform had been set. Evidently, Gorbachev had perceived the depth of the problems Soviet society was facing, and in broad terms he formulated the new tasks. From the outset, he led the reform from the front. After having become General Secretary on 11 March 1985, Gorbachev developed some of his themes in four big speeches from April to June 1985. His preoccupation was immediate improvements and the ensuing five-year plan which must have demanded a lot of top-level attention. He concentrated on the technocratic agenda, but added reactionary elements and in each speech Gorbachev alluded to fundamental reform, too. He reached a peak at the CC Conference on the acceleration of scientific-technical progress on 11 June 1985.

These speeches can be summarised by the slogan 'acceleration of economic development' (*Pravda*, 24 April 1985). A major theme was investment policy, which would be oriented towards more retooling and less construction of new big factories. Gorbachev focused on one branch, civil engineering, of which he had no personal experience. He lashed out against all kinds of wastage, demanding order and discipline. The economic experiment in industry had to go further in order to develop enterprise management. The rights, independence and responsibilities of enterprises and associations should widen, and real economic accountability should be introduced (Gorbachev, 1987a, pp. 141–3). He desired organisational changes and suggested 'the creation of management organs of large national-economic complexes' (Gorbachev, 1985a, p. 24), hinting at some kind of superministries. The intermediary bodies between enterprises and ministries, the all-union industrial associations (VOP) should be abolished, paving the way for a two-tier administration. It was necessary to trim the administration, and some bodies ought to be liquidated. Already at the CC Plenum in April 1985, Gorbachev countenanced the creation of 'an integral economic and management system', involving a perestroika of the highest economic bodies and the introduction of a more flexible price system (*Pravda*, 24 April 1985).

After two months of radical but amorphous speeches, the audience expected more, but the contrary occurred. Starting with his speeches in Dnepropetrovsk (26 June) and Kiev (27 June), Gorbachev sounded considerably more conservative. Something had happened. Gorbachev appeared to be on the defensive and said little of interest for economic reform until the 27th Party Congress. For eight months, he did not even utter innocuous words, such as 'economic accountability' or 'economic experiments', in public. At the same time, Gorbachev avoided saying anything that could be used against reform. He had evidently been forced to a tactical retreat.

At the 27th Party Congress (on 25 February 1986), Gorbachev focused on economic reform, especially in agriculture. For the first time, he used the term 'economic reform', even calling for 'a radical economic reform'. He stated: 'we are approaching the most serious perestroika of the socialist economic mechanism' and outlined changes of the major elements of the economic system. For the first time, outside observers could surmise what kind of economic system Gorbachev envisaged.

Gosplan was supposed to become a scientific-economic staff, devoted to long-term planning and macro-economic matters, but 'relieved' of current economic issues. A flexible wholesale trade should be developed. Through 'a planned perestroika of the price system as one entity', prices were supposed to become more flexible under the influence of quality, efficiency, [market] balance and demand. In a brief reference to foreign trade, Gorbachev suggested 'a perestroika of the structure of foreign trade', but he did not speak of reform of the foreign trade system. He stated the need for democratisation of management, without specifying what he meant (*Pravda*, 26 February 1986). New bodies were to be established for the management of large multibranch complexes, with most operative management functions being delegated to enterprises. Branch ministries should concentrate on technical policies, proportions within their branches, and the satisfaction of needs of high quality products, but it was 'time, at last, to put an end to petty tutelage over enterprises by ministries'. Hence, new and fewer economic 'norms' would be established.

Gorbachev favoured a reinforcement of the territorial approach to planning and management. Enterprise management should be based on 'real economic accounting' and 'self-financing'. Gorbachev commended the experiments with self-financing at the car manufacturing giant VAZ in Togliatti on the Volga and the Frunze engineering association in the Ukrainian town Sumy. He praised the Shchekino method, and its variant, the Belorussian railway experiment. Besides, Gorbachev advocated a rational mix of large, medium-sized and small enterprises, and the development of cooperatives in construction, services and trade, as well as 'individual labour activity' (*Pravda*, 26 February 1986).

Gorbachev's detailed discussion of agriculture—his long-time speciality—indicated that reform would start in this branch. He emphasised the need to raise efficiency and reduce losses, which he said could add 20–30 per cent to available resources. A reorganisation had already started with the establishment of a new superministry—the State Agro-Industrial Committee (Gosagroprom). The organisational integration should be reinforced with a new effective economic mechanism, based on 'a creative utilisation of the Leninist idea of tax in kind, applied to contemporary conditions'. Lenin's 'tax in kind' had replaced the arbitrary requisitioning of agricultural produce and was the start of NEP. In practice, farms were to receive stable procurement plans for each five-year period. (Leonid Brezhnev had made the same promise in March 1965, but had not kept it.) Farms would be entitled to sell surpluses, and a share of the planned volume, of potatoes, fruit and vegetables freely to the state, to cooperative trade or on *kolkhoz* markets at higher prices. The organisation of work would be improved through long-term contracts for brigades, teams and families. Authorities were told to stop their incompetent interference in the work of farms.

Most of this sounded like an advocacy of a socialist market on the margin. Gorbachev envisaged a system with several plan indicators, of which the notorious gross deliveries were the most important; the state would continue fixing prices; ministries were not forbidden to interfere in subordinate enterprises. Gorbachev's protégé Vsevolod Murakhovski, the newly-appointed Chairman of Gosagroprom, actually used the term 'socialist market':

The socialist market must play an important role in the increase of volumes and the improvement of the quality of production. This is nothing to be afraid of. The limits of the market are determined by the socialist system and the key positions of the state in production and distribution (*Pravda*, 3 March 1986).

Murakhovski also hinted at some kind of land rent. We may assume that he spoke on behalf of Gorbachev. At the Party Congress, no one else picked up these ideas, and Gorbachev and Murakhovski stood out as extreme reformers. The resolution of the Party Congress reflected little of Gorbachev's ideas of economic reforms. Presumably, Gorbachev wanted to go even further, but the lack of political support for such a course was evident. Until June 1986, no other Politburo member or CC Secretary appears to have pronounced the word 'economic reform' in public.

In the second quarter of 1986, Gorbachev went to the East German and Polish Party Congresses and received the Hungarian General Secretary Janos Kadar in Moscow. He exploited these occasions to develop his ideas of foreign trade. In East Berlin, he emphasised the need for direct links between enterprises in the two countries and the formation of joint ventures, and called for the establishment of 'a new economic mechanism in our coopera-tion' (*Pravda*, 19 April 1986). At the Polish Party Congress, Gorbachev sounded a strong warning against trade with the West (see Gelman, 1987, p. 58):

We must admit, after all, that we understood too late what kind of traps are laid on the trading routes leading to the West. It has been discussed here what great losses have been suffered by Poland, and not by it alone. The very idea that it is simpler to buy from the capitalist market than to make it yourself has already done harm. Now we are decisively uprooting such inclinations in our country. It is not, of course, a matter of folding up economic links with the West . . . It is a matter of making rational use of them, eliminating excesses and preventing dependence (*Pravda*, 1 July 1986).

Where did Gorbachev look for useful examples? In May 1985, Gorbachev made a curious, seemingly improvised, statement on the GDR, which was broadcast on TV but not printed:

In 1966 I went with a party delegation to the GDR to study the experience of work on the party bodies' management of economic reform. I was greatly impressed by what our friends had accomplished even then. In all the main directions of their output they determined where—in what country—the highest indices and the best quality were, and they set themselves the task of surpassing them . . . (FBIS, 22 May 1985, p. R7).

This statement has been interpreted as support for the present GDR model. However, in 1966 the GDR pursued the most successful Liberman reform, the New Economic System, which was finished off in 1970–1 by the coming General Secretary Erich Honecker. Thus, Gorbachev made a positive reference to a more reformist GDR model which seemed like a reproach to Honecker. During his visit to the GDR in the spring of 1986, Gorbachev was politely complimentary to the East Germans, but in general terms. He avoided saying anything about the East German economic system (*SSSR-GDR*, 1986). This caution contrasted with Gorbachev's words to Janos Kadar: 'The CPSU pays attention to and respects the search for solutions of difficult economic and social problems that is carried out in Hungary and other socialist countries. We . . . try to adopt everything useful' (*Pravda*, 10 June 1986). The Hungarian delegation left Moscow relishing an alleged endorsement of their economic model by Gorbachev. He did not openly approve of one socialist model over another, but his public treatment of Hungary was slightly more positive.

Domestically, Gorbachev lost political momentum in the spring of 1986. At the CC Plenum on 16 June 1986, his irritation was evident. He refrained from using most of the reformist terminology, but instead launched a sharp attack on 'several responsible officials of Gosplan of the USSR and the RSFSR' for having refused to accept new methods and sticking to the old planning system. Previously Gorbachev had stated that the reform should begin with the central economic bodies. Now, on the contrary, he announced that the reform would start with enterprise management and that 'a law on socialist enterprises (production associations)' would be worked out as soon as possible (*Pravda*, 17 June 1986).

Three days later, Gorbachev met a group of Soviet writers. A credible version of his conversation was leaked (e.g. *L'Unita*, 7 October 1986). He sounded more aggressive and embattled than before: 'there is a very profound and serious battle ahead'. His criticism against Gosplan was even sharper than at the CC Plenum: 'For Gosplan there are no authorities, no General Secretary, no Central Committee. They do whatever they want.' Gorbachev also criticised the *apparat*, not only of ministries but also of the party, 'which does not want any reforms or any reduction in certain rights they have connected with privileges'. To judge from the evidence, high-level political resistance was forcing Gorbachev to adjust his reform strategy.

In the summer of 1986, it became clear that Gorbachev had changed strategy. In speeches in Khabarovsk (31 July) and in Krasnodar (18 September), he turned to 'perestroika of the political system' and his language was radicalised. Now, Gorbachev put the emphasis on democratisation and struggle with the resistance against reform. He equated perestroika with revolution, but he also declared that it was necessary to undertake perestroika gradually. His notion of democratisation was still nebulous, involving consultations with the people, a greater role for the Soviets, and less interference by local party organisations in the work of local authorities. He promised clarifications of the role and functions of central economic bodies, such as Gosplan, Gossnab and GKNT, within the nearest future, but these were only adopted one year later (*Pravda*, 2 August 1986). In Krasnodar, Gorbachev cast doubt on all levels of the party: 'Much depends on how quickly the CPSU will restructure itself, all its links from primary party organisations to the Politburo and the CC' (*Pravda* 20 September 1986). Apparently, Gorbachev had concluded that he could not implement a viable economic reform without breaking the entrenched political resistance and for that he needed a political reform, raising the pressure from below.

These two speeches aroused new expectations, but little happened to economic reform in the autumn of 1986. The major economic events were the adoption of the Law on Individual Labour Activity and the introduction of independent state quality control (*gospriemka*). Neither appears to have been particularly controversial within the leadership. The next CC Plenum, that was supposed to deal with personnel issues, was all the more contentious and was postponed three times until 27 January 1987. In fact, this Plenum focused on democratisation and political reform. Gorbachev surprised all with his radicalism, delivering a sharp criticism of virtually the whole communist system: 'The roots of this brake lie in serious shortcomings in the functioning of the institutions of socialist democracy . . .' (*Pravda*, 28 January 1987). He replaced the Brezhnevian concept of 'developed socialism' with the notion 'developing socialism'. In substance, he proposed real elections between several candidates with secret ballots in enterprises, state assemblies and even in the party. Considerable differences of substance between Gorbachev's speech and the resolution of the CC Plenum evidenced that the CC approved of few of his proposals.

In the wake of the CC Plenum of January 1987, a draft Law on State Enterprises was published, and an extensive public discussion followed. In the autumn of 1986, reformers spoke of the law on socialist enterprises as an attempt to cut the feet from the ministries and central economic bodies. However, when the draft law was published, they regarded it as a failure. The central economic bodies and ministries had transformed it to their liking. The debate grew dull, but towards the end of May a new momentum was building up. On 8–9 June, a CC Conference on economic reform was held with the obvious purpose of paving the way for more radical decisions at the ensuing CC Plenum. Gorbachev tried to make it a virtue to begin with a reform of enterprise management: 'Speaking of the past, the perhaps most important mistake was that we started from the top' (*Pravda*, 13 June 1987).

The CC Plenum on economic reform (25–6 June 1987) corresponded to highly set expectations. Gorbachev went through most economic questions. His criticism of both economic performance and system was severe. Four Deputy Prime Ministers, including the chairmen of Gosplan and Gossnab (but also Murakhovski), were criticised by name. Gorbachev linked democratisation to economic reform: 'we shall not succeed with the tasks of perestroika if we do not firmly pursue democratisation' (*Pravda*, 26 June 1987). He outlined the whole reform programme, summarising it in five points:

1.   A considerable extension of the independence of enterprises on the basis of self-financing.
2.   A fundamental perestroika of the centralised management of the economy, concentrating it on the main issues.
3.   A cardinal reform of planning, price formation, and the finance-and-credit mechanism and the adoption of wholesale trade.
4.   The establishment of new organisational structures.
5.   Transition from the excessively centralised command system of management to a democratic one, development of self-management, the creation of a mechanism to activate human potential.

The General Secretary spoke in detail of a reform of all basic elements of the economic system, apart from foreign trade and the political system. The substance of the reform proposals will be discussed in the following chapters.

Much remained muddled and riddled with compromises, but there could no longer be any doubt that Gorbachev himself favoured a radical economic reform akin to the Hungarian model. How far Gorbachev really wants to go remains an open question, because he is still a reformist extremist on the Politburo, but, as we have seen, he has been willing to agree on measures pertaining to other models. His impatient activism appears so great that he seems to prefer a counterproductive decision to no decision at all. He might consider such a tactic expedient, since a new leader can benefit from turbulence.

In August 1987, Gorbachev turned to agricultural reform again, declaring that the new CC Plenum would be devoted to the elaboration of agrarian policy. The crucial issue was his advocacy of leasehold in agriculture (*Pravda*, 6 August 1987). However, the matter faded away as a conservative counter-offensive raged, culminating in the Yeltsin affair in October and November 1987. The agricultural CC Plenum had been postponed for some time. On 13 May 1988, Gorbachev organised a special meeting in the CC on leasehold in agriculture. He spoke categorically for the development of leasehold and cooperatives (*Pravda*, 15 May 1988). However, the response appeared muted and at the 19th Party Conference Gorbachev chose to bypass this topic, but he returned to it with new vigour on 12 October 1988 (*Pravda*, 14 October 1988).

In the autumn of 1987, the implementation of economic reform was faltering because of bureaucratic resistance in the central economic bodies and branch ministries. Then, Gorbachev's focus moved back to political issues and to the very role of the party—a moot point in the reform package. Gorbachev was unequivocal. The role of the party in the running of the economy should be reduced: 'the creation of a new management mechanism for the economy allows for the liberation of party bodies from for them, uncharacteristic, purely economic management functions' (*Pravda*, 17 October 1987).

The 19th Party Conference in the summer of 1988, and the preceding debate, were devoted to political reform. Gorbachev's explicit purpose was to subordinate the party apparatus to popular control and to strengthen the role of the legislature and the president. Besides, the central economic bodies and branch ministries took a heavy beating in the debate, and a new openness in public debate developed (*Pravda*, 29 June–2 July 1988).

In his political strategy, Gorbachev appears to have moved between four major fronts: ideology, agricultural reform, general economic reform, and political reform. He spoke of all four in December 1984, but ideology was the focal point. In the spring of 1985, he hinted at economic reform. At the 27th Party Congress, he discussed economic reform, but concentrated on agricultural reform. After apparently having failed to win sufficient support for these endeavours, he switched his emphasis to political reform in the summer of 1986, without letting economic reform down. This combined strategy led to the endorsement of the package of economic reform measures in the summer of 1987. Gorbachev's attempts to boost leasehold in agriculture, both in August 1987 and May 1988, were unsuccessful. Instead, he turned to political reform, while the economic reforms were being implemented. In his advocacy of political reform, Gorbachev has gone further than Hungarian or Chinese leaders. He has done so in a rational response to political resistance.

A few of the new Soviet leaders 'stuck out their necks' for reform before it was espoused by the party. Apart from Gorbachev, this group of evidently radical reformers in the leadership is limited to Aleksandr Yakovlev, Eduard Shevarnadze, Vadim Medvedev and Anatoli Lukyanov. All these men appear to have forged such close personal links that we may regard them as a faction. Their regional backgrounds vary, though nobody comes from the East, and Yakovlev, Medvedev and Lukyanov have worked in the central party apparatus for some time. These three have impressive academic qualifications in history, economics and law, respectively. A common denominator of all five radical reformers is that none of them is an engineer. Apart from Yakovlev's service in the army during World War II, their contact with the military has been minimal. A worrying fact is that none of them has any direct responsibility for economic affairs.

The Politburo member and CC Secretary for International Affairs, **Aleksandr Yakovlev**, appears to have been Gorbachev's right-hand man and chief ideologue until the CC Plenum in September 1988, when he switched to foreign affairs. His experience is impressive. He is a Professor of History and a corresponding member of the Academy of Sciences. Because of his long tenure in the CC Propaganda Department (1953–73), he is personally acquainted with many radical publicists who have given perestroika momentum. By publishing a forceful attack on 'Great Russian chauvinism' (*Lit. gaz.*, 15 November 1972), Yakovlev became notorious as an enemy of Russian nationalists. As a result, he was sent into diplomatic exile as Ambassador to Canada for ten years, from where Gorbachev apparently recalled him in 1983 for fast promotion. Yakovlev has published sharply anti-American works, but eleven years' experience of North America must have left imprints of many kinds.

Since the spring of 1987, Yakovlev has pronounced his views on a wide spectrum of issues with great clarity, leaving no doubt about his radical reformism (Yakovlev, 1987ab, *Pravda*, 10 April, 28 November 1987, 11 August 1988). He has displayed a knack for always speaking after Yegor Ligachev on approximately the same issues, contradicting Ligachev on basic ideological questions. For instance, when Ligachev has spoken for limited glasnost, Yakovlev has expounded on how great the openness must be; when Ligachev has lauded Soviet history, Yakovlev has brought up the dark sides of Stalin's terror; when Ligachev has criticised the market, Yakovlev has gone further then ever in defence of the market.

In a speech on social sciences in April 1987, Yakovlev criticised most Soviet social sciences, and in particular the Brezhnevian concept of 'developed socialism'. However, he also censured a technocratic approach, favoured by the engineers in the centre of the Soviet leadership. Yakovlev desires a deep qualitative renewal of socialism through open intellectual discussion. His socialism includes far-reaching democratisation and a socialist market. He appears to have supplemented Gorbachev's radical statements with his own, revising much of the Soviet political economy and acting as the ideologue of perestroika. Apart from the concept of a socialist market, he pushes for self-management, cooperatives, and individual labour activity. His radicalism is both far-reaching and open.

The Minister for Foreign Affairs and Politburo member since July 1985, **Eduard Shevardnadze** has the strongest background as an economic reformer. From 1972 until 1985 he was the First Party Secretary of his native Georgia, which excelled as the most innovative and reformist regional party. Georgia has the largest second economy in the USSR. Despite an initial purge, Shevardnadze's strategy was to coopt the unofficial economy, by making the official economy more market-oriented. He also reinforced the economic role of territorial bodies at the expense of branch ministries.[8]

Both the number and the boldness of the experimental reforms in Georgia were impressive. Some will be discussed in Chapter 4. Possibly the most daring experiment was attempted in 1985 at a shoe factory in Batumi which operated with no plan, for profit and with profit-sharing among the employees. The factory used an independent market-oriented pricing, sold through its own retail shops on the basis of market research, and was managed by an enterprise council (*Sots. ind.*, 4 October 1985). It was, in fact, no less than a self-managed enterprise of the Yugoslav type. Other experiments involved the private leasing by families of cafés in the countryside, individual leasing, private handicrafts, and the acceptance of informal work teams (*shabashniki*). The pricing of non-agricultural produce was very flexible and market-oriented, with queues unusual. Certain political developments accompanied the economic experiments, notably the development of opinion polls and the activation of local organisations.

These market-and-profit-oriented experiments were undoubtedly promoted personally by Shevardnadze. He spoke frequently of them, and nothing similar occurred elsewhere in the Soviet Union. Economic science was poorly developed in Georgia, and inspiration for the schemes appears to have come from the unofficial market economy. Shevardnadze's successor as First Party Secretary of Georgia, Dzhumber Patiashvili, reversed the whole economic strategy. He ousted several of Shevardnadze's closest aides, accusing them of economic offences, and launched a ferocious campaign against 'private-property tendencies'. Shevardnadze's most daring experiments ended in 1986.[9]

Shevardnadze's credentials as a reformer appear impeccable (notwithstanding his initial campaign against economic crime in Georgia). In July 1985, it would have been surprising for such an outspoken radical to advance as far as the Politburo. The obvious explanation was support from Gorbachev, who had known Shevardnadze since their Komsomol days and visited Georgia

three times as CC Secretary for agriculture, praising the Georgian agricultural experiments.

The most competent economist in the leadership is **Vadim Medvedev**, who
has been CC Secretary since March 1986 and a Politburo member since
October 1988. Medvedev was known as a reformist political economist before
he became a party official, and he is a corresponding member of the Academy
of Sciences. In the early 1970s he served with Aleksandr Yakovlev as deputy
head of the CC Propaganda Department. Soviet reform economists tend to
look upon Medvedev as 'their man' in the political leadership. He has
published a great deal, and his main topic is economic reform. His reformist
views were publicised with unusual candour in a 1983 publication (Medvedev,
1983). It contains one of the best Soviet analyses of the reforms of 1965.
Medvedev criticises them from a liberal point of view for not having gone far
enough and for not having introduced supervision of the economy. Medvedev
also advocated far-reaching democratisation of management. This book may
be seen as a first programme of perestroika. Even Medvedev's friends were
surprised that he was given the task of liaison with the socialist states when he
was elected CC Secretary. But in fact he became deeply involved in the
impending reform of the CMEA trade system, advocating convertibility of
the ruble and a new pricing and finance system (*Pravda*, 1 and 9 December
1987).

Medvedev's election to the chairmanship of a new CC Commission on
Ideology appeared much more natural. His election and simultaneous
elevation to the Politburo is most likely to have been to Gorbachev's liking.
Now the CPSU chief ideologue is actually one of the leading political
economists of the country. In his first speech on his new job, Medvedev
praised the present market system and also envisaged leaseholding in large
enterprises. In particular, he called for a positive reevaluation of social
democracy (*Pravda*, 5 October 1988).

Anatoli Lukyanov, now candidate member of the Politburo and First
Deputy Chairman of the Presidium of the USSR Supreme Soviet, is the most
qualified legal expert in the leadership with good academic and reformist
credentials, as well as wide experience of working in the CC apparatus, the
Council of Ministers and the Presidium of the Supreme Soviet. He is likely to
have met Gorbachev as a fellow law student at Moscow University.
Lukyanov's reformist credentials were established in Khrushchev's time,
when he wrote his dissertation on the withering away of the state.[10] He has
come out clearly in favour of Gorbachev and his reformist ideas (*Pravda*, 30
October 1987, 2 February and 26 June 1988).

Possibly one should add the young candidate member of the Politburo and
CC Secretary for personnel, **Grigori Razumovski**, who appears connected
with Gorbachev, having made his career in Krasnodar *krai* which is close to
Gorbachev's Stavropol. However, from the time of his elevation to CC
Secretary in March 1986 until April 1988, Razumovski refrained from
making a convincing reformist speech, which suggests that he is cautious or

lukewarm. Somewhat belatedly, on 22 April 1988, he espoused radical reformism (*Pravda*, 23 April 1988).

RYKZHOV: REFORM NOT DISTURBING GOSPLAN[11]

Nearest to the radical reformers come a tightly-knit group of engineers and technocrats with a background in Gosplan: Prime Minister Nikolai Ryzhkov, CC Secretary for economic affairs Nikolai Slyunkov and the Chairman of Gosplan, Yuri Maslyukov. We may call them moderate reformers. In 1987, Ryzhkov and Slyunkov were undoubtedly behind the promulgation of economic reform. At the same time, they have been hesitant about the more radical of Gorbachev's reformist ideas. Their common view appears to be that economic reform involving marketisation is necessary, but they still support the omnipotent role of Gosplan. Although all three have worked in the military–industrial field, there is no military emphasis in their pronouncements although they are preoccupied with machine building.

Ryzhkov, Slyunkov and Maslyukov occupy the three central economic jobs in the country. Any *ad hoc* commission of the Politburo on economic reform issues seems to be headed by one of them. In effect, a major reform measure cannot be legislated without their approval. Therefore, Gorbachev and his associates are forced to compromise with these men on all decisions on economic reform—or remove them, as was the case with Lev Zaikov who was CC Secretary for economic affairs in 1986, and Nikolai Talyzin who was the Chairman of Gosplan from October 1985 until February 1988.

Of these three, **Nikolai Ryzhkov** has declared the clearest views. He was brought to the fore under Andropov through his appointment as CC Secretary for economic affairs in November 1982. After Gorbachev's accession to power, he advanced quickly to full Politburo membership in April 1985 and became Chairman of the Council of Ministers in September 1985. He is probably the most senior economic politician in the administration.

Ryzhkov is an archetypal technocrat. For twenty-five years he worked his way up as an engineer in Sverdlovsk, in the giant enterprise—the Urals machine building association (Uralmash) and became its director general. After four years as a Deputy Minister of the Ministry of Heavy and Transport Machine-Building, he became First Deputy Chairman of Gosplan in 1979. Until then, Ryzhkov had only dealt with a limited area of heavy engineering. Most of his life has been spent in the Urals—one of the most parochial parts of the Soviet Union. His career and reputation suggest that he is a superb Soviet manager. The drawback is that his outlook and concerns are limited.

Ryzhkov has delivered a large number of major speeches, but as they were usually on very official occasions he could not always speak his mind. However, his personal characteristics are easy to discover.[11] For formal reasons, Ryzhkov made some important speeches a few days after Gorbachev had spoken, which drew attention to their differences. However, he later moderated his pronounced views in line with Gorbachev's statements, although he did not do this immediately. He tends to emphasise Soviet capabilities and achievements. Once Ryzhkov said—admittedly addressing a foreign audience—that the only necessary external condition for the success of perestroika was peace: 'We have everything else—a detailed elaborated precise programme of action, qualified personnel, who believe in their abilities and are convinced about the correctness of the ideas of socialism, rich natural resources and a large scientific-technical potential' (*Novoe Vremya*, No. 39, 1986, p. 6). In his belief in the greatness of his country, Ryzhkov reveals a certain ideological innocence: 'We have to show the whole world the advantages and the unlimited possibilities of socialism, we have to achieve the foremost efficiency, product quality and labour productivity in the world' (*Pravda*, 23 April 1987). Admittedly, Gorbachev has spoken in a similar vein, but only rhetorically, while Ryzhkov speaks like a believer.

Ryzhkov has been a strong supporter of a higher growth-rate, intensification and greater efficiency. Since he does not think that the problems are all that great, he believes in an immediate acceleration of economic growth (*Pravda*, 22 June 1986). As an engineer, he sees the following sources of accelerated growth: 'an acceleration of scientific-technical progress, the ensuring of a fundamental improvement of the quality of production, a perestroika of investment process and a fuller utilisation of the production potential' (*Pravda*, 23 April 1987). To his mind, Soviet research is satisfactory, and the major problem is the implementation of its results. Therefore, Ryzhkov advocates the integration of research, development and experimental production into large scientific-production associations, like Uralmash (*Pravda*, 29 June 1985; *Izvestiya*, 18 October 1985). He shows great involvement in the new investment policy, emphasising retooling and a concentration of investment to machine-building. Because of his concern for investment in machine-building, he proposed a major change in construction before any other leading politician (*Pravda*, 4 March 1986).

With his pragmatic approach of problem-solving within the system, it was natural for Ryzhkov to take a positive view of the reduction and improvement of plan indicators. In the pre-election campaign in February 1985, he spoke more favourably of economic experiments than anyone in the leadership, apart from Shevardnadze, creating a reformist impression (*Pravda*, 2 February 1985). He endorsed the experiments with self-financing at Sumy and VAZ at an early stage (*Pravda*, 4 March 1986), and it is likely that he was pivotal in starting them. He appointed the economic director of VAZ (P. Katsura) head of a new department on the economic mechanism at the chancery of the Council of Ministers. In June 1986, it was Ryzhkov who elaborated on changes in enterprise management, but his approach was branch-oriented which suggested limited change. Within an enterprise, Ryzhkov favours team contracts and greater income differentials, with higher incomes for managers and engineers.

Initially, Ryzhkov was less critical of the ministries than Gorbachev, but he has almost caught up and has unequivocally called for their total restructuring and a sharp cut in the size of their staff (*Pravda*, 19 December 1987).

Of all party meetings, Ryzhkov appears to have been most enthusiastic about the CC Conference on 11–12 June 1985 on scientific-technical progress (*Pravda*, 22 June 1985). It dwelt on his favourite themes. Considering that Ryzhkov was CC Secretary for economic affairs at the time, it is likely that Gorbachev's speech on 11 June 1985 reflected Ryzhkov's ideas.

At the 27th Party Congress, Ryzhkov cited Gorbachev's statement that half-measures were not enough and that a radical reform was required, but he stopped short of Gorbachev's proposals on a dozen points. In his big speech to the Supreme Soviet in June 1986, Ryzhkov recovered a lot of reformist ground and went almost as far as Gorbachev. His Lenin anniversary speech on 22 April 1987 had few reformist connotations, but at the Supreme Soviet in June 1987, once again, Ryzhkov almost approached Gorbachev's reformism. In May 1988, he spoke with Gorbachevian candour in favour of reform and cooperatives.

Inside information of Ryzhkov's actions matches this evidence. He chaired *ad hoc* commissions on the Law on State Enterprises and the Law on Cooperatives. The former Law was perceived as a serious set-back for reform, and the latter as an important gain (cf Boris Kurashvili in *Moscow News*, No. 23, 1988). On both occasions Ryzhkov championed the winning cause. Similarly, various evidence suggests that he is a more forceful than consistent decision-maker. In spite of Ryzhkov's transformation, six major differences appear to exist between him and Gorbachev.

First, Ryzhkov avoids attacking the central economic bodies and the basic functions of the economic system. Instead, he admonishes them to improve their work. For instance, Gosplan should 'carry out its activities in correspondence with the new demands, reinforce the complex approach to key tasks and take the full responsibility for a balanced and efficient growth in the economy.' Only certain organisational changes within Gosplan were necessary (*Pravda*, 4 March 1986). In June 1987, Ryzhkov was more critical of Gosplan, but in the end he suggested: 'USSR Gosplan must raise all its balancing to a qualitative new level and increase its role considerably' (*Pravda*, 30 June 1987). Thus, Ryzhkov advocated a greater role for material balancing—the essence of a command economy—while Gorbachev favoured a substantial reduction, or possibly even its abolition.

Second, Ryzhkov shows little enthusiasm for democratisation. At the Party Congress, he mentioned the possibility of establishing enterprise councils, and in April 1987, he pronounced the words 'self-management, electivity, real possibilities of the workers to influence decisions on production and social tasks', but he said little more (*Pravda*, 4 March 1986, 23 April 1987). In June 1987, he went much further, explaining that self-management was a unity of three elements: the active participation of the collective in the making and implementation of all decisions; the election of all managers from foreman up to general director; and the strengthening of one-man management (*yedinonachalie*) in the enterprise. However, one of his justifications for elections of managers was that they 'created a stable base for the strengthening of the authority of the manager, and ... reinforced the principle of one-man management' (*Pravda*, 30 June 1987).

Third, Ryzhkov shows little enthusiasm for the market. At the Party Congress, he avoided Gorbachev's allusions to the market, notwithstanding his mentioning of 'money-commodity relations and the law of value' (*Pravda*, 4 March 1986). A rare reference to NEP was negative: 'Of course, one cannot identify the present perestroika with NEP. That was a policy of the transitionary period from capitalism to socialism' (*Pravda*, 23 April 1987). However, two months later Ryzhkov even took the word 'socialist market' into his mouth: 'The satisfaction of the needs of the socialist market will to a great extent depend on how economic competition between enterprises will be accomplished in practice' (*Pravda*, 30 June 1987). It is difficult to make sense of this turnaround, but the reason might simply be that the problem-solver Ryshkov is not very concerned about ideology.

Fourth, Ryzhkov leaves out a number of economic issues that are presumably distant from his mind. He speaks a lot about problems with quality, but hardly ever of shortages. Until 1988, he barely touched upon private enterprise, cooperatives, and small and medium-sized enterprises and said as little as possible about agriculture and the consumer sector.

Fifth, Ryzhkov is more interested in foreign trade and its reform than Gorbachev. He favours a large foreign trade, particularly in technology. Consequently, he attacks the western technology embargo whenever an opportunity is offered, though he also speaks of the need to improve the efficiency of Soviet foreign trade. He sounds more reformist in this field than on domestic issues. A steady theme of his is the need for joint ventures both with the West and the East (*Ek. gaz.*, No.7, 1986; *Novoe Vremya*, No. 39, 1986). It was he who went public with the Soviet demand for an improvement of the pricing, currency and finance system within the CMEA (*Pravda*, 4 November 1986). He seems to take a keen interest in making the ruble convertible and has reportedly favoured the establishment of free economic zones of the Chinese type.

Sixth, among the top politicians Ryzhkov seems to be least impressed with disciplinary measures. He has said little about the struggle against alcohol and unearned income. He addressed the new quality control after its introduction in this unenthusiastic manner: 'We had to take such a severe step as to adopt the state acceptance' (*Pravda*, 23 April 1987). Whatever the reason, Ryzhkov does not appear to believe in repressive measures, but favours material, professional and moral incentives.

Ryzhkov's basic ideas appear rather clear-cut, but limited. His swift, public transformation on vital ideological issues is confusing. Obviously, Gorbachev is persuading him to go further, but where is Ryzhkov's bottom line? According to a good Soviet inside source, Ryzhkov and Nikolai Talyzin (then Chairman of Gosplan) took issue with Gorbachev over the enterprise law in the Politburo on the turn of 1986, reacting against the circumscription of the powers of the central economic bodies.[12] This information matches the public statements by Ryzhkov and his personal links with Gosplan. However, in December 1987 he is said to have given Talyzin an ultimatum on the reorganisation of Gosplan, which eventually led to Talyzin's removal. As Prime Minister, Ryzhkov has built up a new economic *apparat* at the Council of Ministers, which makes him less dependent on both Gosplan and the CC apparatus.

On the whole, Ryzhkov's economic strategy is both partial and inconsistent. It does not match any of Berliner's models. Its origin is a concern for the development of machine-building, while the adjustments are essentially propelled by Gorbachev. It is difficult to say to what extent Ryzhkov's moves have been motivated by new insights, party discipline or opportunism, but after his speech on 29 June 1987 few differences remain between him and Gorbachev. The last important dividing line is Ryzhkov's commitment to Gosplan, Gossnab and material-balancing—the basis of the command system. This stand is inconsistent with his advocacy of a socialist market, but politicians are entitled to contradictions. The programme Ryzhkov pronounced in 1987 may be described as marketisation with maintained material-balancing or with a minimal reduction of Gosplan's role. Given that Ryzhkov has followed Gorbachev so far already, it would be surprising if he does not follow Gorbachev a bit further. Ryzhkov's effective promotion of the Law on Cooperatives points in that direction.

Nikolai Slyunkov became CC Secretary for economic affairs in January 1987, and full member of the Politburo in June 1987. Beside Prime Minister Ryzhkov, he is the most senior economic politician. It is natural to relate Slyunkov to Ryzhkov. Slyunkov was Deputy Chairman of USSR Gosplan 1974–83, where Ryzhkov was First Deputy Chairman 1979–82. Both were born in 1929 and trained as engineers. Both specialised in heavy machine-building and have spent most of their careers in their respective provinces, though Slyunkov has a broader professional experience including a stint as First Party Secretary of Belorussia from 1983 until January 1987. Ryzhkov and Slyunkov are known to be personal friends, and it is rather obvious that Slyunkov owes his fast promotion primarily to Ryzhkov.

Since Slyunkov enjoyed considerable independence as First Party Secretary of a Soviet Republic, one would assume that his political profile would be easily discernible, but that is hardly true. Slyunkov's speeches are rich in content, but he avoids controversial and ideological issues, while flattering the General Secretary more than most.[13] He neither boasts about Soviet achievements, nor criticises the system sharply. His speeches focus on practical problem-solving within the boundaries offered by the party, and his reasoning is sensible. Slyunkov moves with perestroika, paying respect to all major uncontroversial undertakings, but he does not stick his neck out unnecessarily. The views he expresses appear to depend much more on the situation than on his personality. The more one scrutinises his statements and actions, the more inscrutable he appears. He complies with one stereotype of a senior communist official: the excellent administrator who unquestioningly receives party guide-lines and resolves all issues in an intelligent manner.

Slyunknov was exceptionally successful as First Party Secretary of Belorussia. For years, Belorussia has been praised for its economic achievements. In the stagnation of the first half of the 1980s, the Belorussian NMP grew officially by an annual average of 5.8 per cent (Slyunkov in *Pravda*, 27 February 1986). At the 27th Party Congress, Slyunkov underlined: 'In our republic, economic experiments are carried out in all branches of the economy' (*ibid.*), but at the end of 1984 he did not even mention the ongoing experiments, though he stressed his 'systemic approach'. One of its features was a precise division of functions between party organs, local authorities, economic organs and public organisations (Slyunkov, 1984, pp. 38–9). Party officials were told neither to be drawn into decisions meant for economic officials nor to dwell on petty tutelage of enterprises.

In essence, Slyunkov suggested a rationalisation of the existing control system as in the GDR: since most work was performed during the last days of the month, control should be carried out every tenth day; the analysis of economic results should be comparative; officials of all kinds should try to minimise conferences and paperwork, but improve their contacts with the field as well as their working style; problems should simply be studied and solved pragmatically. Slyunkov appeared to favour a rational corporate organisation, but he avoided specifying what the economic system should look like (Slyunkov, 1984).

At the 27th Party Congress, Slyunkov paid most attention to the construction experiment in Belorussia, which had started in 1982 before Slyunkov returned to Minsk. Its principles were simple: rather than letting the customer pay all costs that occur, a lump sum was agreed from the outset. If actual costs were lower than the negotiated price, half of the savings went to bonuses for all parties involved, encouraging builders to complete projects faster and cut costs. The results were excellent. Construction periods were cut by one third; the number of unfinished construction projects was reduced; costs were cut by 5 per cent (*Pravda*, 27 February 1986; *Sots. ind.*, 14 August 1985; *Ek. gaz.*, No.35, 1986, p. 14). Still, this experiment implied a minimal systemic change, and the inspiration appears to have come from the GDR.

The Belorussian railway experiment was also acclaimed but it was just a variant of the old Shchekino experiment. Slyunkov organised a large-scale certification of work places in order to free superfluous labour and enhance shift-work, which was a purely administrative measure. A Belorussian ministry was among the first five ministries to launch the large-scale economic experiment in industry in 1984, but that experiment was of little economic significance. Slyunkov spoke of 'the acceleration of scientific-technical progress', and he pushed for a massive retooling in Belorussia (*Pravda*, 25 November 1986), though he appears more interested in administration than technology. It should also be pointed out that the authorities in Minsk have regulated the prices at its *kolkhoz* market.[14] The many Belorussian economic experiments were aimed at rationalisation and modernisation of the economic system, not at economic reform.

Slyunkov did not rejoice over the accomplishments in his republic, but stated in late 1986: 'The results have essentially been achieved through the strengthening of labour, state and plan discipline and the introduction of order, that is through reserves which, so to say, lie on the surface.' He spoke in favour of individual house construction, individual labour activity and small cooperatives, though he also supported the struggle against unearned income (*Pravda*, 25 November 1986).

Until June 1987, Slyunkov hardly pronounced the word reform in public, but it was he who presented the guide-lines for economic reform on 8 June 1987, and Soviet reform economists claim that he speeded up the work on reform, when he became CC Secretary for economic affairs in January 1987. The abbreviated published version of his speech contained most of the essential features of the reform that Gorbachev elaborated two weeks later, though his vocabulary was less reformist. Unlike Ryzhkov, he did not state that Gosplan should continue compiling material balances. Two omitted features are worth noticing. First, Slyunkov did not mention the market or any of its euphemisms, although his proposals sounded as market-oriented as Gorbachev's. Second, in his speech on 8 June Slyunkov avoided all talk of democratisation, though he spoke of 'broad self-management' (*Pravda*, 13 June 1987). He had mentioned democratisation, without elaboration, before (*Pravda*, 25 November 1986), and as early as July 1987, more than 2,200 managers of various ranks had been elected in his old Belorussia (*Pravda*, 30 July 1987). During a trip to Estonia in May 1988, he praised Estonia as a 'bold experimenter', suggesting a commitment to the radical reforms conceived there (*Pravda*, 28 May 1988). Reformers tend to pass positive, but imprecise, judgements on Slyunkov.

Slyunkov seems an unusually shrewd politician. In his public appearances, he reveals a minimum of his own preferences, making it difficult to predict what his future course will be. Nor can he be criticised for anything. He appears to have a rather realistic view of the Soviet economy and bothers little about ideology. With his speech on 8 June 1987, he committed himself to radical economic reform in the spirit of Gorbachev. At the same time, nothing suggests that he would take unnecessary political risks to further reform. Nine years in the service of Gosplan cannot have passed without trace, but Slyunkov does not reveal any lingering sentiments. His closest personal connections are with Ryzhkov, but his rapid promotions are likely to have been supported by Gorbachev as well. Gorbachev made Minsk the target of his third journey in the country after having become General Secretary and praised Slyunkov and Belorussia highly (*Pravda*, 12 July 1985). A reasonable guess would be that Ryzhkov and Slyunkov might act more or less in unison, though for slightly different reasons. Ryzhkov wants to safeguard some role for Gosplan, while Slyunkov hopes to avoid risks.

Yuri Maslyukov, the Chairman of Gosplan, First Deputy Prime Minister and candidate member of the Politburo since February 1988, appears to have connections with Ryzhkov and Slyunkov. Maslyukov took over as First Deputy Chairman of Gosplan after Ryzhkov and worked there together with Slyunkov. Maslyukov has risen fast in the secluded military-industrial complex. He appears to be an able technocrat, but little is known of his views.

Maslyukov's predecessor, **Nikolai Talyzin** had a similar background. As Permanent Representative to the CMEA, 1980–5, Talyzin must have had frequent contact with the CC Secretary for economic affairs, who was Nikolai Ryzhkov from November 1982, and the two men are considered closely connected. Talyzin's soft fall in early 1988 was reportedly caused by his stubborn refusal to reorganise Gosplan and his apparent incompetence— widely lamented by Soviet economists. His presentation of the annual plan for 1988 revealed that barely any reform was under way (*Pravda*, 20 October 1987). Ryzhkov is supposed to have found himself forced to remove Talyzin.

ZAIKOV: TECHNOCRATIC RATIONALISATION

A third programme is also supported by engineers and pronounced technocrats with a background in military industry, but this group favours a technocratic rationalisation of the existing system as in the GDR, without envisaging any marketisation. Its chief advocates are Lev Zaikov and Yuri Solovyev, who have both spent most of their careers in Leningrad.

Lev Zaikov represents Leningrad and the military-industrial complex in the Soviet leadership. He replaced Gorbachev's rival Grigori Romanov as CC Secretary for the military-industrial complex in July 1985, and in March 1986 he was elevated to full member of the Politburo. In addition, he supervised economic reform issues in the CC Secretariat from October 1985 until January 1987, when Slyunkov took over this responsibility. Since November 1987, he has also been First Party Secretary of Moscow City.

Zaikov has a background similar to that of Ryzhkov or Slyunkov. Until 1985, he lived in Leningrad, where he advanced in the armaments industry from worker and engineer to director of a large enterprise. In 1976, he became a politician, and in 1983 he replaced Romanov as First Party Secretary in Leningrad *oblast*. It has been assumed that he is a client of Gorbachev, because he was not among the most senior Leningrad politicians, and he was installed by Gorbachev and not Romanov. This hypothesis was reinforced when Gorbachev praised Zaikov on a visit to Leningrad in May 1985, after which Zaikov was quickly promoted. However, Yuri Solovyev, who replaced him in Leningrad had been Romanov's deputy; no purge of Romanov's *apparat* seems to have taken place; Zaikov's political outlook is reminiscent of Romanov's and very different from Gorbachev's.[15]

It is easy to see what Zaikov stands for. He is outspoken and has made a large number of published speeches, which are highly repetitive.[16] Few have proven so consistent, or rigid, during these turbulent years. Zaikov emphasises military and patriotic themes, such as the October revolution, the great patriotic war, defence, and 'the greatness and glory of our Motherland'. He advocates 'a strengthening of the position of the states of the socialist community in the international arena' (*Pravda*, 28 June 1986). Like Ligachev, he often speaks of environmental issues cherished by Russophiles. In Ulyanovsk, he even started a speech in a highly Russophile language: 'There are holy places in Russia' (*Pravda*, 14 February 1987).

Engineering seems to have formed his frame of mind. He speaks in technical terms, as if unaware of economics. From 1983 to 1985, Leningrad developed a territorial complex programme called 'Intensification–90' under Zaikov's stewardship. It is a diverse package of measures (Zaikov, 1984), which Zaikov incessantly refers to and has promoted at union level. By promoting a regional complex programme, Zaikov proved his belief in territorial integration. He has repeatedly complained about departmental barriers and shows little understanding for branch ministries. Even more than Ryzhkov, Zaikov underlines the importance of machine-building and the acceleration of scientific-technical progress.

One of his Leningrad measures was to combine research and development with production in GDR-like associations. Another method was a salary reform, offering higher salaries and bonuses to successful directors and engineers, while increasing income differentials. A third means was simply to certify machinery and workplaces administratively for the sake of rationalisation. Zaikov believed that youngsters could be tied to one enterprise, if they received their final vocational training there. Scarce labour should be concentrated to the most efficient machinery in two or three shifts. Fourthly, Leningrad pioneered the practice of independent quality inspection in civilian industry. Finally, 'Intensification–90' implied an extraordinary belief in minute command planning at regional level. In line with Zaikov's moralistic patriotism, he advocates discipline and order. He even proposed a regional complex programme on 'Organisation of the free time of the youth' (Zaikov, 1984; cf Gendler and Ovchinnikova, 1987; *Izvestiya*, 30 June 1985; *Ek. gaz.*, No. 50, 1986).

Like Ryzhkov, Zaikov appears to have taken to heart the CC conference on the acceleration of scientific-technical progress in June 1985, with its stress on engineering, computerisation, robotisation, electronification, automation and a new investment policy favouring machine-building. The haste and energetic tone fitted Zaikov's style. 'Perestroika of the economic mechanism' is reflected in his speeches without elaboration (*Pravda*, 29 April, 28 June, 9 August 1986).

Since Zaikov held the responsibility for economic reform within the CC Secretariat in 1986, it is of particular interest to see which issues he brought to the fore then. The most striking observation is that Zaikov never pronounced the word 'economic reform' in public. Four measures were legislated that Zaikov had advocated and tried out in Leningrad: namely a complex programme for the development of machine-building, an independent quality inspection, a new wage system and the promotion of shiftwork. All may be described as technocratic and administrative. Zaikov entertained high hopes for the development of technology and quality:

The output of high-quality products grows so that in 1991–1993, [we can] go over completely to the production of machines, instruments and equipment that correspond to the highest world achievements...This task is revolutionary without parallel...the most important economic and political task is to produce 80–95 per cent machine-building products towards the end of this five-year plan that correspond to the world level (*Pravda*, 9 August 1986).

These goals are just impossible. Even according to an exaggerated official estimate, not more than one fifth of Soviet machine-building production corresponded to international standards. Zaikov himself set the plan target for 1987 at 38 per cent (*Sots. ind.*, 12 November 1986). These targets are reflected in speeches by several other senior politicians, but Zaikov repeats them like a believer (*Pravda*, 28 June, 9 August, 30 October 1986; *Sots. ind.*, 12 November 1986). In a traditional Soviet manner, Zaikov is fascinated by the target itself and seems to forget about how to reach it.

Very little of Gorbachev's economic reform programme from the 27th Party Congress has been reflected in Zaikov's speeches. Only at the end of October 1986 did Zaikov refer to economic accountability and self-financing (*Pravda*, 30 October 1986; *Sots. ind.*, 12 November 1986). He spoke up in favour of perestroika of Gosplan and branch ministries, with which he had little connection. He started mentioning the draft law on socialist enterprises without saying much about it. One issue appealed to him: competition between institutes and constructors, which already existed within the military-industrial complex (*Pravda*, 26 April 1987). Considering that Zaikov had worked his way up as an enterprise manager, it is mysterious that he has shown minimal interest in the improvement of enterprise management. He barely used economic concepts, such as prices, profits, competition, markets or shortages, but Zaikov refrained from dogmatic economic statements. In fact, he appears free from economic thinking altogether and was therefore unsuitable for the supervision of economic reform. Zaikov has stayed on the sidelines, repeating his old views. Willingly or not, he seems to have impeded reform in 1986.

However, like Ryzhkov, Zaikov showed great interest in reform of the foreign trade system. In particular, he encouraged socialist integration and joint ventures with socialist countries (*Pravda*, 9 August 1986). He lauded the reform of foreign trade in 1986, and numerous of his favourite enterprises in Leningrad were given foreign trade rights in 1987 (*Pravda*, 30 October 1986). Presumably, both Ryzhkov and Zaikov based their enthusiasm for reform of the foreign trade system on their experiences of military machine-building.

Given Zaikov's authoritarian and traditional outlook, it is somewhat surprising to find that he expressed support for Gorbachev's drive towards democratisation and self-government at an early stage (*Pravda*, 30 October 1986). In his first public speech after the CC Plenum in January 1987, he came out in support of elections of enterprise leaders with multiple candidates (*Pravda*, 14 February and 28 November 1987). The explanation may be that elections reinforced the power of regional party committees (which nominated candidates) at the expense of branch ministries.

Zaikov's successor as First Party Secretary in Leningrad *oblast*, **Yuri Solovyev**, was elected candidate member of the Politburo in March 1986. He is also an engineer, who has lived nearly his whole life in Leningrad. His speeches arouse the suspicion that he and Zaikov share a speech-writer, though Solovyev has shown a certain interest in small and medium-sized enterprises and has promoted individual labour activity to a degree in Leningrad (*Pravda*, 28 February, 23 October 1986; Solovyev, 1986).

It is natural to treat these two top politicians as one separate group, although they have much in common with Ryzhkov and Slyunkov. Together these two groups form a political centre. Both comprise technocrats and engineers, preoccupied with machine-building. They have set out with a programme reminiscent of the GDR. However, Ryzhkov and Slyunkov have gone further, embracing considerable marketisation, while neither Zaikov nor Solovyev show any appreciation of the market, nor developed a comprehensive economic programme. On the other hand, they do not care much about Gosplan or branch ministries, but want to reinforce the economic powers of the regional administration. Zaikov and Solovyev represent Leningrad and the military, Romanov's constituency, and they reflect Romanov's programme. Although Ryzhkov and Slyunkov also have been involved in military machine-building they do not support military interests—including Russophile and patriotic themes—which Zaikov and Solovyev do.

This programme is not likely to be very effective, but, apart from the support for democratisation, it appears quite consistent. It implies energetic modernisation, rationalisation and streamlining, but no marketisation. It does not correspond to any of Berliner's categories. It is closest to his neo-Stalinist model, but it seems too soft and technocratic. It is more similar to the GDR system. The Leningraders appear to have been directly inspired by the GDR, a country with which the large military-industrial sector of Leningrad has many links.

Since Zaikov and Solovyev are the only civilian top politicians who incessantly refer to the interests of the military, we may surmise military support for their programme. In an article in *Pravda* (2 October 1985) Academician V. Trapeznikov proposed the special practices of the Soviet armaments industry for the rest of the economy, and he came very close to Zaikov's programme. However, an analysis of the economic views of the military élite falls beyond the scope of this study.

LIGACHEV: SOCIALIST MORALITY

Berliner's reactionary programme also has supporters in the Soviet leadership, the most obvious one is **Yegor Ligachev**, CC Secretary since December 1983 and Politburo member since April 1985. Born in 1920, Yegor Ligachev is the oldest of the new Soviet leaders. From April 1985 until September 1988, he was Second Secretary—the most powerful politician after Gorbachev—chairing the CC Secretariat (*Le Monde*, 4 December 1987). Since September 1988 his responsibilities have been limited to agriculture.

Although trained as an engineer, Ligachev is the ultimate party official. He has spent most of his career in Siberia, in Novosibirsk (1944–61) and Tomsk (1965–83). His characterisation of Siberians is presumably also a self-portrait: 'Under difficult conditions real communists were forged here, people with strong character and high moral purity' (*Pravda*, 27 August 1987). Thus, he romanticises one of the most backward and isolated parts of the Soviet Union (cf *Pravda*, 2 July 1988).

In Tomsk, Ligachev acquired a certain popularity as a strong-handed and dynamic regional leader.[17] Soon after he became the First Party Secretary of Tomsk *oblast*, he launched an anti-alcohol campaign, trying to convince people to drink wine rather than vodka. He maintained low regulated maximum prices at the *kolkhoz* market, hindering the few Kazakhs who came to Tomsk to make excessive profits at the expense of local Russians. He personally engaged in the struggle against all kinds of unofficial economic activities.

Ligachev stands out as a skilful, cunning politician. His many speeches abound with interesting content, but it is not obvious how to interpret them. A number of recurring themes appear to represent his basic programme, but the variations are considerable. His most controversial views have been spelt out, when he has seemed particularly strong, or when Gorbachev has been on holiday. As a good tactician, Ligachev adopts some ideas introduced by other politicians. On occasions, he mentions an issue in passing once or twice—often at an early stage—as if he does not want to fight over them. His statements abroad are invariably far more liberal than domestic ones. He seems to put up Potemkin villages for foreign consumption. However, back in the Soviet Union, he pursues a more authentic line.[18]

Ligachev tends to diffuse Gorbachev's terms by altering them slightly. For instance, Ligachev avoids Gorbachev's key term 'perestroika of the economic mechanism'. Instead he speaks conservatively of the 'perfection of the economic mechanism', 'perestroika of management (*upravlenie*)' and of investment structure as well as perestroika in general (Ligachev, 1985a). Once he used the phrase 'reconstruction of the economic mechanism' (*Pravda*, 7 November 1986). Later, he began speaking of 'the new economic mechanism' as if it already existed (*Pravda*, 19 November 1987). A reformist term goes 'transition to full economic accounting' but Ligachev twisted it to 'full transition to economic accounting' (*Pravda*, 22 May 1986), which can mean anything. Similarly, Ligachev has an inclination to cite Gorbachev's most conservative statements, even distorting them a bit.[19] Another common Soviet trick is to hijack a reformist term and redefine it in a more conservative way. Obviously, Ligachev has a political purpose for all these plays with words, and all his alterations point in one direction. Besides, like Gorbachev, Ligachev seems to enjoy surprising and confusing people. He is never grey or boring. With all this on our mind, we shall try to extract Ligachev's actual programme.[20]

The principal theme in Ligachev's programme may be labelled 'socialist morality'. He uses terms like 'norms of socialist morals' himself (Ligachev, 1985b, p. 92). He wants in 'every conceivable way to confirm the authority of honest and conscientious labour'. Consumerism is the main evil, and Ligachev calls for 'preparedness for a struggle with bourgeois influences alien to our ideology and morals' (Ligachev, 1985b, pp. 85–6). In one question, Ligachev has synthesised many of his aims: 'What impedes the moral sanitation of society, the overcoming of bureaucracy, wage levelling and the affirmation of a sober way of life?' (*Pravda,* 17 September 1987).

This moralism is intertwined with vivid anti-western sentiments. Ligachev has attacked western morals and ideology in many speechs and his tone is rabid. He seems fascinated by the competition between the Soviet Union and the West, between socialism and capitalism, between collectivism and individualism, and he intermingles these themes.

Bourgeois ideologies of all colours slander the Soviet system and spread distorted notions of the situation of the individual under socialism ... The class purpose of this campaign is obvious. It is ... to diminish the attractive force of socialism (*Pravda*, 2 February 1985).

The class and ideological enemy harbours hopes, that perestroika will weaken the influence of Marxist-Leninist ideology. That is, of course, a completely groundless day-dream (*Pravda*, 3 June 1987).

... among the class enemies, there are those who praise us for perestroika and give it a distorted meaning that is comfortable for them, [they] nurture hopes for the Soviet Union's departure from socialism in the direction of market economy, ideological pluralism and western democracy. Vain hopes. We shall never leave the Leninist road and [we] shall never give up the achievements of socialism (*Pravda*, 27 August 1987).

At the same time, Ligachev realises that perestroika may increase the international stature of his country: 'The processes that are developing in the USSR have an enormous international importance and reinforce the attraction of real socialism to the world.' Ligachev has repeatedly lashed out against any kind of market economy and private enterprise:

The changes in the economic sphere outlined at the [CC] conference [on scientific-technical progress in June 1985] will take place within the framework of scientific socialism, without any aberrations whatsoever in the direction of 'market economy' and private enterprise *(Pravda*, 29 June 1985).

It must be said with all determination: the process of the perfection of our economy occurs and will occur within the framework of socialism. We shall utilise the advantages of the socialist system. There is no talk and [there] will be no talk of a market economy, which always and everywhere brings with it social injustice and social inequality. We need as much socialism as possible, a maximum of socialism (Ligachev, 1986, p. 3; cf *Pravda*, 6 August 1988).

Obviously, these attacks are also designed to castigate domestic liberals, to whom he sometimes vaguely refers. Among the members of the Politburo, only Viktor Chebrikov uses such strong ideological language.

Despite Ligachev's abusive verbage, he reveals little ideological depth, never proceeding beyond slogans. Ligachev's anti-western moralism could equally be called Russophile, and he is preoccupied with Russophile themes. More frequently than any other leader, Ligachev uses the words Motherland and Fatherland. He has spoken in defence of 'national sanctuaries' and dwelt on environmental issues dear to Russophiles (*Pravda*, 28 February 1986). He advocates interchange of personnel and labour between various republics, which would reinforce Russification (*Pravda*, 7 November 1986, 3–4 June 1987). His criticism of Central Asian communists is scurrilous (e.g. Ligachev, 1985a, pp. 17–18). An extreme example of Ligachev's Russophile rhetoric is 'In ancient times, [the town of Voronezh] was a shield, guarding *Rus* from forays by enemies, a reliable custodian of the southern borders of the Muscovy state' (*Pravda*, 10 July 1986).

Ligachev's brand of Russian nationalism does not appear militaristic. He rarely mentions defence and prefers the unambitious term 'reliable' defence, while defence advocates, such as Zaikov, advocate a reinforcement of defence. Ligachev's anti-western rhetoric is aggressive, but it is also isolationist and focuses on ideological competition. Ligachev courts Russophile culture personalities with attacks against 'western so-called mass culture' and rock-music which he labels 'primitive' (*Pravda*, 2 October 1986, 27 August 1987).

As one would guess, Ligachev takes a negative view of foreign trade. He has emphasised the excellence of Soviet technology and lamented that purchases of foreign technology force the Soviet Union to lag behind (Ligachev, 1985b, p. 80, 1986, p. 4). Such statements indicate both his noninterest in technology and ignorance of the level of foreign technology. After a few trips abroad, Ligachev seems to have moderated his views: 'At present the output of video-recorders comprises millions in the West, but thousands here. Moreover, our market is enormous' (*Pravda*, 23 May 1987).

Ligachev's frame of mind has obviously been formed by his long tenure as a senior party official. Besides, he favours all proposals that maximise his personal power. At the top, he has underlined collective leadership (*Pravda*, 29 June 1985, 28 February 1986), as is commonplace for a Second Secretary who has disagreements with the General Secretary. For the rest, he has advocated a strongly centralised party leadership. 'Of course, the basic part of the work on perestroika of management will be carried out in a centralised manner' (Ligachev, 1985a, p. 14). He has underlined that all ministries and regional party organisations 'must be within the zone of criticism and open to party criticism' (*Pravda*, 28 February 1986); 'not one party organisation, not one worker can stay outside control' (*Pravda*, 2 June 1985). But it is evident that the control should be directed from above. Before Gorbachev suggested real elections within the party, Ligachev proposed on the contrary that secret ballots should be abandoned in party elections, with the obvious purpose of reinforcing centralised control:

Now all questions, apart from elections, are decided in party organisations by a show of hands. As you can imagine, conditions are developing in the party to gradually introduce votes by a show of hands also in elections. It will facilitate the confirmation of openness and adherence to principles among communists (Ligachev, 1985b, p. 83).

To Ligachev, personnel policy is the key to everything: 'A successful realisation of all our plans depends directly on the selection, placement and training of the leading cadres' (*Pravda*, 29 June 1985); 'in order to ascertain apt progress in all matters, it is necessary to pursue a hard cadre policy based on principles' (*Pravda*, 2 June 1985). His personnel policy aims at more integration of the regions under the supervision of the CC Secretariat.

He shows surprisingly little interest in organisational changes. In general, he wants to strengthen the centre and enterprises. 'While reinforcing the actual centralised leadership of the economy, the party will ensure a growing role for the basic production link, that is associations and enterprises' (Ligachev, 1985b, p. 90). He does not mind a weakening of regional bodies: 'In the republican, *krai* and *oblast*, organs among enterprises and associations, there are many superfluous links, which without harm to the cause could be merged or relinquished' (Ligachev, 1985a, p. 14). At the lower level, Ligachev has approved of the formation of various kinds of more integrated associations in industry and agriculture and has even encouraged initiative from below to accomplish this (Ligachev, 1985a, p. 90). At the same time, Ligachev approves of rationalisation trimming the administration, but his own power comes first.

Considering Ligachev's values, it is natural that his main approach to economics is to preach discipline and order in virtually every speech. One formulation of his credo is: 'A necessary condition for the acceleration of our movement forwards is the affirmation of conscientious discipline, socialist order and a high degree of organisation in all spheres of social life' (*Pravda*, 2 June 1985). He wants to continue the discipline campaign launched by Andropov in 1983.

In one word, the intention is to carry out an energetic, purposeful attack on indifference and passivity, laxity, irresponsibility, wastefulness, to assert the authority of honest, conscientious labour in every possible way and persistently introduce intensive economic methods (Ligachev, 1985a, p. 11).

Indefatigably, Ligachev calls for 'a consequent, uncompromising struggle against bribery, embezzlement of socialist property, parasitism and favouritism—in short, against everything that contradicts the labour nature of our socialist way of life and the principle of social justice' (*Pravda*, 2 June 1985).

Ligachev's preoccupation with discipline and order may be explained by his belief that the system is good but poorly run. He has a rosier picture of Soviet economic achievements than the other new leaders. Repeatedly, he has limited the period of shortcomings to the end of the 1970s and the early 1980s, and he has even lauded Soviet economic achievements in the 1960s and 1970s (*Pravda*, 6 March, 27 August 1987). While Ligachev is plainly upset by the moral crisis, he does not seem to perceive any economic crisis. Reformers focus on the system, but Ligachev turns his eyes on the human factor and available reserves:

Practice shows that palpable economic results can be attained comparatively quickly, if organisational-economic and social reserves are activated. And here it is especially important to activate the human factor, to have everyone working conscientiously at his place of work at full capacity (Ligachev, 1985a, p. 11).

Ligachev discusses most problems in terms of discipline. Plan discipline is naturally prominent. He favours high plan targets. Resource-saving is perceived as a major disciplinary matter, and Ligachev is particularly upset by the wasting of working hours. Even technological discipline has its place in Ligachev's statements (Ligachev, 1985a, pp.10–12). He has promoted the linkage between bonuses and the fulfillment of contracts (*Pravda*, 7 November 1986). As one would expect, education and training are particular pet topics of this moralist.

Like other new leaders, Ligachev favours greater income differentials and payment in proportion to achievement, but he makes a conservative reservation because of his concern for political stability: 'It is necessary to keep in mind that the political stability of Soviet society and the progress of our country in many [fields] are determined by a correct social policy of the party' (*Pravda*, 28 February 1986).

In practice, Ligachev's drive for discipline and order has resulted in three principal measures: the ousting and prosecution of a large number of senior officials for economic crimes or ineffectiveness; stern measures against alcohol and drinking; and the struggle with 'unearned income' enacted in May 1986. These three themes have been reflected in most of Ligachev's speeches. For the rest, Ligachev does not appear to have initiated any economic policies, leaving him with a poor record of innovations. Instead, he has reacted to proposals by his colleagues, which he does with tactical cunning in a not very predictable manner.

Beside Gorbachev, Ligachev has been the main actor on the political stage.

In the spring of 1985, they were allies, but Ligachev made only one speech that was reasonably close to Gorbachev's line (*Pravda*, 2 June 1985). Soon, Ligachev took exception to Gorbachev's programme. He did so emphatically in his speech on 28 June 1985 (*Pravda*, 29 June 1985) in reaction to the CC conference on the acceleration of scientific-technical progress on 11–12 June 1985, which Ryzhkov and Zaikov have taken to their hearts. For the first time, Ligachev stressed the principle of collective leadership and delivered a diatribe against market economy and private enterprise. He even rephrased a key paragraph of Gorbachev's speech that pointed towards economic reform. Gorbachev's statement read [emphasis added to highlight differences]:

We should go along the line of further strengthening and development of *democratic socialism. An increase of the efficiency of the centralised principles of management* and planning, a *considerable* extension of the economic independence and responsibility of enterprises and associations, *the active utilisation of more flexible forms and methods of steering*, of economic accounting and money-commodity relations, of *a whole arsenal of economic levers and incentives* (Gorbachev, 1985, pp. 22–3).

Ligachev reformulated this passage:

The CC conference confirmed once again that our road goes via *all conceivable*, strengthening of the *centralised* planning with the simultaneous extension of the independence of enterprises and an increase in their responsibility through the development of economic accounting and the utilisation of money-commodity relations *corresponding to the socialist mode of production* (*Pravda*, 29 June 1985).

The first important difference concerned the view of planning. Gorbachev wanted to raise its efficiency, while Ligachev called for its reinforcement. Gorbachev wanted to develop democratic socialism, which Ligachev ignored. Ligachev omitted Gorbachev's liberal words on enterprise management. Probably for tactical reasons, Ligachev accepted the notion of money-commodity relations, but he negated it by adding 'corresponding to the socialist mode of production'. In other words, Ligachev opposed any economic reform involving marketisation or the diminution of central planning, and he went public with his opposition to Gorbachev's ideas of market-oriented reform. The most plausible explanation for Gorbachev's evasion of all reformist allusions during the next eight months is Ligachev's resistance.

Ligachev appears to have developed his stand on enterprise management gradually, without devoting much attention to the topic. His own favourite project reinforced the emphasis on contract fulfillment (*Pravda*, 30 August, 7 November 1986). He embraced the large-scale economic experiment in industry and had long approved of collective contracts with economic accounting (Ligachev, 1985a, p. 15). In November 1985, as the first senior politician, Ligachev came out publicly in support of the Sumy self-financing experiment (Ligachev, 1985b, p. 90). It might be explained in tactical terms. Ligachev recognised this experiment would be expanded and preferred not to fight over it. He has certainly not pushed for self-financing.[21] Still, Ligachev appears tolerant of attempts at the extension of enterprise autonomy.

The differences in the leadership became more obvious at the 27th Party Congress. In an attack on *Pravda*, Ligachev implicitly castigated the newspaper for having published an article against the privileges of party officials, and thus moderated his own stand on social justice. He refrained from pronouncing the word economic reform or adopting Gorbachev's reform ideas, though he avoided a polemic over these issues, and later in 1986 he adopted parts of Gorbachev's terminology in one speech (*Pravda*, 7 November 1986).

Gorbachev pushed for agricultural reform at the Party Congress and it was legislated soon afterwards. In opening a CC conference on this decree, Ligachev stated: 'This important political party document has been worked out on the initiative of and through direct participation of comrade M.S. Gorbachev' (*Pravda*, 6 April 1986). This was undoubtedly the case, but Ligachev avoided expressing his support for the reform. He has repeatedly spoken on agriculture, but he continues to say as little as possible in favour of reform measures, without speaking openly against them. Exceptionally, Ligachev has referred to family contract, but not to family farms or family leasehold (Ligachev, 1987, p. 34). Once he referred to tax in kind and to NEP in an agricultural context, but he has not endorsed the fixed delivery targets, which are the essence of the agricultural reform. He has mentioned private plots a couple of times, but without much approval (*Pravda,* 19 November 1987). *Kolkhoz* markets appear to be absent from his speeches, as well as all discussion of the vital principles of pricing. It is obvious that Ligachev obstructs agricultural reform, but he does not profess any alternative.

One would have assumed that Ligachev would approve of the state quality inspection launched on a large scale in 1987, since it is both an administrative and disciplinary measure, but he appears disinterested. Possibly it is his general disregard for machine-building that averts his interest. He has shown a similar lukewarm attitude to the extension of shiftwork and the Belorussian railway experiment (*Pravda,* 6 March 1987).

Gorbachev stepped up his political rhetoric from the summer of 1986 with words such as 'revolutionary changes', 'democratisation' and 'self-government'. Ligachev accepted the new terms, sometimes with the addition of a weakening attribute such as 'further' or 'socialist'. To attack 'dogmatism' suited him (*Pravda*, 2 October, 7 November 1986). Even 'developing socialism' has been incorporated in Ligachev's vocabulary (*Pravda*, 27 August, 19 November 1987). However, the crunch came at the CC Plenum in January 1987. Gorbachev's concept of democratisation, with secret ballots and multiple candidates, contradicted Ligachev's interest in creating a maximum of centralised control. In an article written immediately afterwards, Ligachev referred to 'the electivity of leaders of work collectives', after which he launched an attack on 'our enemies in the capitalist world', asserting: 'Deep perestroika does not at all mean the destruction of our political system. On the contrary, the issue is to strengthen and develop this system' (Ligachev, 1987, p. 29). Since then, Ligachev has omitted the word 'electivity'. His enthusiasm for the Law on State Enterprises appeared equally muted (Ligachev, 1987, p. 38).

In spite of Ligachev's frivolous liberal gags, there can be little doubt as to where his heart rests. The main planks of his programme comply with Berliner's reactionary model, although Ligachev shows no inclination to praise Stalin (see *Pravda*, 2 July 1988). His brand of reaction is more Russophile than Marxist-Leninist or militaristic. Ligachev's economic programme is simplistic, and his original programme for economic revitalisation appears singularly ineffective, but he is politically astute. He has a habit of opening doors in unexpected fields. Soviet intellectuals are aware of the danger of authoritarian reaction. One young reformer has warned against 'the danger of a false overcoming of bureaucracy in the form of restoration of elements of an autocratic style.' This 'pseudo-alternative can be identified as an image of a stern individual leader, who himself delves into all and himself decides all questions' (Obolonski, 1987, p. 60; cf Nuikin, 1988a).

THE CONSERVATIVE PROGRAMME: A MINIMUM OF CHANGE

All the new Soviet leaders want change, but they find it difficult to agree on what kind of change. It was much easier for Leonid Brezhnev and his allies, who desired a minimum of change, leaving them with few and not very significant choices. Berliner's conservative model is directly applicable to the last Brezhnevites on the Politburo: full members Geidar Aliev, Viktor Grishin, Dimukhamed Kunaev, Vladimir Shcherbitski and Nikolai Tikhonov, and candidate members Vladimir Dolgikh and Petr Demichev. Of these, only Shcherbitski remains in the leadership. We shall only discuss Shcherbitski and Dolgikh. Surprisingly, the economic programme of one of the new rising stars, Viktor Nikonov, Politburo and CC Secretary for agriculture, conforms with the conservative programme.

A conservative approach does not exclude alterations, but promotes change in order to preserve. Because of the reformist pressure, conservatives are forced to simulate change, to accept parts of the reforms and introduce relatively harmless innovations. They are identifiable by their reluctance to support all programmes of economic revitalisation. The speeches by conservatives are mostly tedious, since they have little purpose. They tend to discuss details, production targets and plan fulfillment, as they take the system for granted. After the party has adopted a reform proposal, they repeat some of the changes, but preferably belatedly, partially and in unclear terms. The present reformist propaganda depicts the conservatives as corrupt and incompetent. It is true of some, but not of all, and the new leaders are not necessarily more competent than some old ones.

As First Party Secretary of the Ukraine since 1972, and full Politburo member since 1971, **Vladimir Shcherbitski** (born in 1918) is a seasoned and astute politician. He evades commitment to reform, giving an overwhelming priority to the preservation of his own power, but he manages the Ukranian economy comparatively well. Anyone travelling from the RSFSR to the Ukraine cannot help but notice that he enters a wealthier and better-run republic. The degree of public criticism against the performance of the Ukrainian economy does not appear justified, as long as the more backward RSFSR economy receives much less criticism. The issue is obviously political: to oust Shcherbitski, but he has not panicked.

He has chosen selectively among the new measures. The large-scale economic experiment in industry, launched in 1984, involved the Ukrainian Ministry of Food Industry, which went particularly far towards enterprise autonomy.[22] The Ukraine has pioneered new ways of integrating research and development into production and the utilisation of waste, drawing on GDR and Czech experience. Naturally, Shcherbitski has welcomed the reinforcement of the powers of the republican economic administration. He has encouraged the merger of enterprises into associations, preferably all-Ukrainian associations (*Pravda*, 28 December 1987).

Since he has been under attack from the centre, he has minimised glasnost and even prohibited the circulation of critical central publications in the Ukraine. However, he gladly accepted elections of enterprise directors, in effect empowering the Ukrainian party organisation to control the appointment of directors without much interference from Moscow-based ministers. When necessary, he emulates a bit of the reform vocabulary, but with apparent restraint (see *Pravda Ukrainy*, 26 December 1987). At the 27th Party Congress, Shcherbitski distanced himself from Gorbachev's proposals for economic reform like this: 'In the speech [by Gorbachev it] was justly pointed out, that socialist society and its planned economy possess enormous advantages and opportunities that are far from fully utilised' (*Pravda*, 27 February 1986).

Vladimir Dolgikh stands out as an excellent manager of a traditional Soviet type. He rose as a successful engineer and enterprise director in Krasnoyarsk *krai*, Konstantin Chernenko's domicile, and he was considered a likely future Prime Minister. As CC Secretary from 1972 until 1988, he presided over the stagnation of raw material production, but that was almost inevitable because of rising costs. When acute crisis erupted, for instance when oil production fell in 1985, Dolgikh came out in front, sacked managers on a large scale, mobilised massive investments, and managed to turn the decline in the production, but at a high cost. Thus, Dolgikh is a hard-fisted trouble-shooter. His speeches have typically been devoted to acute problems in production. He has scolded the responsible officials in no uncertain terms, but avoided commenting on the economic system (*Pravda*, 13 March, 28 May 1987). The extraction of raw materials is generally perceived as the least complex branch of the economy, with a limited need for reform. However, the new investment policy is directed against Dolgikh's branches, and the surge of energy investment in 1985–6 ran counter to the new policy.

Viktor Nikonov is no obvious member of any camp. By training an agronomist, he has occupied a variety of party and government posts in the Urals, Krasnoyarsk and Moscow. Since he succeeded Gorbachev as CC Secretary for agriculture (in April 1985) and was in contact with Gorbachev in his preceding agricultural posts, it has been widely assumed that he was chosen by Gorbachev. However, their connection is tenuous. The Chairman of Gosagroprom, Vsevolod Murakhovski, long worked with Gorbachev in Stavropol. It is he, not Nikonov, who has advocated agricultural reform. The differences between Nikonov and Murakhovski have been striking after the adoption of agricultural reform. At the CC Conference introducing the new legislation, Ligachev seemed indifferent, while Murakhovski warmly praised the reform measures. Finally, Nikonov talked about personnel and avoided any endorsement of the decree (*Pravda,* 6 April 1986). Nikonov has continued in that manner, talking about production plans and results, technology and investment. All the old platitudes surface in his speeches, which virtually lack economic thinking (*Pravda,* 8 May, 27 July 1986, 4 February 1987).

In an article in the journal *Kommunist* in March 1987, Nikonov (1987) elaborated his attitude to reform for the first time. The article contains many reformist ideas: collective contract, 'a fundamental improvement of management, planning and the whole economic mechanism of the agro-industrial complex', 'Lenin's ideas about economic accounting ... cooperation and tax in kind', 'full economic accounting', 'self-financing' and 'family and individual contract'. However, Gorbachev and Murakhovski had said all these things one year earlier, making Nikonov's late words appear lip-service. There is a brief mentioning of elections of enterprise leaders and managers, as if Nikonov wanted, but did not dare, to avoid them. Besides, he explained that a unified plan of the agro-industrial complex would imply 'a more tightly centralised coordination of the basic indicators of all its links' (Nikonov, 1987, p. 18). When discussing self-financing, he argued that it could only be introduced on about one fifth of *kolkhozy* and *sovkhozy* since he reckoned that a profitability of 35–40 per cent is necessary. He avoided many reform topics, such as the stability of planned deliveries of agricultural produce, private plots, *kolkhoz* markets, and direct sales to the market. In 1987, the crucial issue in farming was family leasehold, and like a typical Soviet conservative, Nikonov hedged this subject until November 1987 (*Pravda*, 19 November 1987), sticking to yesterday's debate.

Both Ligachev and Nikonov have spoken at several agricultural meetings. Their pronouncements have much in common. They appear to drag their feet on agricultural reform, without offering any alternative. Nikonov dwells on the need for more input into agriculture, which is a dubious conservative preoccupation. His speeches are most prominent for their lack of conceptualisation. They are neither ideological nor Russophile, and certainly not reformist. Nor does he emphasise discipline. Nikonov appears to be merely a traditional conservative party official. His promotion to the Politburo in June 1987, together with Yakovlev and Slyunkov, was probably a boon to Ligachev.

Dolgikh, Shcherbitski and Nikonov do not seem to have close personal links or form any kind of group. However, they all appear to think that no fundamental change is necessary, and thus all earn the label conservative. Their late and partial mentioning of reformist themes is probably a reflection of party discipline and political necessity.

Several senior politicians helped Gorbachev to power, but later fell out with him. The most prominent examples are the Politburo members Viktor Chebrikov, Mikhail Solomentsev and Andrei Gromyko, who for this reason were singled out for praise by Ligachev at the 19th Party Conference (*Pravda*, 2 July 1988). By doing this, Ligachev came very close to declaring his own oppositional faction. None of them has said much about economics from 1985 to 1988, so it has been difficult to distinguish whether they are reactionary or conservative by our classification, though at least Chebrikov and Solomentsev appear to be both reactionary and linked to Ligachev. Both Solomentsev and Gromyko were retired at the end of September 1988, while Ligachev's power was reduced and Chebrikov moved, formally upwards to the CC Secretariat, but away from his power base in the KGB.

Viktor Chebrikov, CC Secretary for legal affairs since September 1988, has made sinister speeches against the West and public disorder (see *Pravda*, 7 Novermber 1985, 11 September 1987). In spite of originally being an old Brezhnevite from the Ukraine, he switched allegiance to Andropov (Medvedev, 1986, pp. 171–2). As Chairman of the Party Control Committee, Mikhail Solomentsev worked in close contact with the KGB. His language was moralistic, and he demanded stricter discipline and the 'honest appearance of a communist'.

The Politburo member **Vitali Vorotnikov** has long been rumoured to have supported Gorbachev on divisive measures. However, in spite of an illustrious career, Vorotnikov's speeches have been lacklustre. They have followed a cautious party line without obvious commitment, giving the impression that Vorotnikov does not push for anything at all. In Gorbachev's autumn coup of 1988, Vorotnikov was demoted from RSFSR Prime Minister to Chairman of the Presidium of the RSFSR Supreme Soviet. It is not clear what stand Vorotnikov actually takes, if any.

A PROGRAMME OF COMPROMISE

We may conclude that at least five different economic programmes have been advocated by leading members of the present Soviet Politburo. The radical reformers Gorbachev, Yakovlev, Shevardnadze and Medvedev favour a far-reaching marketisation, a multitude of cooperatives, an extension of private enterprise and political reform. The moderate reformers Ryzhkov and

Slyunkov have gradually come to accept marketisation, but maintain respect for Gosplan. Zaikov prefers a technocratic streamlining of the existing system as in the GDR. Ligachev's programme is short but ferocious with arduous disciplinary measures. Finally, conservatives like Nikonov and Shcherbitski desire a minimum of change. Assuming that Chebrikov sides with Ligachev, the present Politburo (October 1988) comprises six radical or moderate reformers (Gorbachev, Yakovlev, Shevardnadaze, Medvedev, Ryzhkov, Slyunkov), four reactionaries or conservatives (Ligachev, Chebrikov, Nikonov, Shcherbitski) with one technocratic rationaliser between them (Zaikov) and one indeterminate (Vorotnikov). Until September 1988 the latter two held the balance in the Politburo. However, the division is not so simple. Soviets with some insight allege that there are not such definite factions on the Politburo, and that the majority shifts from issue to issue.

What happens when these programmes and people are confronted with each other? In private, a senior Soviet with knowledge of top-level decision-making stated emphatically: 'All decisions are compromises'. We face an oligarchy composed of several hierarchical bureaucracies which converge in the Politburo. The Politburo (twelve full members) meets almost every Thursday for several hours. The CC Secretariat (nine members) and the Presidium of the Council of Ministers (fourteen members) convene once a week as well, chaired by Ligachev (until September 1988) and Ryzhkov respectively. Both discuss issues that will be decided by the Politburo. More detailed discussions are usually confined to a few members of the Politburo. Soviet insiders underline that politicians are so specialised that only a few of them are influential on most matters. The natural combination preparing a major question is the General Secretary, the Prime Minister, the Second Secretary, the competent CC Secretary, and the responsible Deputy Prime Minister. In the case of economic reform, the first four would be Gorbachev, Ligachev (until September 1988), Ryzhkov and Slyunkov (as of January 1987), while the responsible Deputy Prime Minister would vary with the issue. Each of these officials has such powers that he is entitled to have a say in the final decision. Allegedly, decisions in the Politburo have traditionally been taken through consensus, but now rumours are repeatedly spread about divisive votes on the Politburo. As a result, the majority on the Politburo on each issue would be more important than before. In any case, major reform legislation is likely to be discussed repeatedly in some detail by the whole Politburo, as one can see from its publicised bulletins. Besides, the commitment of a politician and his will to fight for his cause must be important.[23]

On the basis of what various politicians have stated in public, their formal responsibilities, and the decisions taken, we shall try to trace who have been behind various decisions. We shall discuss a mixture of small and big matters, which have the common denominator that they were important economic questions subject to separate decisions at Politburo level.

The original common platform of the new leadership—the old alliance forged around Andropov—was an acceleration (*uskorenie*) of economic growth, which was inscribed into the five-year plan for 1986–90.

The experiment was self-financing, launched at the beginning of 1985, fell under Ryzhkov's responsibility. Both Gorbachev and Ryzhkov praised it at the 27th Party Congress. These two men are likely to have promoted it, but against minimal resistance. Presumably, Ligachev just accepted it, although he was the first leader to endorse it in public.

The reinforcement of disciplinary measures in the spring of 1985, was supported by several politicians, notably Ligachev, but also Chebrikov, Gorbachev, Romanov and Zaikov.

The anti-alcohol campaign launched in May 1985 was Ligachev's special baby, strongly supported by Gorbachev and Chebrikov. Gorbachev (1987a, p.224) waited until the decree was published to acclaim it in public, though he has returned to it numerous times.

The new investment policy incorporated in the new five-year plan with its emphasis on machine-building and retooling was promoted by Ryzhkov, Zaikov and Gorbachev.

Virtually all leaders were in favour of production associations with integration of research and development into production.

The two-tier organisation with superministries was advocated by Medvedev (1983) and pushed by Gorbachev. The bureaux at the Council of Ministers, reminiscent of the Military-Industrial Commission, appear to have been supported by Zaikov and Ryzkhov.

The agricultural reform enacted after the 27th Party Congress was pushed by Gorbachev and Murakhovski alone.

Several decrees on partial reform in various branches passed in 1986 bear witness to a mixture of influences and have little consistency.

The struggle with unearned income and the legislation on individual labour activities seem to have been linked through a compromise. At the 27th Party Congress, Gorbachev mentioned both together. The first Politburo bulletin on both issues coupled them and stated that they would be elaborated simultaneously (*Pravda*, 28 March 1986). Moreover, Ligachev also discussed them in one context (*Pravda*, 10 July 1986). The obvious partners of the deal are Ligachev, who incessantly speaks about unearned incomes, and Gorbachev, who has taken the most favourable view of private enterprise. If there had not been some kind of agreement, Ligachev would probably have obstructed the legislation on individual labour activity more effectively.

In 1986, when Zaikov was in charge of economic affairs in the CC Secretariat, various measures already implemented in Leningrad became subject to union legislation. They included: admonitions to enhance shift-work; a new wage system; and a system of independent quality control. Gorbachev pledged support, particularly for the quality inspection (*Pravda*, 16 November 1986), although these measures were not really part of his programme. Other politicians are likely to have been rather indifferent.

A decree on territorial integration passed in the summer of 1986 was inspired by Georgia. It is likely to have been approved by Zaikov, Gorbachev, Slyunkov and Shcherbitski, but disliked by Ligachev and probably Ryzhkov. Disagreement could explain a very vague wording.

The reform of foreign trade legislated in August 1986, must have been promoted by Ryzhkov, Zaikov, and Medvedev, while Gorbachev probably consented.

The push for democratisation at the CC Plenum in January 1987 appears to have come as a surprise to everyone. The stark discrepancies between the resolution of the Plenum and Gorbachev's speech, as well as the ensuing restrained reactions of leading politicians suggest that the radical reformers forged ahead, trying to overrun their adversaries rather than seeking a broader alliance.

The political approach to the CC Plenum on economic reform in June 1987 contrasted sharply with the January 1987 Plenum. The preceding CC Conference on 8–9 June 1987 was specifically designed by Gorbachev to convince some of his colleagues of the need for radical economic reform with the support of Slyunkov.[24] The Law on Cooperatives appears to have been brought forward by the same coalition in May 1988, with Yakovlev and Gorbachev pushing initially and Ryzhkov making the conclusive speech in its favour.

The politically sensitive issue of family leasehold in agriculture has so far been blocked from mass introduction. It is all too clear that Gorbachev has pushed for it but been stopped by Ligachev and Nikonov.

This brief summary of the protagonists on a score of significant economic decisions helps us to understand the causes of inconsistencies in the economic programme that has evolved under Gorbachev's leadership. It is simply not Gorbachev's own programme, but a programme of compromise. We are facing a collective leadership, in which specialisation provides an inequal distribution of influence, but in the end the Politburo majority plays a major role.

Of the issues we have investigated, only two have been pushed by Gorbachev and his closest allies with little or no support from others, namely agricultural reform and electivity. The former has been stalled because of strife. The drive for real elections has clearly heightened tensions in the Soviet leadership, and Gorbachev needed a long time to prepare for it.

Gorbachev has successfully won support for two controversial projects. The first was the Law on Individual Labour Activity, where he compromised with Ligachev who obtained a devastating struggle against unearned income in return. Thus, Gorbachev appears to have recorded a pyrrhic victory. The other controversial issue was the economic reform package endorsed by the CC Plenum in June 1987 after lengthy and laborious persuasion of reasonably like-minded colleagues. As a result, many principles were left ambiguous. This appears a better political method, but it is so costly in terms of time and scarce top personnel that it can only be exploited in exceptional cases.

For the rest, no project seems to have been sanctioned by the General Secretary alone. The alterations in the collective political line over time can largely be explained with the changing composition of the Politburo and hence the movement of its centre. In 1985, Ligachev presumably covered the middle ground in the Politburo and could tip the balance. His disciplinary measures set the stage and lent a neo-Stalinist character to the economic strategy of the new regime. At the same time, the new investment policy favoured by Ryzhkov and Zaikov was adopted. The organisational changes appear to have had a broad support. Ligachev's frontal attack in June 1985 on Gorbachev's advocacy of reform presumably stalled this issue until the Party Congress in early 1986. There was minimal correlation between actual policies and Gorbachev's rhetoric.

After Nikolai Tikhonov and Viktor Grishin had been removed from the Politburo (in October 1985 and February 1986, respectively) and Zaikov promoted to full Politburo member (in March 1986), Zaikov is likely to have comprised the centre of the Politburo. Moreover, he was CC Secretary for economic affairs and the military-industrial complex, and he benefited from Gorbachev's consent. Zaikov worked for several changes of a not very reformist kind and saw them promulgated in 1986; quality control, a complex programme on machine-building, a new wage system, territorial integration and more shiftwork. In addition, he desired the reform of foreign trade that occurred. However, his lack of interest in actual economic reform halted Gorbachev's reform endeavours for another year. Zaikov appears to have dominated economic policy-making, and 1986 was his year. Still, the campaign against unearned income and the Law on Individual Labour Activity were not primarily of his making, but the apparent result of a compromise over his head.

In 1987, Gorbachev was no longer content to let the centre shape most of the economic strategy. He charged ahead with a minority surprise attack at the CC Plenum in January 1987 and achieved a partial success, but the political sequel was a bitter polarisation, forcing Gorbachev on the defensive from late February until late May. However, the replacement of Zaikov with Slyunkov as CC Secretary for economic affairs broke the stalemate over economic reform.[25]

In June 1987, Gorbachev presumably intended to push as far as possible towards economic reform, while still carrying a majority in the leadership. He accomplished an impressive advance, with the assistance of Slyunkov. A Politburo *ad hoc* commission on the Law on State Enterprises was chaired by Ryzhkov. Apparently, it was primarily with Slyunkov and Ryzhkov that Gorbachev had to compromise. However, all key elements of the reform, especially pricing, were muddled. Compromise had seriously harmed the design of the reform, reflecting the line of Ryzhkov and Slyunkov. Even so, Gorbachev was compelled to go on the defensive again from August until December 1987. The polarisation was aggravated; in particular, Chebrikov came out against Gorbachev's policies (*Pravda*, 11 September 1987); and the CC

Plenum on agricultural reform was aborted. The fall of Gorbachev's close ally Boris Yeltsin as First Party Secretary of Moscow City illustrated the hazards of the political strains.

Again Gorbachev regained political momentum after the summit in Washington in December 1987, and in May 1988 the Law on Cooperatives broke all records of reformism. It appears to have been promoted by all the reformers in the leadership. In comparison with June 1987, one significant difference was that Ryzhkov appeared to be pushing the reformist cause rather than restraining it. Another important factor was that the Law on Cooperatives did not directly target the central economic bodies. There was no institutional kernel of resistance around which the opposition could gather.

On the one hand, the General Secretary does not seem to have been overruled on any occasion, but he has colluded in all changes, with more or less enthusiasm. On the other hand, only in June 1987 had he managed to strengthen his political power enough for the adoption of a reform programme, and even so with important compromises. Yet, in legislative terms, he has been more successful than his adversaries, Ligachev and the conservatives, who essentially disapprove of the very notion of reform.

The differences at the very heart of power are so overwhelming that the Politburo with adjacent bodies should be the centre of our study. There is a gulf of difference between the programmes of Gorbachev and Ligachev. They want to develop the system in opposite directions. Consequently, they swiftly became enemies after the Brezhnevian stalemate was broken,[26] though the rules of Soviet politics compel them to manage their animosity. Our analysis illuminates the powers and restrictions of the leading politicians in the economic field. It confirms the importance of a few key posts, but it also shows that the centre of the Politburo appears more important for the actual decision-making than either the General Secretary or the Second Secretary. It is another matter that gradually these two top politicians may tilt the balance in the Politburo through personnel changes, and the General Secretary seems to formulate most of the agenda.

Gorbachev is committed to a far-reaching economic reform, but at least until September 1988 he was not able to carry the Politburo with him on reform of the state economy. Almost half of the Politburo was comprised of outright adversaries of economic reform. A crucial condition for the advancement of economic reform was a fundamental change in the composition of the Politburo, introducing a reformist majority. Gorbachev's coup at the end of September 1988 certainly tilted the balance in the leadership, but still reformers made up only half, and radical reformers a third, of the Politburo. Strong politicians like Ligachev and Chebrikov are likely to be both threats and impediments for as long as they manage to stay in the Politburo and the CC Secretariat.

The design of economic reform is essentially worked out in strife between reformist academic economists and a conservative Gosplan backed up by other central economic organs. The CC Economic Department (with about 100 professionals) headed by Slyunkov is the obvious referee. Prime Minister Ryzhkov has established an independent economic *apparat* at the Council of Ministers, having one department for the economic mechanism (with some twenty professionals, headed by P. Katsura, formerly director at the car factory VAZ) and one department for economic policy (with at least thirty professionals, headed by Vadim Kirichenko, previously the director of Gosplan's Economic Research Institute). Because of this new *apparat*, the Prime Minister is no longer a hostage of Gosplan's *apparat*. His staff complement the CC Economic Department as referee in the internal economic debate.[27]

The elaboration of new legislation takes place in commissions, which gather expertise both from the administration and the academic world. For each major economic law adopted by the Supreme Soviet, a Politburo *ad hoc* commission is formed, usually chaired by the Prime Minister. The CC Secretary for economic affairs or the Chairman of Gosplan may lead Politburo commissions on other essential economic issues.

On the turn of 1985, the 'Commission for the Improvement of Management, Planning, and the Economic Mechanism' was constituted, officially under the auspices of the Council of Ministers, but in practice under Gosplan (*Izvestiya*, 22 January 1986). It was chaired by Gosplan's Chairman (first Talyzin, later Maslyukov) and Gosplan's *apparat* acted as the Commission's secretariat. It included the heads of the major central economic organs (Gosplan, Gossnab, Goskomtsen, the Ministry of Finance, Gosbank, the GKNT and Goskomtrud) as well as the two top economists, Academicians Abel Aganbegyan and Leonid Abalkin. It meets regularly once a month.

In practice, this commission has become a major obstacle to economic reform, since it is dominated by the institutional custodians of the old system. It has a counterweight in its own 'scientific section' (chaired by Aganbegyan, with Abalkin as deputy), which comprises the director and possibly one more economist from each of the leading economic institutes. Thus, it is dominated by capable reform economists. The scientific section has a score of *ad hoc* working groups on various reform issues. These groups meet with the respective central economic bodies to discuss how they are to be reformed. The differences between the reform economists, who want to reduce the powers and size of the central economic bodies, and the bodies in question which aspire to reinforce their powers, are of course palpable. As long as the Gosplan-controlled commission decides, reform attempts are watered down to a minimum. The CC Economic Department or the *apparat* of the Council of Ministers must intervene in order to tilt the balance in favour of reform (cf Åslund, 1987).

NOTES

1. The last model is the least satisfactory, as it says little about the public bulk of the economy. Berliner finds the GDR closest to this model, but the technocratic streamlining of the whole GDR economy—what Peter Wiles (1988, p. 234) connects with 'centralizing modernizers'—appears a more general characteristic.
2. I have read almost all speeches by Politburo members and CC Secretaries published in the central Soviet press (except *Krasnaya zvezda*) from December 1984 (when Gorbachev made his programmatic speech) until June 1988.
3. Oral information from initiated Soviets; cf Shevchenko (1985).
4. Personal information from Goskomtsen corroborated by personal observations in many parts of the country.
5. Gorbachev's speeches have been published in newspapers, journals, special booklets and his selected works (Gorbachev, 1987abc, 1988). In most cases, I utilise the *Pravda* version. However, from December 1984 through June 1985, Gorbachev's speeches were censored in *Pravda*. For that period, I have turned to booklets and his selected works, though his speech in Leningrad on 17 May 1985 has been heavily edited, compelling me to use the TV version translated by the FBIS.
6. For Gorbachev's background, see especially Brown (1985), Medvedev (1986), and Tatu (1987).
7. As the Brezhnev-Chernenko tradition was to speak in an enlightened manner, but minimise actions, most observers were sceptical at the time. The notable exceptions were Archie Brown (1985) and Jerry Hough (1985) who read Gorbachev more literally and correctly.
8. The following facts were gathered during a most fruitful study tour to Georgia, 24–8 September 1986, kindly organised at our request by the Ministry for Foreign Affairs of Georgia. The tour involved conversations with twenty officials of five ministries and state committees, as well as three enterprise tours. All facts have been checked in different interviews, and many through personal observations.
9. Such was the prevalent view in Tbilisi in September 1986. For political changes in Georgia, see Fuller (1986). In September 1986, there was heavy police surveillance of the central market and at all approaches to Tbilisi, with ruthless controls of anything suggesting the black economy. Patiashvili appears to have joined hands with Ligachev. When the latter visited Georgia in early June 1987, Ligachev incessantly attacked Shevardnadze's period of rule (*Pravda*, 3–4 June 1987). Later, Patiashvili accompanied Ligachev to Paris, at the apparent choice of Ligachev (*Pravda*, 1 December 1987).
10. Personal information from Daniel Tarschys, who has studied Lukyanov.
11. Major speeches and articles by Ryzhkov have appeared in *Pravda*, 2 February 1985, 4 March and 19 June 1986; 23 April and 30 June 1987; *Novoe Vremya*, No. 39, 1986.
12. Something important did happen to the draft law at this time. It was renamed from a law on *socialist* enterprise (*Pravda*, 11 December 1986) to a law on *state* enterprise (*Pravda*, 29 January 1987), implying worse treatment of cooperatives.
13. Major speeches and articles by Slyunkov: Slyunkov (1984, 1988); *Pravda*, 27 February and 25 November 1986; 13 and 28 June 1987; 28 May 1988.

14. Personal observation in Minsk in June 1986.
15. It matters little that Gorbachev referred to both Zaikov and Solovyev during another visit to Leningrad in October 1987 (*Pravda*, 14 October 1987).
16. His most informative speeches are: Zaikov (1984); *Pravda*, 29 April, 28 June, 9 August, 30 October, 16 November 1986; 14 February, 26 April and 28 November 1987; *Sots. ind.*, 12 November 1986.
17. Based on interviews in Moscow with two ordinary Soviet citizens from Tomsk.
18. Ligachev's liberal statements abroad have convinced some analysts to revise their view of him, see Gary Lee's article on Ligachev's trip to Finland (*International Herald Tribune*, 2 December 1986) and Teague (1987) on Ligachev's journey to Hungary. In Paris, he spoke approvingly of pluralism (*Le Monde*, 4 December 1987).
19. In August 1987, Ligachev said: 'Comrade M.S. Gorbachev noticed, that every day of our history that we have lived through is dear to us ... ' *Pravda*, 27 August 1987). He must have referred to a statement by Gorbachev that read: 'We must value (*dorozhit*) every year of our 70-year Soviet history' (*Pravda*, 14 February 1987).
20. For particularly informative speeches and articles by Ligachev, see *Pravda*, 2 February, 2 and 29 June, 22 December 1985; 28 February, 6 April, 22 May, 10 July, 2 October, 7 November 1986; 6 March, 23 May, 3 and 4 June, 27 August, 17 September, 19 November 1987; 18 February, 5 June, 2 July, 6 August 1988; *Sovetskaya kultura*, 7 July 1987, 7 April 1988; Ligachev (1985ab, 1986, 1987).
21. At the time, a senior Soviet economist told me that Ligachev's statement meant that the whole leadership was in favour of the Sumy experiment.
22. Observations from a personal visit to a Kiev brewery in 1985, compared with other visited enterprises involved in the same experiment.
23. This is the aggregate picture based on a multitude of sources. Moreover, it is essentially the decision-making process in Poland, and it is likely to be approximately the same in the USSR. In the 1970s, the Polish system displayed two aberrations. First, the Politburo did not have a say after the top politicians had agreed. Secondly, the Presidium of the Council of Ministers dominated the CC Secretariat (*Protokoly*, 1986). Among western political scientists dealing with Soviet affairs, Peter Reddaway (1987) comes closest to my perception of Soviet top-level decision-making.
24. Reliable information from a senior Soviet insider.
25. This does not necessarily mean that Gorbachev has broken his political ties with Zaikov (cf note 15).
26. Ligachev cannot possibly be useful to Gorbachev, as some observers have suggested (see e.g. Hough, 1987, p. 39). An enemy who wants to block virtually all your proposals and move in the contrary direction is not an asset.
27. Reliable inside information from several sources.

3. Changes within the traditional framework

A communist regime can undertake many measures without departing from the hallmarks of the command economy. In 1985, the new leaders seemed preoccupied with such limited changes. It was a time of activism with changes introduced on a broad front. All conceivable sources of swift improvements were sought. The easiest were attempted first.

Economic policy was an immediate concern, since the five-year plan for 1986–90 was being elaborated, allowing the new rulers to raise growth targets, adjust the structure of the economy, and change investment policy. Their urge to accelerate economic growth and the new investment policy are worthy of investigation. A certain restructuring of foreign trade was desired, particularly a reduction in the imports of food, consumer goods and large turn-key projects in favour of increased imports of machinery alone. Fear of unbalanced trade expansion on the basis of foreign credits prevailed. Foreign trade was not perceived as a major avenue to modernisation, because of failures to modernise through the import of machinery in the 1970s and presumably also the experiences of the American pipeline embargo (cf Gorbachev in *Pravda*, 1 July 1986).

Disciplinary campaigns constituted a second package of traditional measures. They were much appreciated by the new regime. Substantial personnel changes, a struggle against alcohol, a new stricter system of quality control and a struggle against unearned income are the most prominent measures of this kind. In this chapter, we shall highlight the battle with alcohol and the new quality control. The campaign against unearned income will be discussed along with private enterprise in Chapter 6.

A third group of measures may be called technocratic fine-tuning. Such measures had dominated in 1979, but they were not much liked by the new leadership. The introduction of new wage scales, certification of work places, promotion of shiftwork, furthering of complex programmes, and numerous adjustments in management belong to this group. Only the new wage system merits a section. The changes in enterprise management fell in part outside the traditional system and will be discussed in the next chapter.

Reorganisation forms a fourth package of traditional measures. Most organisational changes are futile, but some are preconditions for a real reform. Therefore, we shall concentrate most of the discussion of organisational issues in Chapter 5.

THE URGE TO ACCELERATE ECONOMIC GROWTH

The new leaders took over while the preparations for the five-year plan for 1986–90 were advancing. They desired to raise the economic growth rate. Acceleration (*uskorenie*) of the country's social-economic development was the most prominent demand in Gorbachev's speeches in the spring of 1985. In May 1985, Gorbachev stated that recently the national income had grown by about 3 per cent a year, but 'calculations show that we need a minimum of 4 [per cent] ... or even more' (Gorbachev, 1987a, p. 214). The combined needs of consumption, modernisation of industry and defence caused this craving for a higher growth rate (cf Aganbegyan, 1985a, p. 6).

Today, Soviet economic assessments in 1985 appear dated because of their excessive optimism about Soviet achievements and the possibilities of raising the growth rate. Aganbegyan made a number of boastful statements: 'On the whole, during the last three decades we have developed two or three times faster than the leading capitalist states; this was a manifestation of the advantages of socialism, its planned organisation' (Aganbegyan, 1985b, p. 13). Stating that the Soviet Union needed to raise labour productivity from 3–3.5 per cent a year in the period 1976–85 to 5 and later 6 per cent a year, Aganbegyan (1985a, p. 18) concluded: 'It is easy to calculate that under these conditions already by the year 2000 our country will surpass European capitalist countries in terms of labour productivity and approach the US level.' A completely different picture emerged, when Soviet economists started to acknowledge publicly a sizeable hidden inflation. According to Vasili Selyunin and Grigori Khanin (1987) it averaged about 3 per cent a year. Thus, Aganbegyan (1987b, p. 7) noted: 'In reality, for a number of years, especially in 1979–1982, the actual growth of the national economy came to a halt and there was stagnation.' The whole discussion of growth was confused by the flawed statistics. How were the planned growth rates to be understood? Should they also be deflated by some 3 percentage units each year?

The new leaders had a highly exaggerated view of how much traditional means could accomplish. In his Leningrad speech in May 1985, Gorbachev (1987a, p. 216) sounded confident: 'we can really obtain rapid returns, if we put all organisational, economic and social reserves into operation, activating first of all the human factor, in order to attain that everyone works honestly, conscientiously and effectively at his place of work.' The 'reserves', or inefficiency, were extraordinary, but it was difficult to activate them. In his speech on 11 June 1985, Gorbachev surveyed the means for a swift rise in economic dynamism. The new leaders seem to have thought that the mere replacement of old, incompetent or corrupt cadres would quickly boost production. A lot of slack could be eliminated by administrative means: 'Experience shows that through the certification of work places alone it is possible to reduce labour costs by 5–10 per cent' (Gorbachev, 1985a, p. 17). Admonitions for economising on all kinds of resources were issued. Much attention was devoted to a new investment policy. This was a combination of

Table 3:1   Planned increase in economic efficiency,
1986–90

(average annual increase, per cent)

	1981–5	1986–90 Plan
Utilised national income	3.1	4.1
Labour productivity	3.1	4.2
Capital productivity	–2.3	3.0
Energy intensity	–1.1	–1.7
Metal intensity	–1.9	–2.7

Source: Pravda, 19 June 1986.

a technocratic and a disciplinary policy, but both were intended to favour machine-building rather than consumers.

In June 1986, Prime Minister Nikolai Ryzhkov outlined how efficiency would increase (see Table 3.1), but there was little substance behind the hope for rapidly improved efficiency. The great hopes for improved capital productivity indicates the weight given to the new investment policy.

Senior economists stated that improvements within the system would be sufficient for the acceleration of growth for the rest of the 1980s. In the early 1990s, economic reform would add a new impetus. Such was the optimism of the time. All demands were simply added up, under the assumption that it would be enough to deploy underutilised means.

In western discussion, it has long been recognised that higher growth targets are likely to aggravate shortages and bottlenecks. Therefore economic reform required less arduous quantitative tasks. In the Soviet Union, it was Gosplan under its old conservative Chairman Nikolai Baibakov and Gosplan's Economic Research Institute that advocated moderate targets (and limited restructuring) while mainstream reformers, such as Aganbegyan, favoured high growth targets. As perestroika proceeded, the ambitious quantitative tasks proved to be beyond reach, and even harmful. The radical reformer Vasili Selyunin pointed out that even if growth accelerated, it would have 'a very slight impact on living standards', and a lot of substandard or nonutilised produce was superfluous. Selyunin concluded there was a choice: *'either a boost of output volumes, or a perestroika of the structure of the economy'* (*Sots. ind.*, 5 January 1988; emphasis in original). Nikolai Shmelev (1988, pp. 166–7) agreed and wanted to disband the five-year plan, since market balance, a higher technical level and product quality were more important than quantitative growth. In June 1988, Gorbachev approached this point of view: 'the rates of growth are not important in themselves, but their fulfillment in real terms, the actual satisfaction of the people's needs' (*Pravda*, 29 June 1988).

A NEW INVESTMENT POLICY[1]

Initially, the new leaders devoted great effort to changing the investment plans for 1986–90. Investment resources were considered both carriers of scientific-technical progress and the most easily controlled economic levers. The strife over investment plans appears to have been intense, as evidenced by the retirement of Nikolai Baibakov in October 1985, on the eve of the CC Plenum devoted to the next five-year plan. Later, Gorbachev revealed that the plan had been sent back to Gosplan three times. Despite bureaucratic resistance, the five-year plan was significantly altered. As many times before, the key slogan was to switch from extensive to intensive growth. It had many corollaries, ranging from more emphasis on re-equipment and modernisation to an overwhelming priority for machine-building. Important aims were to raise quality and the technical level of production.

However, one main feature of the new policy could be perceived as extensive, namely the planned increase in the annual growth of gross investment to 4.9 per cent, from 3.7 per cent in the period 1981–5 (*Narkhoz 1986*, p. 55). The share of accumulation in the national income was supposed to rise from 25.0 per cent in 1985 to 27.6 per cent in 1990 (Faltsman, 1987, p. 12). Conversely, the share of consumption in the national income would fall. Ryzhkov defended this: 'The acceleration of the economic growth and the increased efficiency of social production allow an increase in the productive potential and the solution of a larger circle of social problems at the same time . . . ' (*Pravda*, 19 June 1986). The conflict between increasing investment and consumers' demands was glossed over.

The rate of investment might appear reassuring, but experts like Delez Palterovich and Vladimir Faltsman of TsEMI argued that the hidden inflation in equipment incorporated in investment was about 3 per cent a year from 1979 to 1984 (Palterovich, 1987, p. 590), and their estimates were conservative. There was a significant hidden inflation also in construction, where real investment might have stagnated. The Novosibirsk economists K.K. Valtukh and B.L. Lavrovski (1986) saw a reduction in production capacity during those years. In this light, the new five-year plan could be seen as an attempt to attain a real growth of investment.

A similar confusion surrounded scrapping rates. On the basis of official statistics, Tigran Khachaturov (1988, p. 9) argued that 'service periods [of equipment] were unfoundedly long, and amortisation rates low'. The overall retirement rate of 1.8 per cent of fixed assets in 1985 was supposed to rise to 3.1 per cent in 1990. At the same time, the annual retirement rate of machinery and equipment was planned to increase from 3.2 to 6.2 per cent, and in machine-building from 2.2 per cent to 9.7 per cent (*Pravda*, 19 June 1986). Because of the long service life of equipment, repair costs had grown excessive. However, already a decade earlier Ya. Kvasha had calculated that the scrapping coefficient was almost twice as large as official statistics alleged (Rumer, 1984, p. 258). Valtukh and Lavrovski (1986, pp. 20–1) showed that

6–8 per cent of the nominal capacity had been tacitly scrapped. Retirement ratios were even considered wastefully high in agriculture, construction, and parts of raw-material extraction (Palterovich, 1988, p. 120; Kushnirsky, 1987, p. 266).

Another major aim was to raise the share of investment devoted to modernisation and retooling of already existing factories, from 38.5 per cent in 1985 to 50.5 per cent in 1990. Re-equipment was regarded as more efficient than new investment, with a 50 per cent higher output-to-capital ratio (Kushnirksy, 1987, p. 266). The age-old Soviet inclination towards mastodontic projects was to be overcome. Consequently, the projects on the turning of northern and Siberian rivers were abandoned, and no new gigantic project was launched. These policy changes were sensible, but they proved difficult to implement. For construction organisations, it was still more beneficial to erect buildings than to install equipment, since specialised supplies were uncertain. For enterprise managers, disruption through reconstruction augured the threat of not reaching plan targets, and reserves were still needed to counter unexpected increases in plan obligations.

An eternal problem of command economies is long construction periods and excessive numbers of ongoing projects. In 1985, there were about 350,000 construction projects employing a total of 4.5 million workers, that is an average of thirteen workers per project (Khachaturov, 1988, p. 4). Faltsman (1987, p. 83) notes that the average construction period of 800 large machine-building projects amounted to about thirteen years, which guaranteed their obsolescense. A significant share was under construction for more than twenty-five years. Nikolai Ryzhkov stated that the normative construction period for a new production enterprise was 3–3.5 years, while the real time was nine years (*Pravda*, 19 June 1986), and 25 per cent of the investment projects that were transferred to the new five-year plan had been designed 10–20 years earlier (*Pravda*, 4 March 1986). A traditional reaction to these problems was to call for a higher investment rate, in order to cut construction periods (Chernikov, 1986, pp. 68–9). In July 1986, Gorbachev declared that the ministries had been told to review all technical investment projects in order to abort already obsolete projects. He assumed that this review process would last for one or two years (*Pravda*, 2 August 1986). It is difficult to reconcile this delay with the great rush to boost investment.

The tardy introduction of the production of new machines was a related problem. The average length of the innovation cycle from fundamental research to serial production had reached nineteen years. The intention was to speed it up after a slow-down during the preceding two decades. The share in total production of commodities produced for more than ten years had increased from 16.2 per cent in 1967 to 30.6 per cent in 1981 (Faltsman, 1986, p. 56).

The new regime wanted a rapid restructuring of investment. Its first priority was to accelerate scientific-technical progress. For this purpose, machine-building, in particular computerisation, electronification, robotisation and automation, were promoted. Prime Minister Ryzhkov called machine-building 'the material base of the acceleration of scientific-technical progress and the technical reconstruction of the national economy'. Its production was supposed to increase by 43 per cent from 1985 to 1990, and investment in civilian machine-building by no less than 80 per cent (*Pravda*, 19 June 1986).

Ryzhkov expressed the desire to concentrate incremental investment on four major 'complex programmes' for food, energy, machine-building and electronification, and the production of chemicals. 'For their realisation more than 80 per cent of the whole increment of investments will be allocated as opposed to 50 per cent in the eleventh five-year plan' (*Pravda*, 19 June 1986). Second order priorities were housing and social investments. Table 3.2 illustrates that the three heaviest investment posts, the agro-industrial complex, energy and housing construction, accounted for 33, 18 and 15 per cent, respectively, of total planned investment for 1986–90. The modern branches, machine-building and chemical industry, were not getting all that much.

Table 3.2:   Distribution of planned investment 1986–90

	Total (billion rubles)	Annual increase (per cent)
Total	994	4.3
Agro-industrial complex	330	4.1
Energy complex	180	6.2
Civilian machine-building	63	12.5
Chemical industry	25	8.5
Housing construction	150	. .
Transportation	62	. .
Light industry	14	4.6
Others	189	. .

Note: Most figures are compiled from Nikolai Ryzhkov's speech on 18 June 1986 (*Pravda*, 19 June 1986). Numbers from different sources tend to vary because of different definitions and revisions of plans. The figures for light industry are cited from Leggett (1988, p. 245).

Contrary to declarations, a great deal of investment remained in raw-material extraction. Agriculture was subject to ineffective overinvestment (Faltsman, 1987, p. 12), but its investments were planned to grow almost in line with the Food Programme, though within the agro-industrial complex investment would be reallocated from agriculture proper to food-processing and infrastructure. Despite severe criticism, the Ministry of Water Economy, with almost two million workers and an annual budget of more than 10 bn rubles, continued to pursue works that were unncessary and even harmful

(Shmelev, 1988, p. 171). The decline in oil production in 1985 probably reassured the energy complex of its investment resources. There is a logic behind these figures. Energy production provided the country with most of its hard currency earnings, and agricultural failures had necessitated large hard currency imports of food. With half the investment volume tied to two raw material producing branches, little was left for modern branches.

Agricultural and energy investment were also supported by long-term complex programmes. The idea of programme planning had gained support in the 1970s and was strongly endorsed in 1979. It remained popular with the new leaders. Since departmental barriers were criticised, the uneven development within broadly defined branches or complexes was exposed. Programme planning was seen as a solution, and a large number of so-called complex programmes were adopted. By definition, they last for more than five years, involve several branch ministries and have broadly defined purposes. Of the three major complex programmes adopted before March 1985, the Food Programme (adopted in May 1982) and the Energy Programme (November 1982) remained in force, while the Irrigation Programme was abandoned. It had been adopted at the CC Plenum in October 1984, by the Brezhnev alliance against obvious opposition from Gorbachev. New principal complex programmes were the Consumer Goods and Services Programme (September 1985), the Chemicals Programme (October 1985), and the Machine-Building Programme (June 1986). Other important complex programmes concerned housing and computerisation. Besides, there were plenty of regional complex programmes.

Because of the high priority of major complex programmes, small means were left for the strained infrastructure, with the exception of housing. Transportation and communications were neglected both in public statements and budget assignments. The indifference to infrastructure was even worse than under Brezhnev. Consumers were also disregarded, although the party's proud new target was to 'assure practically every family a separate flat or individual house by the year 2000' (*Pravda*, 19 June 1986). It was an ambitious goal, considering that 'in most provinces of the country the shortage of housing comprise 20–25 per cent of the needs' (*Pravda*, 1 March 1988). A frequent complaint was that the social sector had traditionally been planned as a residue. More resources were allotted to, for instance, health, but the prior neglect was great, and the consumer sector as a whole remained a low-priority area.

Many of the shortcomings in the old investment policies were easily detected, but it proved difficult to amend them. Statistics were so poor that macro-policy was reduced to guesswork. The economy was rigidly moulded by its existing structure. Any attempt at a quick change would be restricted by bottlenecks. The mere speed of the planned restructuring of investment made it unfeasible. Valtukh and Lavrovski (1986, p. 32) argued that the investment complex itself needed to have its share of investment raised from 10–11 per cent to at least 15–17 per cent.[2] The most obvious bottleneck was machine-building. Kushnirsky (1987, p. 265) and Malygin (1985, p. 34) have calculated that planned new investment and retooling required a growth in machine-building output of more than 70 per cent from 1985 to 1990, but the planned growth was only 43 per cent. Kushnirsky identifies the shortage of equipment as the most important reason for low retirement ratios. Contrary to intentions, the share of machinery and equipment in actual investment fell in 1986–7, because of this bottleneck (cf *Planecon*, 29 January 1988, p. 6).

An obvious alternative would have been to increase imports of modern machinery. However, Gorbachev and Ligachev were opposed to such a course (cf Gelman, 1987, p. 58). Faltsman (1987, pp. 72, 143) argued against larger imports, which already accounted for one third of the new machinery and equipment in the country. One of his arguments was that these imports were caused not only by the low domestic technical level, but also by overall shortage; another that their quickly rising prices boosted costs of investment. Neither argument sounds convincing, but from 1985 the fall in Soviet exports resulted in a decline in imports of machinery. Domestic machine-building failed to fill the gap both quantitatively and qualitatively. Here the Soviet government has an option, if it is prepared to accept a greater indebtedness or larger sales of gold, which Nikolai Shmelev (1988) has proposed.

The attempts at a concentration of investment resulted in the abandonment of some major projects, confused delays and admonitions. In 1986, the stock of unfinished construction soared (*Narkhoz 1986*, p. 332). Gross investment increased by 8.4 per cent while the commissioning of new assets rose only by 5.9 per cent (*Narkhoz 1986*, p. 51). In machine-building a hike in investment of 15 per cent resulted in an increase in new assets of just 3 per cent (Gaidar, 1988, p. 45). There was no balance between plan targets and means. The hasty investment campaign in machine-building brought about a 'diversion of enormous resources without regard to economic and technologically rational proportions between the traditional and radically new technology' (Rumer, 1986, p. 28). A certain improvement took place in 1987, since the authorities had moderated their ambitions. A growth of gross investment of 4.7 per cent was matched by an increase in the commissioning of new assets of 5.0 per cent (*Pravda*, 24 January 1988).

One important result of the new activist investment policy was that the traditional shortcomings of the economic system were exposed. The selection and design of investment projects could not become economically rational without a reasonably accurate price system. As the economy grew more complex, it became ever more difficult without producer markets to identify weak links in production. With the predominance of gross production targets, constructors had little incentive to check costs, to reduce the number of current projects or to diminish construction periods. Little could be achieved through administrative intervention based on common sense. The new Soviet leaders much have realised that their high hopes for economic improvements through a better investment policy had been exaggerated.

A RUTHLESS STRUGGLE AGAINST ALCOHOL

A campaign against alcohol was one of the first measures enacted by the Politburo after Gorbachev became General Secretary (*Pravda*, 5 April 1988). On 17 May 1985, the Soviet press published a CC decree 'On Measures to Overcome Drinking and Alcoholism'. It was accompanied by more concrete decrees by the Council of Ministers and the Supreme Soviet. A multitude of restrictions on sales and consumption of alcohol were imposed. Most actions were determined locally, causing considerable regional differences.

The basic idea was that it should be difficult to buy alcohol. Sales were limited from 2 p.m. until 7 p.m.; the number of shops selling alcohol was reduced to less than half the original number; simple drinking places were closed and most cafés lost their right to serve alcohol, leaving Moscow with seventy-nine restaurants entitled to serve alcohol. As a result enormous queues lasting for two to three hours were formed in many places. Since the production of alcohol halved from 1984 until 1987, a substantial shortage arose. Sales of alcohol to young people under twenty-one were forbidden, as drinking among the young had caused great concern. Another important aim was to bar drinking from places of work. Large fines were set, and a drunk at work could easily be sacked. In order to stop drunkards from appearing in public, the police started picking them up on a large scale, detained them for sobering up and fined them.

It was a full-fledged disciplinary campaign of the old style, staged with impressive stamina, though the punishments were limited to fines and dismissals. Commissions for the struggle against drinking were established in a traditional manner. A propaganda campaign against alcohol was launched, and soft drinks were promoted as an alternative; societies for sobriety were propagated. A significant price rise occurred, but official prices were far below the rising black market prices of illegal homebrew (*Pravda*, 28 September 1987).

The short-term effects of this campaign were extraordinary. Sales of alcohol fell by 25 per cent during the last seven months of 1985, by 37 per cent in 1986, and by another 13 per cent in 1987 (*Pravda*, 26 January 1986, 18 January 1987, 24 January 1988), leaving the volume of alcohol sales at 46 per cent of their level in 1980 (*Narkhoz 1986*, p. 463). Drinking was undoubtedly reduced. Alcohol-related diseases, crimes and accidents declined sharply—by 25–40 per cent within two years (*Izvestiya*, 10 March, 2 June, 3 December 1987). Evidently, drinking at work and in the streets had been sharply reduced. Even the death-rate and infant mortality sank, and life expectancy rose (*Pravda*, 18 January 1987). However, in the short term no positive impact on economic performance was apparent.

After the first shocks, drinking habits were reestablished as moon-shining developed. According to the Minister for Internal Affairs, A.V. Vlasov, 72 per cent of revealed cases of illegal distilling occurred in the RSFSR, and particularly in the Urals and Siberia. Previously, moon-shining had been typically rural, but now some 40 per cent of these violations were revealed in towns. They assumed mass proportions. During one and a half years, the militia confiscated no less than 900,000 distillers (*Izvestiya*, 10 March 1987). The number of sentences of home-brewers grew more than six times from 1984 to 1986. The expansion of moon-shining showed up in a rapid increase in sugar sales from 1987, which led to the rationing of sugar in many areas (*Izvestiya*, 8 April 1988). The previous achievements were partly reversed. While 117,000 cases of drunkenness at work were reported in 1986, the number surpassed 250,000 in 1987 (*Izvestiya*, 3 December 1987). The underground economy was compensating for much of the shortfall of official alcohol sales. Nikolai Shmelev (1988, pp. 162–3) has even argued that home-distilling probably made up for the whole reduction in official production, though that is doubtful given the high price of home-brew. He has warned that the restrictive policies could cause the appearance of large-scale organised criminality as in the USA during prohibition in the 1920s.

The decline in official alcohol sales had important effects on the economy. Other sales did not make up for this reduction, so shortages on consumer markets were aggravated, weakening incentives to earn more. Since turnover tax accounted for 85–90 per cent of alcohol sales, total turnover tax revenues fell by 6.2 bn rubles or 6.3 per cent from 1985 to 1986 (*Narkhoz 1986*, p. 628). The national income was reduced accordingly (since it included turnover tax), through this was covered up though the manipulation of statistics (Hanson, 1986b; Vanous, 1987; *Ek. gaz.*, No. 3, 1988). In 1984, alcohol sales had amounted to almost 17 per cent of total retail sales. The halving of alcohol sales kept total retail sales down, which increased in current prices by 2.6 per cent in 1985 and 2.4 per cent in 1986 (*Narkhoz 1985*, p. 464; *Narkhoz 1986*, p. 456). Essentially as a result of this, the national income at current prices grew only by 1.6 per cent in 1985 and 1.5 per cent in 1986 (*Ek. gaz.*, No. 3, 1988). According to Nikolai Shmelev (1988, p. 163), the deficit in the state budget grew sharply because of the reduction in alcohol revenues and was covered through the printing of more bank notes.

Whatever the exact figures, the campaign against alcohol had aggravated market imbalances severely; a large, but undisclosed, budget deficit had been created; the campaign required the attention of a large police force; and it was likely to be less successful in the long run. Even the most justified administrative campaign had caused such problems that its value was in doubt. The state could not offer any alternative to drinking, neither spiritually nor economically.

REINFORCED QUALITY CONTROL

The quality of Soviet produce appears to have been declining steadily since the 1960s, as a result of a permanent excess demand, regardless of technical progress (cf Nuti, 1986, p. 76; Bim and Shokhin, 1986, p. 69; Birman, 1983, p.

178; Kushnirsky, 1984, p. 49; *Izvestiya*, 27 March 1987). Outside the military sphere, there has been no potent state authority in charge of quality control. The State Committee for Standards (Gosstandart) has set technical standards, and all production enterprises possessed large organisations for quality control, but they were subordinate to the director of the enterprise. If plan fulfillment was endangered, the director ordered controllers to cease their activities. As technological development proceeded, the declining quality grew into an ever more serious problem. It was one of the main themes of Leonid Brezhnev's speech to the 25th Party Congress in 1976, but little happened.

The Brezhnev regime preferred carrots to sticks, and its approach was bureaucratic. Gosstandart assessed whether a commodity equalled a western counterpart. If so, it was awarded a quality mark, and its producer could raise its price and obtain special bonuses, but only 10–15,000 types of commodities were evaluated each year. Furthermore, the inspection was considered both inaccurate and excessively bureaucratic. A revision in 1985–6 reduced the share in total commodity production with the quality mark from 16.3 per cent to 14.7 per cent (*Sots. ind.,* 14 August 1987). In early 1988, a Deputy Chairman of Gosstandart declared that 14.2 per cent of total production conformed with current world standards (*Izvestiya*, 23 January 1988). More plausibly, Nikolai Shmelev (1987, p. 154) states that according to the most cautious and pessimistic estimates, only 7–8 per cent of Soviet manufacturing corresponds to world standards.

All the time the military had its own independent quality control at armaments manufacturers, rejecting substandard arms in large quantities. In the spring of 1985, an experiment with a similar civilian quality control was initiated at nineteen large enterprises concentrated in Moscow, Leningrad, the Ukraine, Belorussia and Armenia (*Ek gaz.*, No. 29, 1986). In parallel, regional programmes for the improvement of quality were elaborated, notably in Latvia, Belorussia and Leningrad (*Ek. gaz.*, No. 30, 1986; *Izvestiya*, 25 December 1986, 16 December 1987). On 12 May 1986, the CC and the Council of Ministers adopted a decree 'On Measures to Fundamentally Raise the Quality of Production' (*Ek. gaz.,* No. 28, 1986). They decided to 'create a special organ of extradepartmental control—a state acceptance (*gospriemka*)' subordinate to Gosstandart. From 1 January 1987, it would introduce 'state acceptance' (or control) at enterprises producing the most important commodities and also consumer goods.

From the summer of 1986, Lev Zaikov, CC Secretary for economic affairs and military machine-building, pursued a virtual crusade for state acceptance, setting very high targets: a complete transition to 'the production of machines, instruments and equipment that correspond to the highest world achievements in 1991–93' (*Pravda*, 9 August 1986; see Chapter 2). It was abundantly clear that his targets were nothing but wishful thinking, but Zaikov has kept repeating such goals. They appear to constitute a main plank of the unpublished complex programme on machine-building, implying that it is equally unrealistic.

Towards the end of 1986, *gospriemka* emerged as the dominant theme in the economic propaganda. On 14 November 1986, a particular CC Conference launched the new quality control. Among the speakers were three CC Secretaries, Gorbachev, Zaikov and Dolgikh. Gorbachev underlined the poverty of Soviet quality and the importance of raising it. *Gospriemka* was supposed to be a harsh measure, with shortfalls mercilessly reflected in the earnings of all workers concerned. Still, Gorbachev worried that the new controllers would behave too bureaucratically, and he remarked realistically: 'I am generally far from the naive thought that tomorrow or the day after tomorrow all one hundred per cent of the output produced by machine-building will correspond to world standards' (*Pravda*, 16 November 1986). The ensuing propaganda emphasised the severity of *gospriemka* and exaggerated the benefit to consumers. The aims differed widely. Zaikov spoke of catching up with the West in a few years' time, as did Gosstandart's leading spokesmen, while a writer in *Literaturnaya gazeta* (17 December 1986) considered the task to be 'to introduce elementary order' since 'we have to start the attack on quality practically from zero'. Similarly, Academician Leonid Abalkin observed: 'State control can stop the output of what is not needed, but it cannot rectify the situation by itself ... The introduction of state control can be regarded as an intermediary measure' (*Moscow News*, No. 5, 1987).

In July 1986, the pronounced intention had been to start with 740 enterprises and associations (*Ek. gaz.,* No. 29, 1986), but by November 1986 the number had doubled to 1500. They belonged to twenty-eight different ministries and accounted for one fifth of industrial production (*Pravda*, 29 September 1987), and perhaps as much as 60 per cent of machine-building production.[3] The new quality inspectors were directly subordinated to Gosstandart, so that they would not be influenced by enterprises, their ministries or local authorities, including the party. In order to attract competent people and reinforce their integrity, they were very well paid. Their bonuses (of up to 60 per cent of their salaries) were related to a fall in complaints from customers, while they had no direct interest in the plan fulfillment of the firms they scrutinised (*Pravda*, 15 December 1986). Four out of five controllers had previously worked in the factories they examined. Almost one third had formerly been senior managers, and 28 per cent had headed their factory's old quality control departments (*Ek. gaz.,* No. 7, 1987). They numbered slightly less than one tenth of a factory's own quality controllers, but their capacity was considerable, as they utilised sampling. In order to facilitate the introduction of the new control system, it started gradually in the autumn of 1986. *Gospriemka* was supposed to complement, not replace, the old departmental quality control.

The new controllers had been ordered to act severely. The problem was that they did. Only 82–5 per cent of the output passed the first inspection, while the rest was returned for improvements. In 1987, output nominally worth about 6 billion rubles was rejected altogether.[4] The impact on output volumes was dramatic. In January 1987, the production of civilian machine-building fell sharply by 7.9 per cent, while industrial production as a whole declined by merely 0.1 per cent (*Ek. gaz.*, No. 8, 1987). The hard winter, that prompted other poor results, could not be blamed for the extraordinary shortfall in machine-building. A considerable recovery occurred in February 1987, as machine-building production grew by about 1.2 per cent and industrial production by 1.8 per cent, but the growth figures were still very low (*Ek. gaz.*, Nos. 8 and 12, 1987). *Gospriemka* was the obvious villain. Alarming reports appeared in the newspapers about controllers who stopped production for days (e.g. *Pravda*, 9 March 1987).[5] In many places, output targets were not reached and workers were deprived of their bonuses. Complaints of bureaucracy and unjustified production delays were raised. Some directors resisted the introduction of *gospriemka*, not least since 80 per cent of the detected shortcomings were caused by defective inputs, according to Gosstandart's Chairman (*Izvestiya*, 16 December 1987). Obsolete equipment, including German machine-tools captured as war reparations, were blamed (*Lit. gaz.*, 25 February 1987). The improvements of returned products turned out to be very costly, raising labour intensity by 15–20 per cent in parts of machine-building. The ultimate criterion was whether any significant amelioration of quality had occurred. After one year, the First Deputy Chairman of Gosstandart, Boris Sokolov concluded: 'No, no fundamental breakthrough has occurred as yet; inertia is still great.' The most evident achievement was an advancement in technical documentation (*Izvestiya*, 16 December 1987).

Gospriemka was the major economic theme in Soviet media from November 1986 until March 1987. The campaign was launched with the vigour characteristic of the new Soviet leadership. It was initiated with intimidating headlines, such as 'Without Concessions!' (*Lit. gaz.*, 17 December 1986) and 'And If without Compromises?' (*Izvestiya*, 8 January 1987). Soon they were replaced by more conciliatory or hesitant headlines: '*Gospriemka*: Two Approaches: Allies—Conflict' (*Ek. gaz.*, No. 8, February 1987), 'The Drama of *Gospriemka*' (*Lit. gaz.*, 25 February 1987), 'To Demand, and to Help' (*Sots. ind.*, 18 March 1987), and 'Common Sense and Campaign' (*Izvestiya*, 20 April 1987). What had begun as a fierce campaign to improve quality had fizzled out within a couple of months. The publicity about *gospriemka* was sharply reduced in March 1987, and the control eased.

Untypically, both Gorbachev and Zaikov swiftly acknowledged the problems. Gorbachev declared: 'During the first quarter, when we introduced *gospriemka*, economic accounting and a new [economic] mechanism, matters were difficult, in particular with the *gospriemka*.' At the same time, he made the implausible allegation: 'The working class does not want wages for production of low quality' (*Pravda*, 11 April 1987). Zaikov commented: 'But even the boldest project, the most advanced construction can be discredited, if storming and irresponsibility flourish in the production and [if] technological and work discipline are not maintained. That was especially manifested with the introduction of state acceptance of production' (*Pravda*, 26 April 1987).[6] Two months earlier he had optimistically stated that *gospriemka* 'has become the most important component in the struggle for a high technical level and quality of products. It has literally smashed old stereotypes about the necessity of low quality and has become a powerful factor in the forming of the new thinking of people at all levels ... ' (*Pravda*, 14 February 1987). Rarely has a senior Soviet politician turned so quickly against his own creation without demotion.

The emphasis of quality inspection moved from the final product to design, organisation and the quality of inputs, but the idea was such as not discarded. In October 1987, Gorbachev spoke strongly in defence of *gospriemka*, pointing out how useless substandard products were and how well state acceptance functioned in the defence sector (*Pravda*, 2 October 1987). Zaikov followed suit, praising 'the enormous organisational, explanatory and educational work' that *gospriemka* had performed and the many hidden shortcomings in production that had been uncovered (*Pravda*, 28 November 1987). *Gospriemka* was extended in 1988, but not much—to 727 more industrial associations and enterprises and to housing construction in twenty big cities (*Izvestiya*, 13 August 1987; *Pravda*, 18 March 1988). The caution suggests that the quality control was perceived as a failure, but the responsible politicians did not want to give it up entirely. Ironically, in the summer of 1988, the Party Control Committee reproached the leaders of Gosstandart for the scant impact of *gospriemka* (*Pravda*, 25 June 1988).

To judge from newspaper comments, the new controllers were highly qualified and uncommonly conscientious. Although Gosstandart had difficulties pinpointing quality improvements, *gospriemka* appears both more effective and less bureaucratic that the certification of products and the quality premiums that had existed before. It delivered a well-deserved shock to producers and might have promoted elementary order. In the absence of the checks of a market, some external quality control appears necessary, notwithstanding that sooner or later it will become corrupted and that overdemand always depresses quality. However, the ensuing declines in gross output and the accompanying cuts in bonuses turned out to be politically unacceptable. It is difficult to establish the precise reason for the quick reversal, but the overall social strains appear to have become intolerable. One possible explanation is strikes that erupted in the wake of eliminated bonuses. Did the advocates of *gospriemka* not understand what the effects would be, or were they prompted to moderate the campaign by sceptical colleagues? *Gospriemka* was advocated almost entirely by Zaikov and Gorbachev, and the other leaders were not overtly committed to it. Presumably, a Politburo majority desired high production figures, even if they were fictitious. Alternatively, it could be argued that the system itself rejected the new quality control as an alien body, since it endangered plan fulfillment on a large scale.

PERFECTION OF THE WAGE SYSTEM

A number of decrees on wages and social benefits were passed from 1985 to 1987. They barely branched outside the traditional framework. Probably the most important was a revision of wage tariffs. It was based on an experiment in Leningrad under Lev Zaikov's rule. A first decree issued in the summer of 1985 concerned the wages scales of 1.1 million research and development staff in industry (Kostin, 1987, p. 49; *Izvestiya*, 16 July 1985). Similar decrees covering scientific staff, university teachers, medical staff and school teachers—a total of 10 million people—followed (*Izvestiya*, 30 March 1986, 28 March 1987; *Pravda*, 4 January 1987; Kostin, 1987, p.48). Further wage increments were given to workers in the far north and far east (*Pravda*, 23 January 1986). The selection of favoured groups indicates the priorities of the new regime. It wanted to raise both the status and salaries of the intelligentsia in order to stimulate people to raise their qualifications. Research and development needed more effective incentives, and education and health care had long been neglected.

On 17 September 1986, the CC, the Council of Ministers and the trade unions adopted a major decree on new wages and tariffs for all workers employed in the productive sphere. It was to be introduced gradually over the period 1987–90 and would affect 75 million workers—two thirds of those employed in the state sector.[7] The last revision of tariffs in these branches had occurred in 1972–5, and a number of shortcomings had accumulated. A major concern was wage-levelling: 'The wage differences between qualified and unqualified work have been reduced ... If in 1965 the average salary of specialists in industry comprised 146 per cent of the average wage of workers, it was only 110 per cent in 1986' (Kostin, 1987, pp. 41–2). The wage system had grown ever more complicated, causing bureaucracy and reducing incentives. 'Bonuses and increments have to a large extent lost their stimulating role' (SP, No. 34, 1986). In industry alone the number of bonus systems amounted to fifty-six (Kostin, 1987, p. 43). There was hardly any relation between performance and income. Finally, the wage sum tended to rise faster than labour productivity.

A large number of fashionable goals were formulated. The socialist principle of distribution 'to everyone according to his work' was a principal guide-line. The new tariffs were supposed to stimulate all workers more effectively, promoting efficiency, social justice, research and development, quality, thrift and training. Hence, wages would be set in strict relation to 'the quality and quantity of work, to the final results of production' (SP, No. 34, 1986). 'The prestige of engineers' would be raised. The wage increases would be limited to the means earned by the work collective. All this may sound good, but how was it accomplished? There were too many maximands, but that problem appears to have eluded the activist officials of the State Committee for Labour and Social Affairs (Goskomtrud) who elaborated the new system.

Some changes were straightforward. The wage system became more unified. Irrelevant bonuses were abolished and transferred to wages. Thus, the basic wage share was supposed to grow from 50 to 70-5 per cent of the total wage. Income differentials were to be increased both between engineers and workers, and within each profession. Basic wages of blue-collar workers were to rise by 20-5 per cent, but salaries of 'leaders and specialists' by 30-5 per cent. A number of increments for able workers were introduced. They were based on both formal qualifications and actual performance. The number of wage classes was increased in order to boost income differentials. Ceilings on bonuses and total income were abolished. Far-reaching powers were given to directors to re-evaluate the abilities and performance of workers at all levels and remunerate them accordingly. Directors were encouraged to sack superfluous staff through a statute that relieved them of their prior duty to find them alternative jobs (*Ek. gaz.*, No. 44, 1986). The well-known Shchekino experiment, launched in 1967, had allowed directors to reduce their labour force and to distribute the retained wage fund among the remaining workers, if plan targets were met (Rutland, 1984; Norr, 1986). Now, it was propagated with new vigour. The wage reform was supposed to be financed by cuts in staff, increased production and the abolition of inefficient bonus systems.

During the first year (1987), the new wage system was applied to about 26 million workers, notably in the whole of Estonia and relatively successful branches (*Pravda*, 24 January 1988). The main achievement was a large reduction in the work force concerned—4–10 per cent (Kostin, 1987, p. 46). The Belorussian railway experiment, that had been praised by Gorbachev at the 27th Party Congress, led to a quick reduction of the labour force by 12,000 people (*Pravda*, 3 November 1986). It spread to all railways, whose labour force was reduced by as many as 280,000. Labour productivity rose by 14–15 per cent (Kostin, 1987, p. 47), but this was a dubious achievement since railway transportation declined in 1987 (*Pravda*, 24 January 1988), rendering a slim bottleneck even more slender. The certification of workers was often fictitious, though among research and development staff it led to a reduction of 60,000 employees, as much as 7.3 per cent in industry, while 20,000 people found their salaries reduced and about as many were demoted (Kostin, 1987, p. 50). Frequently, engineers did not receive higher pay rises than labourers. Changes in bonus sytems were even less significant. In July 1987, the Council of Ministers expressed their dismay with the unsatisfactory introduction of the new tariffs (Kostin, 1987, pp. 47–8; cf V. Shcherbakov in *Ek. gaz.*, No. 7, 1988).

The limited impact was not surprising. The wage rules were riddled with ambiguities and contradictions. Wages were supposed to be related to final results of work, but an outstanding feature of a command economy is the absence of a relevant measurement of final results. Verbally, qualitative improvements were emphasised, but the wage decree stated that enterprise directors could only obtain their bonuses for fulfillment of contracts if they were fulfilled to 100 per cent (SP, No. 34, 1986, p. 618). Thus, gross production remained the key indicator for bonuses, so little qualitative improvement could be expected. It was stated that each individual would be paid in accordance with his 'labour contribution' but, contrary to this principle, 'the role of labour collectives in the organisation of an efficient system of material and moral stimulation' would be raised (*ibid.*, p. 605).

One fundamental question was whether the principle of equal pay for equal work should be imposed, or whether earnings should depend on the performance of each enterprise. The wage decree stated both, without making the necessary choice: one stipulation was 'to assure the unity in payments to workers of the same profession, who carry out work of the same complexity in different branches' (*ibid.*, p. 607), and another: 'To widely practice the distribution of the collective earnings in brigades with regard to a coefficient of labour participation' (*ibid.*, p. 611). The wage decree was an attempt by the central authorities to impose their ideas of what the income structure should look like, but at the same time the decree abounds with assurances of 'a widening of the independence of associations, enterprises and organisations in their disbursement of the wage fund' (*ibid.*, p. 605). Although the movement of labour has been reasonably free in the Soviet Union, the relative shortages of different kinds of labour were hardly mentioned in the many articles on the new wage system. The goal was to encourage certain professions in the long term, but the authorities apparently neglected the short-term balance on the labour market.

Economics was disregarded. Soviet economists have discussed remuneration systems extensively, but they tend to depart from the present system. The First Deputy Chairman of Goskomtrud, L. Kostin (1987, pp. 42–3), complained that 'the contributions of scholars to the elaboration of proposals for the restructuring of wages are still insufficient. It has been necessary to use primarily non-scientific works' from practitioners. He admonished academic economists to work out a theoretical basis for the most efficient and socially-just wage system. However, leading Soviet economists did not think that task could be solved within the traditional parameters. Kostin (1987, p. 45) retorted:

Recently a number of academic economists have asserted that in the conditions of transition to self-financing no tariff system ... is needed. This is a stark example of how we occasionally not only in practice, but also in theory jump from one extreme to the other. A rejection of a tariff system, according to our view, is an anarchistic, anti-scientific position.

Goskomtrud had tried to design an intermediary link in the system before they knew what chain it was supposed to fit into. Little wonder that professional economists were taken aback. The elaboration of the new wage scales appeared to be a premature act of over-active bureaucrats.

The new wage system favoured the intelligentsia and directors. It had little in store for blue-collar workers. Many of them had already been deprived of bonuses by *gospriemka*, although they could barely influence quality. Their long-standing job security was tampered with, as directors' rights over employment and wage-setting were extended (*Izvestiya*, 6 June 1986). Dismissed workers could count on two months' notice, possibly two months' pay, for unemployment, and only the ineffective local job offices were obliged to assist them in their search for a new job (*Ek. gaz.*, No. 44, 1986).

On 12 February 1987 a decree on the promotion of shiftwork was adopted. The intention was to concentrate labour to the most efficient machines, but it offered relatively limited benefits to shiftworkers—wage increments of 20 per cent for evening work and 40 per cent for night work (*Ek. gaz.*, Nos. 10 and 26, 1987).

As if to mitigate negative reactions among workers, it was announced that the wage decree had been discussed in more than 150 work collectives by thousands of people (*Trud*, 30 August 1986). The Politburo bulletin on the adoption of the wage decree apologetically expressed 'the conviction that workers will accept the intended measures with understanding ... ' (*Pravda*, 19 September 1986). A decree on 'the efficient employment of the population ... and the reinforcement of social guarantees' (*Pravda*, 19 January 1988) indicated official concern, but its scant content offered the population little consolation.

In parallel, social benefits to those in particular need were raised. One of the first major measures of the Gorbachev regime was a significant rise of minimum pensions—first to thirty rubles a month (*Pravda*, 21 May 1985), and later to 40 rubles a month (*Pravda*, 4 December 1987). A complete pension reform, which would raise all pensions from their very low level of a maximum of 50 per cent of the salary during the month of official retirement, was envisaged (Bim and Shokhin, 1986; Pavlova and Rimashevskaya, 1987). A series of decrees raised the social benefits of other poor groups, such as families with many children and university students (*Izvestiya*, 20 October 1986; 29 March 1987). For the first time in many years, serious attempts were launched to improve the miserable state of Soviet health care. The CC Plenum in February 1988 was devoted to school reform. In addition, housing construction expanded. Social issues had risen on the agenda, but there was to be no compassion for poorly-performing workers.

THE INEFFECTIVENESS OF TRADITIONAL MEASURES

The new leaders lost no time in implementing a large number of changes within the traditional framework of the command economy. Their energy and activism were impressive. Similar measures had given significant results under Andropov's brief rule (Kontorovich, 1985), but not this time. An average annual growth in the net material product in current rubles of 1.5 per cent in 1985–6 was a very poor result indeed, especially if we deflate it by a probable hidden inflation of about 3 per cent a year.

It turned out that the 'enormous reserves' were not easily activated within the old system, whose combination of bottlenecks, rigidity and vested interests prevented most attempts at improvement. The jacking up of the growth targets in the new five-year plan was unrealistic, and is likely to have aggravated imbalances in the economy. The restructuring of investment was impeded by bottlenecks and inherent rigidities. As long as the price system was not fundamentally improved, rational criteria for the efficiency of an investment could hardly be found. The campaign against alcohol appears to have had several positive effects in the short term, but it was difficult to sustain it and market imbalances were exacerbated. In the longer run, an extensive criminality appears to be an inevitable result. The new quality control was possibly one of the best designed measures, but it appears to have been repelled by the system, since it jeopardised plan fulfillment and hence bonuses in many enterprises. Anyone who believed quality control on its own would raise quality decisively, should have been convinced to the contrary. The changes of the wage scales were neither well-considered nor effective.

The failures and ineffectiveness of the many traditional measures were spectacular. There was no reason to expect a better performance in the long run. Most means had been tried before, though not so energetically for the last two decades. The view that the system was good, but poorly managed, received a serious blow. The futility of these efforts probably taught many Soviet citizens that the traditional system had reached a dead end, and that economic reform was necessary. It should have been sufficiently clear by March 1987, when *gospriemka* had backfired, improvements in investment were absent, and the recoil against the anti-drinking campaign was apparent.

The outstanding negative effect was the aggravation of already severe market imbalances. Table 3.3 shows how the population's official money incomes from the public sector grew by 4.4 per cent in 1986, while retail sales at current prices stopped at an increase of 2.4 per cent. A flow of some 8 billion rubles were added to the inflationary gap. The campaign against alcohol is a sufficient explanation for this shortfall. The government's response was a reduction in income increases in 1987, but even so the inflationary gap grew more than usual. In its ambitious search for improvements, the regime neglected one of its most fundamental tasks: to maintain some balance between supply and demand.

Economists played a very limited role in designing these measures. They were only involved in the discussions on growth rates and investment, but their arguments were flawed and groping because of poor statistics. Still, they should have known that high investment rates and economic reform tend to be incompatible, and that shortages and bottlenecks would hamper any radical shift in investment resources if imports did not increase greatly. The quality control and the new wage system were worked out by the responsible authorities, Gosstandart and Goskomtrud, respectively. Apparently, economists were not consulted on the quality control, while Goskomtrud's ideas of

Table 3.3: The population's public money incomes and retail purchases

(*Bn current rubles*)

	1980	1985	1986	1987[1]
Population's money incomes[2]	291.5	351.6	367.2	378.9
Retail sales[3]	270.5	324.2	332.1	341.1
Money incomes ./. retail sales	21.0	27.4	35.1	37.8
Saving deposits	10.3	18.7	22.0	24

Annual Increase (per cent)	1981–5	1986	1987[1]
Population's money incomes[2]	3.8	4.4	3.2
Retail sales[3]	3.7	2.4	2.7

1. Preliminary and partly estimated figures.
2. Salary, wages, pensions and social benefits in cash. Private sales to the socialist sector and illicit cash flows from enterprises to individuals are not included.
3. State and cooperative sales.

Note: This is not the complete picture. Officially, retail sales accounted for 91 per cent of the population's money incomes in 1986 (*Sovetskaya torgovlya*, No. 11, 1987, table 5, transl. in JPRS-UEA-88-011). Several kinds of private payments to the public sector are not included, notably services other than catering, direct taxes and rents. On the other hand, private sales to the public sector, primarily agricultural produce, are omitted, and illicit payments take place in both directions.

Sources: Calculated from *Narkhoz 1986*, pp. 300, 412, 431, 435–7, 448, 456; *Narkhoz 1985*, p. 448; *Pravda*, 24 January 1988; Grossman (1986) p. 185.

a wage reform ran counter to the thinking of most senior economists. The anti-alcohol campaign barely involved either economists or economic administration.

The sudden demise of *gospriemka* is somewhat enigmatic. Its advocates should have been prepared for negative reactions, but they were not able to sustain the arduous quality control. Ironically, it fell on its own merits. Unlike so many other Soviet measures, *gospriemka* appears to have functioned as intended. The wage system, on the contrary, was poorly designed with many contradictions and unrealistic assumptions. Several of the contradictions might be the results of political compromises, but the many newspaper interviews indicate serious misconceptions in the thinking of responsible officials. The anti-alcohol campaign was a programme of party activism, with the regional party apparatus as the principal executive. Possibly, that explains why this campaign could be maintained even when plan targets were jeopardised. Another possible explanation is that this campaign enjoyed more high-level support than *gospriemka*. Moreover, the quality control antagonised the interests of the powerful machine-building ministries, while the campaign against alcohol primarily harmed weaker bodies, such as the Ministry of Finance, the Ministry of Trade and republican food-processing ministries in the South.

NOTES

1. The main source on the new investment policy, when no reference is given, is Nikolai Ryzhkov's speech at the Supreme Soviet on 18 June 1986 (*Pravda*, 19 June 1986).
2. Selyunin, on the contrary, pointed to unnecessary and unused equipment and favoured a reduced investment rate until the reform had been implemented (*Sots. ind.*, 5 January 1988).
3. At a press conference on 30 January 1987, the First Deputy Chairman of Gosstandart, Boris N. Sokolov, stated that *gospriemka* covered half of the industrial production of the country—a figure that has circulated in the Soviet and western press (e.g. *Ek. gaz.*, No. 7, 1987). However, he had apparent problems coming up with a number, so he was probably inaccurate.
4. These figures were given by Gosstandart's First Deputy Chairman, Boris Sokolov, in *Izvestiya*, 16 December 1987. Numbers vary widely, but it is not plausible that goods worth just 53 million rubles were finally rejected, as the annual plan fulfillment report alleged (*Pravda*, 24 January 1988). Yegor Gaidar (1988, p. 44) states that on average 8 per cent of industrial output did not pass the first inspection.
5. When visiting a factory in Vilnius in February 1987, I noticed from a graph on the wall that one workshop had stood idle for three days in November 1986. It turned out that state quality controllers, who had started working at the factory in September 1986, had stopped production for the readjustment of lathes.
6. 'Storming' is the notorious Soviet practice of concentrating production at the end of a plan period (month, quarter or year). It leads to hasty work and poor quality.
7. Published in SP, No. 34, 1986. The new wage system has been explained extensively in interviews with senior staff at Goskomtrud and the trade unions in *Trud*, 30 August, 4 October 1986; *Ek. gaz.*, No. 43, 1986; *Sots. ind.*, 4 and 31 October, 26 November 1986; *Izvestiya*, 25 September 1986, 13 April 1987; as well as by Kostin (1987). These materials, that are largely duplicative, are the sources of the ensuing exposé.

4. Changes in enterprise management[1]

Economic experiments have long been a feature of Soviet enterprise management. An economic experiment can be anything, but most of them involve tentative changes in enterprise management with minimal impact on the economic system at a national level. Many experiments have been local and of little consequence. However, from 1984, a number of centrally-initiated experiments came to dominate the stage. They were obviously designed to be forerunners of a prospective economic reform, comprising the focal point of Soviet economic debate until the 27th Party Congress in 1986. Today, the years 1984 and 1985 are sometimes referred to as the period of experiments.

Our intention is to highlight the most prominent experiments, with a selection based on political importance and impact on future changes. The first national experiment in this wave was the 'large-scale economic experiment in industry' which was introduced on 1 January 1984. It was closely connected with Yuri Andropov's demands for a perfection of economic management. Half a year later, an experiment in consumer services came into being. In 1985, two large machine-building production associations, the Frunze works in Sumy and VAZ in Togliatti, started an experiment with 'self-financing'. It was considered the second step after the large-scale experiment. The Law on State Enterprises adopted in June 1987 summed up the results of these experiments and may be seen as the third step. After the 27th Party Congress, a number of branch-oriented decrees were adopted. They concerned primarily enterprise management and reorganisation. The first and most important of them dealt with agriculture. In addition, a multitude of experiments or changes in enterprise management touched upon most branches of the economy. In certain areas of the country, notably Georgia, Estonia and Belorussia, economic experiments were particularly numerous and innovative. Many variations or experiments appeared within some experiments.

There are many ways of looking upon the economic experiments, and our evaluation of them will depend on which perspective we choose. A short-term economic evaluation would be negative. Most changes were too insignificant to make much difference, but their pedagogical value was considerable. They promoted economic thinking and showed that changes at the enterprise level were not enough.

Many experiments were so technically complex that only trained economists could understand them. As a result, economists started playing a greater role both within enterprises and at the national level. Chief economists replaced chief engineers as deputy directors at enterprises. A reformist vanguard was formed by progressive enterprise directors, academic economists and politicians. They were backed up by radical journalists. Several directors and officials made their careers on economic experiments. Commissions for various experiments were established centrally, developing an institutional and personal framework for future reforms.

The mobilisation of reformers, together with a growing insight into the difficulty of achieving economic efficiency bred a liberal radicalisation. New experiments probed the limits of the permissible. An economic and political snowball effect had arisen. In the 1960s, the experiments preceding the reform had been more radical than the reform, since they had aroused a conservative reaction. Now the contrary was happening. The initial experiments were cautious and embraced by a reasonably broad political consensus. They attracted radical criticism, prompting more far-reaching changes, though the independent momentum of the experiments should not be exaggerated, since a general political radicalisation prevailed.

From a reformist point of view, it was advantageous to move ahead along a broad, varied front. Branches perceived as particularly conservative, notably raw material extraction and the military-industrial complex, were avoided. Experiments could go surprisingly far in branches and regions with favourable economic and political conditions. The breadth of the experiments made it impossible to check them. A creeping reformism had arisen. The economic variety increased, and the ground was laid for greater economic pluralism, but it was not a smooth ride. Ineffective half-measures would sooner or later invite conservative criticism. The seemingly spontaneous changes at the micro-level sharpened systemic inconsistencies, which could worsen economic performance. The conservatives might even have laid traps by not opposing experiments that they thought would provoke public, anti-reform reactions.

In line with this reasoning, we shall focus on the essence of the qualitative changes involved in each experiment; its size; apparent economic results; institutional and political effects. What mattered in the end was the impact of an experiment on the future development of economic reform.

THE LARGE-SCALE ECONOMIC EXPERIMENT[2]

The origin of the 'large-scale economic experiment' was a decree adopted by the CC and Council of Ministers in July 1983 (*Ek. gaz.*, No. 31, July 1983). It was cautiously named: 'Decree about complementary measures to widen the rights of production associations (enterprises) in industry in planning and economic activity through the reinforcement of their responsibility for the results of their work.' Five ministries with 700 enterprises were singled out as guinea pigs from 1 January 1984. Two of them were all-union ministries for machine-building: the Ministry for Heavy and Transport Engineering and the Ministry of Electrotechnical Industry. The other three belonged to western republics: the Ministry of Food Industry in the Ukraine, the Ministry of Light Industry in Belorussia and the Ministry of Local Industry in Lithuania.

This experiment focused on plan indicators and bonus systems. Like the reforms of 1965, it aimed at a simplification of management. One basic feature was a considerable reduction in the number of plan indicators, but the extent of reduction varied between the ministries and enterprises involved.[3] In general, the consumer-oriented republican ministries appear to have cut the number of plan indicators more than the all-union machine-building ministries.

For the rest, most features of the experiment originated from 1979, but had never been implemented. One example was the attempted elaboration of more adequate plan indicators. The most important task became the fulfillment of planned deliveries. If an enterprise fulfilled all its contracts, its bonus fund ('for material stimulation') was to be increased by 15 per cent. In the case of failure, this fund would be reduced by 3 per cent for each missing 1 per cent of the planned deliveries. Thus, the experiment reinforced the emphasis on gross production. The intention was to make planning more detailed, but also more horizontal. In reality little changed.

Otherwise, a desire for more synthetic plan indicators prevailed. The significance of profits grew. An enterprise's 'fund for the development of production' (for locally-financed investment in production) became more dependent upon the growth of profits, but this fund was of little consequence to employees. It became easier for enterprises to manipulate prices, because they were permitted to raise prices by up to 30 per cent on the grounds of alleged improvements. Plan targets were supposed to be 'normatives', which expressed a relationship between output and input (for instance, labour productivity, material intensity, and capital productivity). Normatives were intended to be stable for five years, offering enterprises a more predictable economic environment. The wage fund of each enterprise was to be determined on the basis of 'stable normatives', related to final results. This gave enterprises an incentive to cut their labour force, because the wage fund would not be cut accordingly, assuring pay rises for the remaining workers. It was a mild version of the Shchekino experiment. Plans should be elaborated earlier to that they would reach enterprises in time. In addition, a large number of minor, ineffective changes occurred.

The political treatment of this experiment was more significant than its economic content. A special commission, 'the Commission for the General Guidance of the Experiment' was established to supervise it. It was chaired by Lev Voronin, a First Deputy Chairman of Gosplan, and met as frequently as twice a month to discuss the experiments that started mushrooming. The Voronin Commission gathered a score of senior academic economists, essentially the director plus one leading economist from each of the major economic institutes. These were the people who were to take the lead in the further development of the economic reform. The large-scale economic experiment offered them a welcome platform. Voronin himself advanced to the chairmanship of Gossnab in November 1985, after which this commission was left hanging in the air.[4] In due course, however, the ministers of the two pioneering machine-building ministries were dismissed after severe criticism for poor performance.

This experiment expanded quickly. In August 1984, the Politburo evaluated its initial results, and decided to expand it in 1985 to 21 ministries: five central ministries for machine-building and a selection of republican ministries for light industry, food-processing and local industry (2,300 enterprises, providing 12 per cent of Soviet industrial production). On 12 July 1985, the CC and Council of Ministers passed an extensive decree on the amendment and broadening of the large-scale experiment. Now it was called 'new economic methods', and the emphasis had turned to 'the acceleration of scientific-technical progress' (*Ek. gaz.*, No. 32, August 1985). The new economic methods would involve half of industrial production in 1986, and the whole of industry in 1987. This decree was extraordinarily unclear and looked like a political stalemate. A reactionary stipulation was the extension of planning in physical terms to 'fundamental kinds of new technology'. The most progressive amendment was that enterprises would be allowed to accumulate profits.

The economic results were insignificant. The most notable effect was an improvement of 1–2 per cent in accomplished delivery, but it dwindled during the course of the experiment, and it can be explained by preferential supplies and transport. The consumer-oriented republican ministries showed better results than the central machine-building ministries. The probable explanation is that there the experiment had gone further (see Voronin, 1984, p. 10; Yasin, 1986). The other notable change was that the experimenting ministries broke with their tradition of hoarding labour and cautiously began to reduce their labour force—by 0.5–0.8 per cent in 1985—presumably by not replacing all retiring staff (Voronin, 1985, p. 13), easing the tension on the labour market a little. No advances could be noticed in quality, technical development or economy.

The obvious conclusion was that the large-scale experiment had proved impotent and that a more substantial reform was necessary. In August 1985, Vasili Selyunin based a far-reaching criticism of the Soviet economy on a scrutiny of this experiment. He demanded the introduction of one single plan indicator, profit: 'All sides of the activity of the collective are really reflected in it' (Selyunin, 1985, p. 192). This was an early harbinger of what was to come, and the large-scale experiment provided an excuse for raising such arguments. Most leading Soviet economists commented on this experiment, praising it in principle, but contending that the changes must go further. The large-scale experiment had got the reformist ball rolling. It had legitimised sharp systemic criticism. Reformist economists were being mobilised both organisationally and intellectually.

THE SERVICE EXPERIMENT

At the beginning of 1984, before Konstantin Chernenko had become General Secretary, the CC and Council of Ministers adopted a decree initiating an economic experiment in the consumer service sector (*Pravda*, 10 February 1984). The purpose was to increase the volume of consumer services and raise quality, without allocating more resources. On 1 July 1984, the service experiment began in eight provinces in the RSFSR. In 1985, it was extended to the three Baltic republics, Belorussia and numerous provinces in the Ukraine and the RSFSR. Finally, in 1986, these new economic conditions were imposed throughout the country.

In principle, the service experiment went much further than the large-scale experiment in industry. It aimed at a considerable independence of enterprises. The central plan indicators for enterprises were radically cut from thirty to four. The most important target was gross sales of services to the population, followed by profits, quality and service. A straight correlation between gross sales and wage sum was introduced. When gross sales of an enterprise expanded by 1 per cent, its wage sum rose by 0.8 per cent (*Izvestiya*, 16 February 1984; *Pravda*, 7 January 1985).

One major novelty involved the distribution of profits. Enterprises were to pay a fixed share of their profits to their ministries and the state budget (*Ek. gaz.*, No. 39, 1984). The enterprise disposed of the rest. According to the decree, the remaining financial means could not be withdrawn by superior bodies, but the RSFSR Ministry of Finance did so anyhow (*Pravda*, 26 August 1985).

Different forms of work organisation were envisaged. The main idea was to promote a series of contractual obligations. Upwards, a service enterprise could conclude a contract with its republican ministry, internally with small work collectives or even individuals. A contract could either specify bonuses in return for a production obligation or be a leasehold agreement. A contractual agreement could become complex with intermediary calculation prices (*Ek. gaz.*, No. 38, 1985). If a small number of workers leased a workshop, they established a *de facto* cooperative, sharing the proceeds in accordance with a mutual prior agreement. In particular in Estonia, such collective leaseholds developed in repair workshops and catering. The successes of publicised cases were spectacular, both in quantitative and qualitative terms, with labour productivity doubling in no time (*Izvestiya*, 18 August 1985, 28 August 1986). Less publicised examples of individual and family leasehold were also excellent. Labour productivity did not increase by less than 50 per cent.[5]

The reported achievements in the service experiment were as striking as they were few. Essentially, they originated from Estonia, Georgia and Lithuania. Press reports, as well as travellers' observations, made plain that little had changed in most of the country. Even in Estonia, the vanguard of the service experiment, only about one tenth in the employees of the republican Ministry for Consumer Services (*Minbyt*) were involved in leasehold in the summer of 1986.[6] Articles in *Pravda* and one CC resolution (10 January 1986; 7 January 1985) bitterly complained that little had happened. Even so, during the second half of 1984, the volume of services in the eight experimenting provinces of the RSFSR rose 3.3 percentage units more than in the republic as a whole (*Pravda*, 7 January 1985).

Unlike the large-scale experiment, the service experiment marked a departure from Brezhnevian economics. It augured the introduction of a new economic thinking. The fixed profit tax-rate could facilitate real autonomy of enterprises. The notion of negotiated contracts between all economic actors was reminiscent of the Hungarian economist Tibor Liska's concept of an 'intrapreneurial' system. Experimental cooperatives, leaseholds and individual enterprises were legitimised by the experiment. Its economic results were excellent.

A combination of reasons conditioned the early application of these liberal ideas on the service sector: here the socialist sector had virtually collapsed, and the state was not prepared to provide additional resources; the service sector was perceived as naturally small-scale, technically backward, and market-oriented, rendering the market and enterprise more acceptable; the ministries in charge were weak republican institutions with little power.

EXPERIMENTS WITH SELF-FINANCING

The economic experiments at the Frunze production association in the Ukranian town Sumy and VAZ in Togliatti on the Volga, have been described by the prominent economists Abel Aganbegyan and Pavel Bunich as 'the second step', after the large-scale economic experiment. Its essence was 'self-financing' (*samofinansirovanie*). It was launched in January 1985 at Sumy and later that spring at VAZ.

The decision to initiate this experiment had evidently been taken under Konstantin Chernenko's rule, but the Sumy experiment was first mentioned in the central press just after Gorbachev's elevation (*Lit. gaz.*, 20 March 1985). From July 1985, a press campaign lauded the Sumy and VAZ experiments. It was spearheaded by the most reformist newspapers, notably *Izvestiya*, and *Literaturnaya gazeta*, but even *Pravda* joined in (17 July and 27 October 1985). At the end of 1986, a mass propaganda book was published on the Sumy experiment (Shramko, 1986). The obvious purpose was to disseminate a new form of economic thinking and to convince people that a radical economic reform was necessary. Both VAZ and the Sumy association were outstanding, well-equipped producers of cars and equipment for extracting natural gas, respectively. The choice of these industrial leaders for an 'experiment' indicated that the aim was to achieve a propaganda success, not to test the viability of certain economic measures.

This experiment addressed the notorious planning from the achieved level, which compelled enterprises to advocate low production targets and avoid exceeding them. Another purpose was to encourage enterprises to economise and exploit their reserves. A third, related, aim was to offer predictable financial conditions. For instance, in 1986 the Gorki car production association (GAZ) paid the Ministry of Finance through fourteen channels and received money back through four. It paid its branch ministry through almost ten channels, and obtained returns in eight ways (*Ek. gaz.*, No. 6, 1987). In addition, its ministry could demand funds at will from successful undertakings and reallocate them to loss-makers. Self-financing was seen as the solution.

In practice, self-financing meant the establishment of a set 'tax' rate on the profits of the Sumy and VAZ associations of 29 and 52.5 per cent, respectively, though the word 'tax' was not used for ideological reasons. This tax was to be paid partly to the Ministry of Finance, partly to their branch ministries. Unpredictable payments to superior bodies were supposed to cease. The bonuses of the preceding year would no longer be guaranteed, but depend on the profit. Fixed shares of the profit would be distributed to three unified funds within the enterprise (for investment in production, for material stimulation, and a social and cultural fund). The label 'self-financing' was not quite appropriate, because some investments in production were still financed out of central funds (Bunich, 1986b, p. 582). A stricter correlation between labour productivity and wage increases was supposedly imposed (*Ek. gaz.*, No. 18, 1986).

The results of the Sumy association in 1985 were widely advertised and appeared impressive. The profit had risen by 32.4 per cent (to compare with an annual average of 18.4 per cent in 1981–4), labour productivity by 13.6 per cent (about 10 per cent a year in 1981–4), and gross production by 14.4 per cent (12 per cent a year in 1981–4), while its debt was reduced by 44.2 per cent (Bunich, 1986b, pp. 583–4). In 1986, its profits even grew by 68 per cent (*Pravda*, 27 January 1987). Similarly, VAZ aspired to cut its work force slightly (by 1,300 men), after having previously suffered from a chronic shortage of labour (*Izvestiya*, 28 July 1985). These two industrial leaders had been given extraordinary attention by supply and transport organisations. Still, the published results suggested that at least the Sumy association operated with a new concern for its profits, and the experiment seemed successful.

The political significance of the Sumy experiment was manifested by the formation of a permanent working-group under the Voronin Commission for this very experiment. Its leading economist was Pavel Bunich, a corresponding member of the Academy of Sciences (*Lit. gaz.*, 6 November 1985). The Director General of the Sumy plant, Vladimir Lukyanenko was swiftly promoted to minister. The economic director of VAZ, P. Katsura, who had published the first extensive articles on the VAZ experiment (*Izvestiya*, 27 and 28 July 1985), became the head of a new department at the chancery of the Council of Ministers on the improvement of the economic mechanism and a senior adviser to Prime Minister Ryzhkov.

While the large-scale experiment primarily drew attention to shortcomings in enterprise management, the Sumy/VAZ experiment exposed flaws in the economic system itself, prompting economists to call for reform. Pavel Bunich exploited it for his advocacy for radical reform (*Lit. gaz.,* 12 February 1986; Bunich 1986ab; Bunich and Moskalenko, 1986). Basically, self-financing meant profit-steering and self-planning, but Bunich (1986a, p. 587) pointed out that the Sumy association was still governed by more than 230 plan indicators. The experiment had focused on financial issues, but an enterprise could not buy anything without an authorised purchasing order from Gossnab, and such orders were based on the plan. This inconsistency aroused new calls for wholesale trade instead of centralised allocation. Prices were still based on costs plus a mark-up, offering enterprises little incentive to save inputs. Such cost-savings could paradoxically lead to a reduction in enterprise profits. Indeed, conservative critics of self-financing argued that the apparent success was caused by hidden inflation, and they called the experiment a bluff (*Lit. gaz.,* 24 July and 6 November 1985). The reformers, on the other hand, grew more explicit in their demands for market pricing.

The perspective of the Sumy directors Lukyanenko and Moskalenko was more power-oriented. They considered the complete amalgamation of individual enterprises into their highly centralised association vital. On the one hand, they needed bargaining power to be able to resist their ministry. On the other hand, they desired autarkic control over the resources of sub-ordinate units (Moskalenko, 1986, p. 102; Lukyanenko in *Izvestiya*, 1 January 1987).

Curiously, unlike other prominent experiments, self-financing was not expanded after one year. Bunich voiced disappointment with its slow development (*Lit. gaz.,* 12 February 1986). Soon afterwards, Gorbachev and Ryzhkov gave it a political boost at the Party Congress, but the expansion of self-financing was sluggish. Only in 1987 did it expand—to five whole ministries and thirty-seven associations belonging to seventeen other ministries, in total contributing over 20 per cent of Soviet industrial production. Of the five ministries, three dealt with machine-building, one was the Ministry for Petrochemical Industry, and the last one was the Ministry of the Maritime Fleet. In 1988, self-financing embraced enterprises with a labour force of 51 million, accounting for over 60 per cent of the industrial and agricultural production, all communications, 88 per cent of transport, 97 per cent of retail trade, and half of consumer services (*Pravda*, 26 April 1988).

However, in 1987 the enterprises engaged in 'self-financing' did not display better result than other enterprises. Their single positive accomplishment was that they shed some workers (*Pravda*, 14 July 1987). Many problems were caused by the branch ministries and the Ministry of Finance, which did not respect the rules of the experiment. VAZ seemed to experience all the traditional problems of a Soviet enterprise: the Ministry of Automotive Industry altered its plans and normatives; detailed instructions were handed down in the old fashion; the Ministry confiscated funds belonging to VAZ; two thirds of its currency earnings were in transferable rubles and there was no mechanism for using them (*Izvestiya*, 30 January 1987). Because of demands from the Ministry of Finance, the unified profit tax in Sumy was abolished and replaced by a profit tax and a capital fee (*Lit. gaz.*, 22 October 1986). In 1987, visitors to Sumy reported the actual profit tax had risen by about 20 percentage units to some 50 per cent of the profit.

With the two model associations being treated so badly, it is doubtful whether self-financing was even introduced at the other enterprises. As the experiment expanded, it appears to have provoked an open struggle between the branch ministries and the Ministry of Finance on the one hand, and the enterprises on the other. The poor economic performance was probably the outcome of this battle. Besides, there were many unsolved technical questions. One was what to do with enterprises operating at a loss. They constituted 13 per cent of all industrial enterprises, and a much larger share— over 60 per cent—suffered from insufficient profitability (V. M. Ivanchenko in *Ek. gaz.*, No. 32, 1986).

Oddly, self-financing developed furthest in an experiment initiated at sixty-nine *theatres* in 1987. They were told to mind their own business, elect directors, choose plays and set wages, within their current level of funding and with fixed ticket prices (*Izvestiya*, 17 August 1986; *Lit. gaz.*, 11 June 1986). The leading reform economist involved in this venture, Nikolai Petrakov, stated: 'Theatre is production' and compared it with industrial production (*Teatr*, No. 1, 1987, p. 27). It was a strange idea to let commercialisation develop furthest at theatres, which are non-commercial in many capitalist countries. Soviet critics claimed that the result was an instance decline in quality. The basic intention might have been to give theatres more political independence, and actors could benefit from higher incomes, but suspicion lingers that this was a trap laid by conservatives.

EXPERIMENTS AND REFORM IN AGRICULTURE[7]

Ever since the collectivisation in the early 1930s, agriculture has been an outstanding weakness of the Soviet economy. No other branch appears so riddled with economic absurdities (see Hedlund, 1984). A variety of experiments have budded and died in different regions of the country. Brezhnev's policy granted agriculture an abundance of resources, but inadequate incentives.

Old reform proposals have included a reduction of the size of agricultural work collectives; the economic independence of work teams with full responsibility for one area of land; the dependence of earnings on profits; and some revision of the price system. The names of the experiments changed, but the same ideas kept reappearing. One of the most far-reaching earlier experiments was normless links—a small group of workers who practically leased an area and shared the profit among themselves. Gorbachev had lent his support to this model in the mid-1970s (Weickhardt, 1985, pp. 253–4).

Yet, agriculture was supervised by an immense bureaucracy, and, to a much greater extent than industry, by the local party apparatus (Nove, 1977, pp. 127–8). Any kind of economic independence threatened local party power, abruptly ending many a successful experiment. Moreover, collectivisation had left a legacy of large-scale, collective or state farming. Gorbachev endorsed the collectivisation as late as 2 November 1987.[8] In addition, the confused Food Programme of May 1982 appears to have been sincerely supported by Gorbachev and remained sacrosanct. No branch was subject to as many local experiments as agriculture. A multitude of reorganisations and changes in the incentive system took place.

The conflicts between different departments were particularly profound in agriculture. The apparent reason was that Stalin's old desire to control the farms in detail had minimised local integration. In each area, the organisations in charge of agriculture, technical supplies, water and material inputs, respectively, were at loggerheads. The apparent solution was to merge all local organs dealing with agriculture into so-called RAPOs (*raion* agro-industrial associations). This was pioneered in Abasha in Georgia in 1974. Estonia followed suit, and the creation of RAPOs became compulsory through the Food Programme. However, the RAPOs received contradictory orders from a plethora of superior bodies. The logical next step was to amalgamate republican ministries dealing with agriculture, first in Georgia in 1982, and the next year in Estonia and Lithuania (*Pravda*, 13 July 1985). In 1986, a major fusion of central agricultural ministries took place, and similar mergers occurred in all republics (see Chapter 5).

RAPOs caused an expansion of local bureaucracy. Since they turned out to be ineffective, the search for efficient local integration continued. Three alternative models of agro-industrial associations developed. Each included a large number of enterprises; aimed at integrating all economic links 'from the field to the shop'; aspired to reduce the RAPO administration, which they more or less replaced; and implied a reduction in the number of compulsory plan indicators from about forty to three. Their differences revolved around the degree of economic independence of enterprises involved and internal accounting rules. The first type of association, the *kombinat* Kuban in Krasnodar *krai*, started in accordance with a decision by the Politburo in 1985 (*Ek. gaz.*, No. 34, 1985). The alternative 'agro-industrial association' in Novomoskovski *raion* in Tula *oblast* was further integrated. A third model, the 'agrofirm' Adazhi in Latvia, involved fewer enterprises. At the beginning of 1988, there were forty-nine agro-industrial *kombinaty* of the Kuban type, nineteen agro-industrial associations of the Novovmoskovski type, and

fourteen agrofirms of the Adazhi type (*Pravda*, 24 January 1988). Neither
kind was encouraged in the most reformist republics, Estonia and Georgia.
Estonian reformers opposed all these agglomerations, which they saw as a
new outburst of gigantomania, threatening enterprise autonomy. They
desired smaller, not larger, economic units. The publicised economic
achievements of all these associations appear mediocre.[9]

In 1985, the most far-reaching and fashionable experiment with small,
autonomous work units was pursued at the Altai *krai* in Siberia under the
leadership of Academician Tatyana Zaslavskaya, with support from
Academician Abel Aganbegyan (*Izvestiya*, 31 May 1985; Aganbegyan, 1985a,
p. 12). Since 1982, small agricultural teams had tended a specific area with full
economic accountability. During the first three years, the results were
excellent. Gross agricultural production rose by 58 per cent, capital
productivity by 55 per cent, and labour productivity by 34 per cent, while
prime cost fell by a third (Aganbegyan, 1985a, p. 12). Soviet agriculture
as a whole was more or less stagnant during these years. This experiment
became a favourite of *Izvestiya* (29 March, 31 May 1985; 12 March, 4 April
1986, 23 February 1987), and *Pravda* honoured it with an editorial on 24
September 1985. Even so, it did not catch on as intended. The regional party
committee tried to stall it in opposition to central authorities. Finally, the CC
adopted a resolution that sharply criticised the party committee of Altai *krai*
for not promoting progressive forms of work (*Pravda*, 21 April 1987).[10]

Collective or brigade contract (*podryad*) had long been promoted, but
usually it did not mean much.[11] It implied a search for smaller more
independent work units, with bonuses related to the gross production of a
team of workers. In rare cases, small collectives were effectively leasing land
and equipment, prompting production and personal incomes to rise instantly
to incomprehensible heights. In one year, the leader of a small brigade
working on leasehold in Uzbekistan earned no less than 23,000 rubles (twenty
times the ordinary wage), arousing protests against profiteering (*Izvestiya*, 6
January 1988).[12] Normless links reappeared and won praise (*Pravda*, 24
January 1987).

At the 27th Party Congress, Gorbachev and Murakhovski put family
contract, and even individual contract, on the political agenda. Like other
forms of collective contracts, 'family contracts' may be divided into a kind of
bonus system and leasehold (see *Izvestiya*, 26 April 1987). As usual, the less
radical form dominated. It is often difficult to distinguish them from one
another in Soviet accounts, but family leasehold are frequently called 'family
farms'. All of a sudden, the press revealed that family farms already existed in
various parts of the country, primarily in Estonia, Latvia, Lithuania, Vologda
and Moscow (*Izvestiya*, 16 January 1986), but their number was tiny—ninety
in Estonia where the number was supposed to be the largest. Their economic
results were outstanding, as were the personal incomes (*Pravda*, 2 November
1986). Besides, in parts of Caucasus and Central Asia actual family farming
had long existed. Now many of them were legalised.

The radical economist Anatoli Strelyani wrote a widely-appreciated television documentary called 'The Arkhangelsk Peasant' about an able, hard-working peasant in the Russian north who concluded a contract with a state farm to lease a poorly used old farm. He achieved excellent results, which prompted local bureaucrats and politicians to cancel his lease, since he exposed their own inefficiency (*Moscow News*, No. 5, 1987). This film showed what could be accomplished on the worst Russian soils without additional resources, and it appealed to the Russian nationalists who disapproved of collectivisation, but otherwise tended to object to market-and-profit-oriented reforms.[13]

Soon after Gorbachev's call for agricultural reform at the 27th Party Congress, the Politburo approved of a Decree 'On further perfection of the economic mechanism in the country's agro-industrial complex' (*Pravda*, 21 March 1986). In spite of its modest title, this document spells out changes that may be labelled economic reform. Obligatory deliveries to the state remained, but plan targets were supposed to be stable for a whole five-year period. Production above plan targets, and 30 per cent of the planned production of potatoes, fruit and vegetables, could be sold by state and collective farms through any channel at going prices. Farms were supposed to pay income tax that would be related to land rent, fixed assets and labour force (*Pravda*, 29 March 1986; *Izvestiya*, 13 September 1986). Strangely, plan indicators were not specified, but after the fulfillment of planned deliveries, profit was meant to become the dominant indicator. The decree 'allows' state farms, but 'recommends' collective farms, to utilise family and individual contract 'as one of the forms of collective contract'.[14]

The most remarkable feature about Soviet agriculture during the next two years was its lack of development. Gross production developed well in 1986, though it stagnated in 1987, but it has been argued that statistical fraud rose grossly over this period (*Lit. gaz.*, 11 May 1988), so the officially-claimed improvement may not have taken place. When asking Soviet agricultural officials in Moscow about the stability of plan targets, I was invariably told that it should not be taken literally. One should not be dogmatic but adopt a pragmatic approach. They never concealed their intention to continue changing targets as they pleased. In 1986, public farms only sold 0.8 per cent of their potato harvest, and 3 per cent of their fruit and vegetables, through consumer cooperatives or on *kolkhoz* markets (Lacis, 1987b, p. 61). The main reason was that officials had juggled plan targets. The bureaucracy had been cut at the top but reappeared at the lower rungs of the agricultural hierarchy (*Pravda*, 3 August 1987), allowing little independence of farms to emerge (*Pravda*, 8 March 1988). Newspapers reported that detailed orders about sowing and harvesting were still passed down to the farms.

The development worsened from 1986 to 1987, presumably because the bureaucratic resistance had been mobilised. The number of leaseholds remained small. Only the Baltic republics managed to calculate land rent—on the basis of the pre-war land prices. The single improvement that came to light was that *kolkhozy* and *sovkhozy* had refused to accept about 30 per cent of the tractors and combine harvesters they had been offered (*Pravda*, 19 July 1987; *Izvestiya*, 13 April 1987). This equipment was both superfluous and of poor quality. Since the farms were overloaded with substandard equipment, it was a good sign that they started bothering about expenditures.

By early 1987, it should have been clear to the rulers that the reform attempt had essentially failed (see Lacis, 1987b). A new start was needed. Two options that had been tried in Hungary and China, respectively, were the abolition of all plan targets handed down from above and family leasehold. At the CC Conference on economic reform (8–9 June 1987), Academician Oleg Bogomolov advocated that economic reform should begin in agriculture, pointing to the experiences of Hungary, China and Czechoslovakia (*Pravda*, 13 June 1987).[15] At the CC Plenum in June 1987, Gorbachev suggested that the almost 800,000 deserted farm-houses north of the black soil area should be utilised and leased with land to town-dwellers (*Pravda*, 26 June 1987). A decree to this effect was adopted, but the plot of each house was limited to 600 square metres, rendering full-time private farming impossible (*Pravda*, 1 August 1987).

In August 1987, Gorbachev argued strongly in favour of family contract, family teams and *arenda*, the correct Russian word for leasehold. He said 'we have agreed in the Politburo on the preparation of the new CC Plenum in order to work over the agricultural policy taking account of the new situation and the accumulated experience' (*Pravda*, 6 August 1987), but the Plenum was postponed into a distant future. In September 1987, a CC Decree on 'urgent measures to accelerate the solution of the food question in accordance with the stipulations of the June (1987) CC Plenum' appeared in print (*Ek. gaz.*, No. 40, 1987). It contained two important novelties. First, all agricultural organisations should introduce self-financing in 1988–9. Secondly, it favoured long-term leases in agriculture (for ten to fifteen years), but it did not contain the necessary operative provisions, so little happened.

Agriculture remains the subject of an inordinate number of big meetings, notably the *Kolkhoz* Congress (March 1988) and two CC meetings on leasehold (13 May and 12 October 1988) where there was much reform verbage, but a decisive reformist push is not yet apparent. The most important development was the formal abolition of plan targets for collective farms through the adoption of the new Law on Cooperatives by the Supreme Soviet in May 1988. As food shortages have worsened, the time might have come for a large-scale introduction of leasehold. However, the legal basis of leasehold remains skimpy. Gorbachev has stated that a law on leasehold—allowing long-term leases—is being formulated (*Pravda*, 14 October 1988). Such legislation appears necessary for the development of leasehold.

Agriculture is moving from state production targets towards self-financing and small-scale, long-term leasehold, but to be convincing, these ideas need to be endorsed by a special CC Plenum. Besides, the complex price system has not been changed and distorts decision-making; it has proved problematic to establish the new tax rates; the intrusive power of superior bodies remains overwhelming. An outstanding problem is that 14.6 per cent of all state and collective farms operated at a loss in 1987, and only 23 per cent were considered to be sufficiently profitable to become really self-financing (*Izvestiya*, 14 January 1988).

SUNDRY EXPERIMENTS

Elsewhere in the economy, a large number of experiments and changes in enterprise management emerged. Self-financing and full economic account-ability (*khozraschet*) had become the catch-words, but the concepts were more common than their application.

The poor state of Soviet light industry could hardly escape anyone's attention. Too few commodities of a narrow assortment and low quality were provided at inflated prices, at the same time as stocks of unsaleable goods piled up. Every conceivable improvement was needed. Some republican ministries were involved in the large-scale economic experiment. The Ministry of Light Industry of Estonia became the favourite of the media (*Sots. ind.*, 18 August 1985; *Trud*, 11 July 1986; *Izvestiya*, 10 April 1986). The peculiarity of the Estonian experiment was primarily that it had taken over supply agencies, the wholesale trade of final products and some retail outlets. The number of plan indicators for the enterprises had been reduced from twenty-three to six in 1985 (Bunich, 1986a, pp. 14–15), and in 1987 to three (profit, gross production in physical terms and an investment limit). The return to a gross output target in physical terms was provoked by enterprises' tendency to limit their contracted sales and to raise prices without authorisation. Estonia could point to good results—a rise in labour productivity of 5.5 per cent a year in 1985 and 1986, compared with 1 per cent in 1984 (*Sots. ind.,* 1 May 1987).

The Estonian model was supposed to be extended to the whole country through a decree by the CC and the Council of Ministers passed on 24 April 1986 on 'improvement' of planning and incentives in light industry (*Pravda*, 6 May 1986; SP, No. 20, 1986). Profit became the principle plan indicator, supplemented with gross output in physical terms, an investment limit, and the fulfillment of contracted deliveries, though additional plan targets were not explicitly prohibited. The decree envisaged stable normatives for the rest of the five-year period for the distribution of the profit, as in the Sumy/VAZ experiment. Still, the decree was too vague to convince, and ensuing official statements were both few and conservative (see the interview with Minister V.G. Klyuev in *Ek. gaz.*, No. 36, 1986). The reform appeared insincere, and it came as no surprise that light industry showed a minimal official growth in 1987.

Because of the prevalence of the seller's market, it was abundantly easy to sell anything. Consequently, the main concern in retail trade was to boost sales as much as possible. By tradition, the costs of trade had been minimised, and losses were not much noticed. Service was atrocious, but trade remained a low-priority branch. Misallocation was a problem, but as long as centralised allocation prevailed, retail traders could not be expected to track large supplies themselves. Since gross sales were the overwhelming preoccupation, radical experiments in retail trade did not appear likely, and little happened. On 17 July 1986, the CC and the Council of Ministers issued a decreee on the 'perfection' of planning, incentives and management in state trade and consumer cooperatives (*Pravda*, 5 August 1986; SP, No. 29, 1986). The number of plan indicators would be reduced, but gross sales (excluding alcohol sales) would become even more important than before. Stable, differentiated normatives for the distribution of profits were envisaged. A Soviet analysis makes clear by implication that twenty additional legal documents entailed little but technocratic 'perfection' of the old command system (Yazev, 1987). No significant changes occurred in the functioning of socialised trade. It is inappropriate to speak of self-financing in retail trade, though an experiment of this nature was introduced in Belorussia, Estonia and Latvia in 1987 (*Pravda*, 26 December 1986; 15 May 1987; *Izvestiya*, 3 April 1987).

Construction was one of the most problematic branches of the economy. It was well-endowed with capital, but highly inefficient. Sheer squandering of resources was striking; the completion of construction projects was very slow; hidden inflation was particularly great in construction; the quality was miserable. The most urgent demand was to raise efficiency of available resources, and thus increase actual capacity, and complete projects faster. Construction had seen a continuous stream of minor changes in plan indicators and organisation (see Komarov, 1984; *Sots. ind.*, 3 October 1985). Leaving aside organisational changes, the future interest focused on two experiments, the Belorussian construction experiment, which has been discussed in Chapter 2, and another in Moscow *oblast*.

The latter started in 1985 at the trust *Mosoblselstroi* No. 18. Its director Nikolai Travkin, who had advanced from foreman, became a Stakhanov of perestroika. He received ample public praise and was frequently interviewed.[16] This experiment started with stable, negotiated prices, as in the Belorussian experiment, but its essence was collective contract with self-management, reminiscent of the once renowned Zlobin system (cf Weickhardt, 1985, p. 258). From July 1986, full economic accountability was introduced. The trust, with about 300 workers, was governed by a purportedly democratically-elected economic council of twenty-nine people. In effect, this constituted a transformation into a self-managed enterprise. The economic results were impressive. In 1985, labour productivity rose by 20 per cent and average wages by 11 per cent, while prime costs fell by 12 per cent and the engineers and technical staff were reduced by 28 per cent. After having been a chronic loss-maker for fifteen years, the trust suddenly became highly profitable. The prominent economic journalist Ruslan Lynev predicted that such new forms of work in construction would bring about a growth in labour productivity by 50–80 per cent (*Izvestiya*, 17 January 1986).

On 14 August 1986, the CC and the Council of Ministers adopted a Decree 'On measures to perfect the economic mechanism in construction' (*Pravda*, 13 September 1986). The Belorussian experiment was explicitly endorsed, and self-financing was supported, but the new rules were unclear. Soon afterwards, the CC issued a recommendation to spread Travkin's example of collective contract (*Pravda*, 31 October 1986). This was not a very authoritative document. Apparently, Travkin's successful experiment had not obtained sufficient political support. Conversely, applied rules made the Belorussian regulations compulsory, while Travkin's experiment was recommended, and a recommendation means little in the Soviet Union (*Byulletin Minyust*, No. 3, 1987, pp. 12–20).

Road transport had long appeared one of the most wasteful and corrupt parts of the Soviet economy. Lorry drivers tried to maximise their achievements in tonkilometres without any consideration for costs, undertaking unnecessary transportation, choosing long routes, falsifying transport documents, and selling about half of their fuel on the black market. From the beginning of 1984, twenty-four road transport enterprises in the RSFSR started an economic experiment to amend this situation.[17] They belonged to eight different ministries, and the experiment was run by Goskomtrud. As in the case of construction, a price was negotiated for a certain transport, and earnings were related to the fulfillment of this task and reductions of costs. To make the incentives more effective, they were applied to small brigades. The results were good. In 1985, the enterprises involved in the experiment fulfilled their contracted deliveries to 99.8 per cent, compared with 86 per cent in 1983. The amount of lorries diminished by 4.7 per cent, the number of drivers by 2.7 per cent, and the cost of fuel by 18 per cent. Labour productivity and wages grew accordingly. The incentive to commit fraud diminished, and thus the experimenting enterprises admitted a reduction in the volume of transported goods of 20 per cent and a decline in tonkilometres of 14 per cent. These excellent achievements led to a proliferation of the new system of road transport.

During Eduard Shevardnadze's long rule as First Party Secretary of Georgia—from 1972 until July 1985—Georgia excelled as the centre of economic and political experiments. The agricultural experiments have already been discussed. At the end of 1981, an experiment started in the small town of Poti.[18] A 'territorial inter-departmental association' was established. Its task was to redistribute means of local enterprises belonging to different ministries in order to raise efficiency and to reinforce the local infrastructure through a proft tax on all enterprises in the area. The experiment existed in two versions, one administrative and one commercial. As the experiment gradually spread through Georgia, the commercial principle gained the upper hand. It implied that the territorial associations were profit-oriented, carrying out their redistribution for a commission fee. In the summer of 1986, this experiment was promoted union-wide as part of a decree on the increased role of the Soviets (*Izvestiya*, 30 July 1986).

The most astounding experiment was launched in 1985 at a shoe factory in Batumi. In effect, the factory was transformed into a self-managing enterprise of the Yugoslav type. This experiment was approved by the Georgian CC in 1984. The council of the firm became its governing body. Since 'one of the shortcomings in the existing economic mechanism in our branch is that enterprises determine their tasks for a full year', the firm abolised annual plans, and declared: 'What to produce and how much, we decide ourselves.' Wages were supposed to be set in accordance with the final result, which appears to have been profit. In order to produce what the market demanded, the shoe firm acquired its own retail outlets and established a department for business cycles and demand. It had the right to set its own prices (*Sots. Ind.*, 4 October 1985).

In 1984, the buses in Tbilisi were effectively leased to the busdrivers' brigades, which paid for fuel, spare parts and repairs themselves. In return, they obtained all fares (Fedorenko and Perlamutrov, 1987, p. 9). These brigades were really profit-sharing enterprises. Since these and similar experiments (including family cafés) were swiftly closed down by Shevardnadze's successor in Georgia, Dzhumber Patiashvili, they had little impact on the future of reform. Georgia stands out as an example of how a new reactionary regional party leader could turn the clock backwards, regardless of a tilt towards reform in Moscow.

THE LAW ON STATE ENTERPRISES

The Law on State Enterprises (Associations), adopted by the Supreme Soviet at the end of June 1987, may be seen as the conclusion of the first round of experiments with enterprise management (*Pravda*, 1 July 1987). At the same time, it was a general programme for economic reform to which the next chapter will be devoted. At the inception of the Law, reformist economists had spoken of it as a means of cutting off enterprises from the harmful influences of superior bodies. In its final form, the law was a compromise, encountering considerable liberal criticism.[19]

The law endorsed a 'combination of centralised management and independence of an enterprise', which implied that enterprises would not be independent. Even the legal independence of enterprises was threatened by their amalgamation into large state production associations (GPOs). The reformist slogan 'self-financing' was incorporated into the law, but its meaning was ambiguous. Four categories of plan indicators survived. Delivery targets were to be replaced by state orders, which were supposed to be limited to the most essential production. For the rest, profits or revenues would be the principal objective, distributed in accordance with stable normatives as at Sumy or VAZ. In addition, there would be investment limits and, ominously, control figures, a remnant of the old system, although they were not supposed to be of directive character.

The most radical elements of the law concerned self-management. Enterprise managers and directors were supposed to be elected by their workers, who would also elect a work council that would confirm the enterprise's plans. There is little mention of the organisation of work within the enterprise, as if this topic was not covered by the law.

The implementation of the law offered unpleasant surprises. State orders turned out to be old commands under a new name and tended to cover 100 per cent of the production capacity of most enterprises. Capital charges varied from 0 to 12 per cent; and profit tax rates from 0 to 90 per cent. Nor were the new normatives stable, but adjusted by the branch ministries at will. Thus, well-run enterprises were assured of a great financial burden, while the loss-makers were relieved of concern.[20]

Still, the agonising implementation of the Law on State Enterprises made clear that little could change in enterprise management without a fundamental reform of central economic bodies, branch ministries and the very mechanisms of the economic system. Through its failure, the Law had produced a forceful argument for radicalisation.

AN EVALUATION OF THE CHANGES IN ENTERPRISE MANAGEMENT

The experiments with enterprise management were pursued along a broad and differentiated front. They were launched in echelons, as political conditions matured. Their design, development and results allow us to draw a wide range of conclusions.

The changes differed in their degrees of reformism. To begin with, it was only a question of establishing more accurate gross production targets in order to restrain hidden inflation, through the return to more physical targets, the promotion of stable norms or a switch to the fulfillment of contracted deliveries. By themselves, none of these old ideas appeared to offer any significant improvement.

A second, more reformist trend was to reduce the number of plan targets radically to about three—profit, gross deliveries and an investment limit. The intention was to simplify, to emphasise the most important targets, and to make enterprises more independent of their ministries. Some shedding of labour and cost-cutting took place, but these changes did not bring about any significant improvement, which they had done in the 1960s. One reason may be that ministries ignored the new rules. However, it does not appear a sufficient explanation. It is more likely that ever more complex regulations tied enterprises so much that a partial deregulation did not help. Then, the conclusion would be that a major deregulation would be necessary in order to liberate initiative.

A third, clearly reformist endeavour was the introduction of self-financing. When it actually was implemented, it seemed effective, but it immediately exposed the limitations of the system, in particular the absence of wholesale trade. In the prolongation of self-financing, profit-sharing emerged. However, self-financing was effectively resisted by branch ministries and central economic bodies, since it worked against their interests and reduced their powers. Also this resistance evidenced the need for reform.

Fourthly, apart from making enterprises independent, reformers strove towards ever smaller work units, and eventually families or individuals, who were autonomous in their search for economic surplus. These endeavours, together with some kind of profit-sharing, appeared to bring about the most evident improvements. Yet, any comparison between autonomous profit-oriented teams and ordinary state enterprises was embarrassing for the latter, provoking their resistance. Finally, the most radical experiments involved a political element—self-management with elected managers and work councils.

The changes in enterprise management proceeded by branch, going much further in some branches. The economic situation in each branch may explain these differences. The neglected public service sector had all but collapsed, inviting far-reaching changes in the direction of small leaseholds. Agriculture, construction and road transport were conspicuous for their inefficiency. In order to impose thrift, self-financing and smaller economic units were promoted. In retail trade and raw material extraction, the biggest problem was simply to boost gross sales and gross production, respectively, which required no reform. For machine-building and light industry, the main task was to raise quality and technical standards. The large-scale experiment and self-financing were attempted, but no qualitative amelioration occurred. Little was even tried in military machine-building, where competition between designers was considered a satisfactory solution (see Academician V. Trapeznikov in *Pravda*, 2 October 1985). For civilian manufacturing, the traditional system did not appear to have any solution whatsoever. The crucial problem of product quality delineated the limits of the possibilities of the old system. As qualitative aspects had grown more important, minor adjustments within the system had become fruitless.

Regional differences were also significant. The reformist experiments developed earlier, faster and further in certain republics, notably in Georgia, Estonia, Lithuania and Armenia, in that order. These republics appeared to strive towards a Hungarian economic model with a socialist market. Also, Belorussia, Leningrad and Latvia undertook many experiments, but they tended to be oriented towards the rationalisation of the existing system, as in the GDR, though the dividing lines were not clear-cut. Odd initiatives occurred in parts of the RSFSR and the Ukraine, but they were few in relation to the size of these republics. At an early stage, there were no experiments whatsoever in the five Central Asian republics, Azerbaijan and Moldavia.

The most obvious reasons for this disparity are economic: the relative shortage of labour and the level of economic development. Labour shortages in most of the European part of the USSR pressed the authorities to economise on labour. Central Asia was swamped with surplus labour, making the absorption of labour the prime issue, for which the command economy was excellent. Furthermore, the experimenting republics were economically the most developed, where the need for qualitative improvements, which the traditional system could not deliver, was paramount.

The degree of market balance is a related factor. Crisscrossing the USSR, one is left in little doubt that shortages of commodities and services are greater in the RSFSR than elsewhere, which might be one explanation for the passivity in Russia proper, where the simple need to fill the shops is overwhelming. In particular, Georgia had the additional problem of absorbing an enormous second economy. Nationality issues played a role. The urge to reduce the demand for labour was particularly strong in Estonia, where it caused the immigration of Slavs, undesired by the indigenous population. There was also a regional factor. Lithuania followed Estonia, and later Latvia followed both. Armenia adopted some Georgian measures. Belorussia and Leningrad—both important centres of the military-industrial complex—pursued similar experiments and exchanged experiences. Finally, regional politics should not be neglected. The Georgian experiments were spearheaded by Shevardnadze and lost momentum when he departed, illustrating the extraordinary power of the Georgian First Party Secretary. In Estonia, on the contrary, the reformist pressures came from below, inspired by Estonian traditions and the neighbouring capitalist Finland. Presumably, the passivity in the RSFSR and the Ukraine can be explained by conservative political leaders and a conservative population.

The further experiments developed, the more they exposed the intrinsic shortcomings of the command economy. All changes had to be defended against intimidating branch ministries; shortages of supplies emasculated attempts at cutting costs and devalued the benefits of additional profits; no sensible principles of pricing or effective means to raise quality could be found; the isolation from export prices on foreign markets nullified the interest in exports; the problems of stimulating labour aroused questions about the alienating effects of centralised state ownership.

The experiments served to mobilise the potential vanguard of economic reform: able enterprise directors, reform economists and progressive politicians. A network of reform commissions and working groups was established in the wake of the experiments. The media attention suggests a great deal about the reformist strategy. It was concentrated on a few experiments, with the large-scale experiment in industry receiving more publicity than its economic content justified. This experiment suited conservatives who wanted to simulate change. To reformers it was a platform for take off. The Sumy/VAZ experiment was called the second step. It was controversial, and reformers apparently thought it a good issue to fight over. In order not to be beaten politically, they had selected two of the best Soviet machine-building enterprises. Agricultural reform probably attracted most publicity, with its many alternative designs, and agriculture has traditionally been given a lot of media attention. Travkin's experiment in construction and the Belorussian railway experiment were neat, comprehensible success stories. At the same time, some sizeable experiments were not much publicised. The service experiment was neglected for long. In its radical versions, it was controversial, and reformers found services too unimportant for a battle, until cooperatives added another qualitative dimension to the picture. The half-hearted changes in light industry could hardly inspire anyone.

A common western objection to economic experiments is that they are carried out under artificial conditions, but then the assumption is made that experiments are undertaken to find the ideal regulations. Our observation, on the contrary, is that at least the reform economists saw experiments as pikes for breaking the conservative ice. The actual economic results were of little interest, while their political impact was everything. Many experiments were designed as to perfect the system, while leading Soviet economists and the Gorbachev camp wanted to replace it with a more market-oriented system. Hence the reformers ought to select the best enterprises and pamper them with preferences in order to further their political cause, which they did.

The reformers seized the initiative, but they were not alone on the stage. The central authorities could accept limited experiments, but as the reform movement advanced, the institutional resistance was mobilised. Previously, the branch ministries had stood out as the disobedient, conservative villains (see Gorlin, 1985). Now, almost all central economic bodies were exposed as fundamentally conservative. Goskomtsen, the Ministry of Finance, Gosplan and Gossnab became regular targets. The reformers had chosen to attack along a very broad and divergent front.

This tactic had been good for getting the ball rolling, but as the struggle between reformers and bureaucracies intensified, the bureaucracy benefited from its greater capacity and information. Many decrees were barely implemented. Each additional decree offered bureaucrats one new lever in their struggle to emasculate reform. Systemic inconsistencies might have become aggravated by the scattered changes. When the reform process got moving, reformers had obvious reasons to switch tactics and go for more concentrated efforts. At this stage, they would gain more from a few good laws. They needed a more comprehensive approach, superseding the branch approach. The Law of State Enterprises was a first attempt in this direction.

NOTES

1. Much of this chapter is based on interviews and study tours. From 1985 to 1987, I undertook study tours of 4–5 days to Estonia, Georgia and Lithuania with packed programmes including visits to the republican Gosplan, a couple of ministries involved in experiments, a few enterprises pursuing experiments and some economic institutes. I participated in a UN tour to steelworks in the USSR, and

made less extensive study tours to relevant institutions and enterprises in the Ukraine, the RSFSR and Belorussia.

2. The Soviet literature on this experiment is immense. Voronin (1984, 1985) presents official evaluations at early stages, Selyunin (1985) and Yasin (1986) early criticisms, while Brus (1985) and Hewett (1988, pp. 260–73) provide valuable western assessments.

3. In June 1985, on a visit to the large Novolipetsk steelworks, I was told that their central plan indicators had been reduced from twenty-three to thirteen, while in September 1985, at a Kiev brewery, I learnt that the number of its centrally-set plan indicators had fallen from twenty-eight to nine, and a further reduction to three (delivery plan, profits and quality) was envisaged for 1986.

4. Of less importance was a corresponding commission at the Politburo level, with Prime Minister Nikolai Tikhonov as chairman and Boris Gostev, first deputy head of the CC Economic Department, as secretary. It met infrequently to supervise the work of the Voronin Commission and was presumably disbanded when Tikhonov retired in September 1985.

5. Oral information from Gosplan in Estonia in 1986.

6. Personal information in Estonia in 1986.

7. This section is to a large extent based on interviews with officials and economists in Moscow, Estonia, Georgia, Lithuania and Belorussia, though in most cases references to published sources will be given. I have also drawn on Karl-Eugen Wädekin's current reports for Radio Liberty.

8. *Pravda*, 3 Novembr 1987. This was a statement approved by the CC. Presumably, Gorbachev did not care much for the collectivisation himself, given his previous call for the adaptation of the agricultural policy under NEP to present conditions. Apparently, he had not the political strength to denounce the collectivisation just after Ligachev and Chebrikov had explicitly endorsed it (*Pravda*, 27 August, 11 September 1987). Gorbachev's personal views are likely to be closer to those of Viktor Danilov (1987), simultaneously published in the authoritative journal *Kommunist*.

9. On the Kuban *kombinat*, see *Ek. gaz.*, No. 34, 1985, No. 49, 1986; *Pravda*, 13 October 1986; on Novomoskovski, *Ek. gaz.*, No. 47, 1987; on Adazhi, *Kommunist*, No. 9, pp. 14–23, No. 10, pp. 77–86; *Ek. gaz.*, No. 52, 1986; *Izvestiya*, 17 December 1987.

10. An additional problem was that the workers involved found nothing to buy but vodka for their larger earnings, and even that benefit disappeared with the anti-alcohol campaign.

11. Darrell Slider (1987) offers a good account of the brigade system. For a useful survey of experiments, see *Ek. gaz.*, No. 36, 1985, but most of them are too insignificant to concern us. In *Ek. gaz.*, No. 8, 1985, the future Chairman of Gosagroprom, Vsevolod Murakhovski describes the details of collective contracts in his and Gorbachev's home area, Stavropol *krai*.

12. The popular reaction might have been reinforced by the fact that these shock workers were Koreans—a national minority disliked in the Soviet Union for their habits of excessively hard work.

13. An otherwise Stalinist article in the Russian nationalist journal *Nash sovremennik*, praises the Arkhangelsk peasant as a good example (Ochkin, 1987, p. 159).

14. For an excellent reformist analysis of the situation in agriculture after the decree had been passed, see Otsason (1986).

15. According to one participant in this meeting, Bogomolov was interrupted by Ligachev when arguing in favour of family leasehold, but Gorbachev clarified his support for Bogomolov's idea.

16. The following is based on *Izvestiya*, 13 February, 12 March, 31 October 1986; *Pravda*, 31 October, 17 December 1986; *Sots. ind.*, 6 February 1987; *Moscow News*, No. 8, 1987.
17. This account is based on *Pravda*, 20 May 1986, 17 February and 25 October 1987; *Ek. gaz.*, No. 48, 1986.
18. This account is based on interviews in September 1986; cf *Pravda*, 24 June 1985; *Sots. ind.*, 15 February 1986.
19. See the disregarded criticism of the draft law presented by Tatyana Zaslavskaya (*Sovetskaya kultura*, 24 March 1987) and by VAZ workers (*Ogonek*, No. 23, 1987).
20. Bunich (1987) took an early lead in the criticism of the Law on State Enterprises and its implementation, but from November 1987 virtually every issue of *Ekonomicheskaya gazeta* contained a couple of articles with detailed criticism.

5. Reform of the economic system

The meagre results of the vigorous changes within the traditional framework and in enterprise management suggested that significant improvements of Stalin's system were no longer feasible. One natural conclusion was that a reform of the system itself was necessary. Sixteen months after Gorbachev had called for 'radical economic reform' an extensive package of reform legislation was passed. In June 1987, the principal documents on the reform of the state economy, the Law on State Enterprises (Associations) and Basic Provisions for Fundamental Perestroika of Economic Management, were adopted by the Supreme Soviet and the Central Committee, respectively. In July 1987, the Law on State Enterprises was complemented by ten decrees on major functions in the economic system and their executive organs: planning, the management of scientific-technical progress, material supplies, financial mechanism, price formation, banking, statistics, branch ministries, republican organs, and social policy (*O korennoi perestroike*, 1987).[1] An eleventh decree on the Council of Ministers was promised, but never appeared.[2]

In spite of its comprehensive character, this package should not be perceived as a blueprint for economic reform, but rather as a first attempt at a comprehensive approach. It was impressive that the Soviet leadership could produce such an integral package of economic reform measures considering that this was its first detailed plan for economic reform to emerge in public, but many basic principles were left unclear, muddled by evident compromises. The outline of the reform compares poorly in quality, clarity and consistency with the Hungarian economic reform of 1968 which it resembles.[3] At a press conference on 26 June 1987, Abel Aganbegyan noted that the Law on State Enterprises was the best that could be achieved under present circumstances, implying that it was not satisfactory. Our view is that it should be regarded as an intermediate political compromise rather than a final reform design. A change in the balance of the political leadership will presumably result in an altered reform strategy. The ensuing struggle over the implementation of the reform legislation will influence both the political strife and the future design of the reform.

Notwithstanding its similarity to the Hungarian economic reform, Soviet economists are anxious to underline the Soviet nature of their reform. To some extent, this is a reflection of the persistent Russian desire to be original, but the reform does have many special Soviet features, and the parallels with Hungary might have been caused more by the similarity in the problems encountered by both regimes than by a diligent study of Hungary. Soviet reformers have primarily sought their inspiration in two Soviet experiences: the reforms of 1965 and NEP. At the CC Plenum in June 1987, Gorbachev cited a programmatic article, published by Academician V. Nemchinov in the journal *Kommunist* in 1964 and reprinted in July 1987 (Nemchinov, 1987).

Many Soviet economists have advocated a Hungarian-type reform since the mid-1960s, but in the last decade of Brezhnev's rule, little appeared in print. The most outspoken radical reformer was probably Boris Kurashvili, a legal scholar of the Institute of State and Law at the Academy of Sciences. In five articles from 1982 to 1985, Kurashvili developed a comprehensive economic reform along Hungarian lines (Kurashvili, 1982, 1983ab, 1985ab; cf Amann, 1987). His ideas are more radical than the current reforms, but they represent an influential stream in Soviet reformist thinking.

Professor Gavriil Popov of Moscow University displays an economic thinking close to Kurashvili's, but Popov is more policy-oriented. He outlined his ideas in a dozen newspaper articles from 1980 to 1985 (Popov, 1985a, p. 334). Three weeks after Gorbachev had become General Secretary, Popov submitted a book manuscript for publication (Popov, 1985a), which was almost a blueprint for economic reform,[4] soon supplemented with a hastily-written action programme (Popov, 1985b). While less radical in their appearance, many of the ideas proposed by Popov are found in Vadim Medvedev (1983), which might be seen as the original reform programme. Still, no one went as far in the direction of a socialist market as Gennadi Lisichkin did in 1966 (Lisichkin, 1966).

Popov (1985a) was probably the only major economic manuscript lying in a drawer prepared for publication. The odd liberal article that has been lying about for a few years can be found (Kosenko, 1986), but otherwise all reformist articles were newly written, although the ideas they contained had matured for a long time. Soviet economists were poorly prepared for economic reform. The reformist top academic economists tended to criticise shortcomings in the present system and offer limited solutions.[5] Medvedev, Kurashvili and Popov stand out as the daring few who conceptualised and wrote about a comprehensive reform before it was politically acceptable. Much of the reform legislation adopted in the summer of 1987 appears inspired by Popov (1985a) and Medvedev (1983).

Crucial questions on economic reform at the macro-level are: To what extent are enterprises dependent on superior bodies? Does the centre decide what enterprises are to produce? Are material supplies to be allocated centrally or purchased on a market? Are prices and money active or passive? Is foreign trade integrated into the domestic economy? What role does the party play in the economy? A comprehensive question is whether enterprises are subject to competition in a market.

ORGANISATIONAL CHANGES[6]

Reorganisation can mean many different things. Any bureaucratic system tends to indulge in organisational changes, which can offer new rulers opportunities to promote their clients. Any organisation needs a shake-up from time to time in order to be revitalised. Such restructuring should not be confused with reform. Still, each economic system needs particular forms of organisation. The traditional Soviet system favours a streamlined hierarchy with ever fewer separate enterprises, while a market system needs independent enterprises that compete. The organisational changes comprised a protracted process, which had started in 1985. Its length has led to a fluid mixture of ideas.

Most present organisational changes are reactions against the structure established in 1965, but some continuity is also noticeable. In 1965, Khrushchev's *sovnarkhozy* were replaced by branch ministries. During the 1970s and early 1980s, the number of branch ministries grew through successive partitions. While 'localism' was the main complaint in 1965, the prevalence of highly centralised branch ministries had rendered 'departmentalism' and 'departmental barriers' major issues in 1985. Other criticism focused on overcentralisation and excessive bureaucratisation (Gvishiani and Milner, 1987, p. 10). All these concerns point towards a streamlining of the existing system.

A reformist aim entered the agenda: to eliminate the operative and directive parts of the branch ministries and central economic bodies, since they were no longer supposed to command subordinate enterprises. At the 27th Party Congress, Gorbachev spelt out the ambition to establish new general schemes of administration, and at the 19th Party Conference in June 1988, he declared that such schemes had been approved (*Pravda*, 29 June 1988).

The basic reformist aim, however, should have been to guarantee the operative independence of enterprises from interference by superior bodies and the party. Now they only demanded 'a considerable increase in the economic independence' of enterprises (Gvishiani and Milner, 1987, p. 90), and nonsensically advocated 'an optimal relationship between the central management and the operative independence' of enterprises (Milner in *Sots. ind.*, 10 April 1986). In order to assure enterprises independence, massive cuts in the intrusive state bureaucracy were needed. In 1986, public administration involved 17.7 million people, of whom 2.4 million worked in managerial positions above enterprises (Boris Milner in *Argumenty i fakty*, No. 11, 1988).

Departmentalism may be subdivided into two issues. The first regret was that closely related branches did not cooperate. The response was to reinforce the coordination at the highest level through the establishment of super-ministerial bodies. The second issue was the relative influence of branch and territorial organisations, respectively. The principal justification for branch ministries was that they focused on technical progress, which Khrushchev's *sovnarkhozy* had failed to do. Conservatives defended the branch ministries, while some outspoken reformers (Kurashvili, Popov and Lacis) more or less endorsed *sovnarkhozy*. Otto Lacis (1987d, p. 267) stated: 'I consider even today that *sovnarkhozy* were useful.' Academician Yuri Nesterikhin punctured the conservative argument for branch ministries: 'The main hindrance against the achievement of the world level in many scientific-technical directions is the monopoly positions of departments' (*Izvestiya*, 30 June 1986).

The idea of the need for some kind of superministerial bureaux was already well-established at the end of the 1970s.[7] Gorbachev (1985a, p. 24) declared in June 1985 that 'the question of the creation of bodies for the management of large economic complexes' was on the agenda. The concepts of super-ministries differed. Boris Kurashvili (1985a, p. 73) made the ultimate proposal: to merge all branch ministries into one 'Ministry of the National Economy'. The ministerial staff could be cut by 90 per cent, facilitating a far-reaching marketisation. However, the prevailing idea was to strengthen coordination within some ten traditionally-defined 'complexes' or groups of branches. Each superministerial body would be led by a deputy prime minister. There was a choice between three types of superministerial bodies.

The first alternative was a 'commission' with limited powers and minimal *apparat*, coordinating through discussion rather than direct commands. An example of this was the Commission of the Presidium of the USSR Council of Ministers on the Agro-Industrial Complex which existed from 1983 to 1985 but had minimal impact. Despite this failure, one new commission with similar status and functions was established in September 1986, namely, the State Foreign-Economic Commission (Gvishiani and Milner, 1987, p. 117). Its future appears uncertain after its two main subordinate bodies, the State Committee for Foreign Economic Relations (GKES) and the Ministry of Foreign Trade, have been merged into a Ministry for Foreign Economic Relations possessing virtually the same competence as the Commission (*Pravda*, 17 January 1988).

A second kind of superministerial body would be a bureau at the Council of Ministers. Such a bureau would have a small *apparat* with some rights to give direct orders to subordinated ministries and to transfer production and investments. Similar bureaux had existed after the war (Popov, 1985a, p. 217). The Military-Industrial Commission (VPK) is a long-standing success story of this kind, hardly ever mentioned in Soviet literature. Five such bureaux at the Council of Ministers have been established, covering most of industry. As a parallel to the VPK, a Bureau for Machine-Building was set up in October 1985, above a dozen civilian machine-building ministries. In March 1986, a Bureau for the Fuel-Energy Complex was established. A Bureau for Social Development followed in the autumn of 1986, and later on a Bureau for the Chemical-Forestry Complex. A Bureau for the Metallurgic Complex appears to exist as well.

The third alternative was the direct merger of a group of ministries into a veritable superministry, with a simultaneous strengthening of the regional organisation. It would amount to a return to the pre-war Stalinist structure with few, large branch ministries (Popov, 1985a, p. 217). One argument against fusions was that the prime task of the ministries was to safeguard technical policy which required specialisation. Other reasons were the reformers' limited political leverage and fear of economic disruption. This solution was chosen for the agro-industrial complex and construction and has been intended for the transport sector, which is the only complex that has not yet been reorganised (Gvishiani and Milner, 1987, p. 118). All these branches need a great deal of regional coordination. The agro-industrial complex has suffered particularly badly from departmental barriers (Lisichkin, 1985). As early as April 1985, Gorbachev coined the slogan: 'there must be one single master on the land' (*Pravda*, 24 April 1985).

Three alternatives were elaborated. One was the establishment of a bureau, the second was the amalgamation of half the ministries, and the third was a radical fusion of all thirteen ministries and state committees within the agro-industrial complex.[8] The second option won, and five ministries and one state committee were merged in November 1985 into the State Agro-Industrial Committee (Gosagroprom; *Pravda* 23 November 1985). No less than 47 per cent of their approximately 7,000 union-level employees were displaced (V. S. Murakhovski in *Lit. gaz.*, 22 January 1986). Similar mergers took place at all levels within the agro-industrial complex. However, soon complaints appeared that the bureaucracy was being recreated at a lower level, particularly at *oblast* level. The reductions in staff at republican level were around 30 per cent, but varied greatly from republic to republic.[9] The reorganisation has been followed by endless bureaucratic in-fighting. Gosagroprom has failed to become an effective decision-making body and is considered an ungovernable bureaucratic mastodon. In its present form, it is not likely to survive.

A similar hybrid was chosen for construction with a superministerial State Construction Committee (Gosstroi) and four subordinate regional construction ministries. A few branch-specialised construction ministries remained (*Pravda*, 20 August and 13 September 1986). The number of ministries did not change, but the intention was to cut the labour force at the central level by 45 per cent and the administrative staff of construction trusts by 40 per cent (*Izvestiya*, 26 September 1986). The argument against the reorganisation had been specialisation, but in practice the construction ministries had refused to specialise (Gvishiani and Milner, 1987, p. 138). However, all the four regional ministries were located in Moscow, resulting in complaints about increased bureaucracy, hierarchy and uncertainty (*Pravda*, 18 January 1988). The problem addressed could not be solved by reorganisation. Considering these experiences, it would not be surprising if no more superministries are attempted.

Instead, the decree on branch ministries of July 1987 recommended gradual mergers of related ministries. Such an approach would dissipate both resistance and disruption. Two pairs of machine-building ministries were combined immediately (*Pravda*, 21 July 1987). One state committee (on the supply of oil products) and one machine-building ministry were abolished (*Pravda*, 30 December 1987, 25 February 1988). Six basic industrial ministries—those of electricity, coal, steel, non-ferrous metals, geology, and oil refining—were singled out for transformation from union-republic ministries to union ministries (*O korennoi perestroike*, 1987, p. 203), implying that republican ministries were abolished and each branch became more centralised. The same transformation occurred in the Ministry of Construction materials (*Pravda*, 9 April 1988). In forestry an old strife over the right to forests was mediated through a contrary transformation of the State Committee for Forestry and the Ministry of Forestry Industry into union-republic organs (*Pravda*, 17 March 1988; *Sots. ind.*, 28 August, 12 September 1985). A few other changes in the ministerial structure occurred, but the trend towards a reduction in ministerial bodies was not unambiguous. After the Chernobyl catastrophe, a new branch ministry for nuclear energy was created.

Under the reform, the branch ministries were supposed to concentrate on long-term planning and technical development, while the centre of operative economic work was to be transferred to enterprises, permitting 'substantial cuts in the administrative branch *apparat* and the abolition of superfluous links' (Gorbachev, 1985, pp. 24–5). Hence, the decree on 'perestroika of the activity of ministries. . .' adopted in July 1987 sets the task 'to cut the staff of the ministries considerably', without specifying numbers (*O korennoi perestroike*, 1987, p. 203). Reportedly, all branch ministries were given a common rate of reduction, but they were allowed to choose how to cut. A Politburo commission for the restructuring of central economic bodies, ministries and departments of the USSR was set up to supervise the reductions (*Leningradskaya pravda*, 26 April 1988). It was reportedly led by Prime Minister Nikolai Ryzhkov.[10] In June 1988, Gorbachev announced that the *apparat* of the union departments had been cut by 40 per cent (*Pravda*, 29 June 1988).

Numbers vary with definitions. It is a common practice to count vacancies and to transfer administrative staff to purported 'research institutes' attached to ministries. In 1986, the central management apparatus, including all ministries, comprised 108,000 individuals (Milner in *Argumenty i fakty*, No. 11, 1988). In the ministries alone, 39,000 people actually lost their jobs (*Moscow News*, No. 10, 1988). In fact, about half of the employees who were laid off had passed the retirement age. So far, the nature of the Soviet ministerial structure has not changed, but its staff has been reduced considerably. The number of ministries at the union level has been reduced from sixty-four in 1979 to fifty-five in March 1988 (*Argumenty i fakty*, No. 11, 1988).

The functional central economic bodies remain the same, though they have undergone limited reorganisation, with cuts in their branch organisation and staff. Gosplan itself was hit rather hard with a cut of 1,095 in its staff of 2,560

(*Moscow News*, No. 10, 1988), but the establishment of a new institute cushioned the effect. Gosplan's many branch departments were simply fused into departments for economic complexes corresponding to the new superministerial bureaux, while Gosagroprom and Gosstroi took over some of Gosplan's responsibilities. Gossnab experienced a similar reduction of 2,500 people when thirty *glavki* (main directorates) were eliminated (*Lit. gaz.*, 30 March 1988). Goskomtsen has pleaded that its staff of 500 cannot be reduced, since it has to prepare a price reform. This is consistent with the intention to weaken branch organs and strengthen functional organs, but in reality most of the 'functional' organs are hardly more supportive of reform than the branch ministries.

One of the decrees adopted on 17 July 1987 dealt with 'the perfection of the activity of republican management bodies'. The USSR possessed no less than some 800 republican ministries and departments — about thirty ministries, fifteen state committees, and twenty other departments in each republic (*Argumenty i fakty*, No. 11, 1988). Under this decree rapid cuts were envisaged in the republican and local administration, although no figures were specified. According to Gorbachev, the reductions at republican level would amount to half and to one third at *oblast* level (*Pravda*, 29 June 1988). Reportedly, the republican authorities were ordered how much to cut, but they could freely choose how. In April 1988, all republics apart from Armenia and Azerbaijan adopted new republican organisation charters.[11] Each republic chose its own structure. A Politburo commission, led by Gosplan's Chairman Yuri Maslyukov, has scrutinised and confirmed all the schemes.[12] The three Baltic republics, spearheaded by Estonia, have chosen to abolish a large number of ministries and replace them with state committees for large complexes, industry, agriculture, transport, culture, education, etc. The organisational schemes chosen by Estonia and Lithuania were explicitly confirmed by the Politburo (*Pravda*, 29 April 1988). In Central Asia, the republican authorities have preferred to cut the number of *oblasti* by thirteen. The most limited changes and reductions have occurred in the Ukraine and the RSFSR (*Izvestiya*, 16 January 1988; *Pravda*, 21 April 1988).

As a consequence of this reorganisation, the organisational pattern varies much more between republics than before. The previous lines to union ministries in Moscow have been cut or confused, dissipating central branch powers. This was the intention, according to an initiated Soviet source. Moreover, by not directing the cuts themselves, the leaders hoped to sow strife in the local administration, while avoiding conflict between the centre and the republics. Thus, the premise was to 'divide and rule', primarily between union and republican ministries. The natural outcome would be increased economic independence of the republics from the centre. However, the radical Estonian reorganisation was not sufficient for the Estonians, who complained that only two centrally-managed enterprises were transferred to republican supervision. Their demand was regional self-financing (*khozraschet*), which the first party secretaries of Estonia, Latvia, Lithuania and Komi ASSR proposed at the 19th Party Conference (*Pravda*, 1–2 July 1988).

Reformers like Gavriil Popov (1985b, p. 52) have long advocated 'the creation of a system of competent bodies for territorial economic management'. One type has been 'territorial production complexes', of which eight have long existed around major raw material deposits, but they have not got any recent boost (Popov, 1985a, pp. 237–8). The Poti experiment with its 'territorial inter-departmental associations' has been another form discussed above. In the wake of the current reorganisations, the *oblast* administrations are being reinforced with both agro-industrial and general economic departments, waiting for tasks. This could augur a far-reaching regionalisation of the Soviet economy.

A traditional problem in Soviet administration has been how to link enterprises to ministries. After the branch ministries were re-established in 1965, a proliferation of *glavki* (main directorates) within them ensued, since a large administration was required to deliver all detailed commands to enterprises. The reorganisation of 1973 aimed at the replacement of *glavki* with so-called all-union industrial associations (VPO), production associations (PO) or scientific production associations (NPO), with their own research and development units.

VPOs embraced all enterprises within a narrowly defined branch in one branch ministry. They became meaningless bureaucratic intermediaries. A typical judgement was: 'VPOs did not solve one single significant question.' Even so, their administration expanded and administrative barriers arose between VPOs, which divided and multiplied (*Pravda*, 8 December 1987). It is merely a sign of indecisive inertia that these harmful bodies survived for so long. In June 1985, Gorbachev (1985, p. 25) announced the self-evident aim to liquidate the VPOs. His preference was a 'two-tier system of management' with no intermediary body between ministries and production associations or enterprises. The abolition of VPOs started immediately, but a new problem was that the old *glavki* were reinstated in the branch ministries, absorbing a large share of the former VPO staff (*Izvestiya*, 11 July 1985).

The emphasis on the abolition of VPOs aroused an urge for mergers of enterprises into production assocations, and specially NPOs, which aimed at vertical integration, like East German *Kombinate*. They had long enjoyed official favour, but their formation required integration between branches, which all branch ministries resisted. At the time of Brezhnev's death, only about 100 NPOs had been organised (Gvishiani and Milner, 1987, p. 83). Gorbachev (1985, pp. 21, 25) urged an energetic agglomeration of enterprises and organisations into POs and NPOs, regretting that the country possessed only 250 NPOs. At the end of 1987, the number had risen to 500 (*Pravda*, 24 January 1988). The old communist yearning for more concentration and larger scale continued. More NPOs were formed, but slowly, and the departmental barriers were not broken.

In June 1987, Gorbachev suggested a large-scale merger of the 37,000 industrial enterprises into several thousand large associations, although he also spoke of the necessity 'to avoid monopoly positions of associations' (*Pravda*, 26 June 1987). This was an overt contradiction, since such a concentration would cause stifling monopolisation. The decree on the branch ministries of 17 July 1987 set out the task to elaborate a statute on a new kind of state production association (GPO) (*O korennoi perestroike*, 1987, p. 206). Such a statute was quickly adopted on 23 September 1987 (SP, No. 47, 1987), and the agglomeration of enterprises into GPOs began, although it ran counter to the essence of the reform. However, half a year later (on 2 April 1988), the Council of Ministers revoked the statute on GPOs, thus stopping their formaion (SP, No. 17, 1988). The main complaints were that certain ministries had tried to recreate the intermediary bureaucracy in Moscow and that the principle of voluntary assocation had been violated (*Sots.ind.*, 28 April 1988). According to Soviet economists, the concept of GPOs had no support among them but was pushed by ministerial representatives. At the 19th Party Conference, Gorbachev explained:

In the course of the practical implementation of the reform, we really feel the resistance from forces of inertia, and sometimes this leads to the adoption of ambivalent, compromise, and sometimes erroneous decisions. It is a fact, comrades, that under the guise of creating state production associations an attempt was made to revive the system of the former bureaucratic ministerial *glavki* (*Pravda*, 29 June 1988).

Both the rise and demise of GPOs are curious. Gorbachev must have been against them in June 1987, given his warning against monopolies in the same context, but apparently he found a need to compromise on this point. Other politicians might have become convinced of the harmfulness of GPOs, when they saw their appearance, or Gorbachev might have strengthened his power so that he dared to reverse the decision. The understanding of the dangers of monopolies had certainly spread. Other attempts at the creation of large associations appear to be of limited significance. The attraction of the GDR *Kombinate* has faded. It is noteworthy that the new legal act is called the Law on State Enterprises (Associations) with associations in brackets rather than the other way around. The number of independent socialist enterprises, organisations and institutions remains very large—514,300 at the beginning of 1987. Therefore the dangers of monopolisation might be less than in Hungary and Poland, though in a large branch like machine-building, there are only 6,600 enterprises (*Narkhoz 1986*, p. 115).

At the enterprise level, the basic question has become: who is to rule enterprises? At present, branch ministries virtually own their enterprises. Khrushchev's alternative was territorial control, and the party can always step in. The reformist answer is that enterprises should be independent and governed by their work collectives. Vadim Medvedev (1983, p. 82) wrote that 'a broader inclusion of workers in the management of production and a deep and all-round democratisation of management is of the greatest importance'. The Law on Labour Collectives adopted in 1983 purported to include workers in management, but it was of no consequence (Slider, 1985). In his December 1984 speech, Gorbachev (1987a, p. 82) observed: 'Marx, Engels and Lenin thought of a transition to self-management by the workers as a practical task for the proletariat from the moment it assumed power. To them, the main content of this idea was to assure an ever larger mass of workers real, practical participation in management.'

The idea of self-management was a vital part of the Law on State Enterprises, which stipulates elections of directors and all managers down to foremen, elections of a work council and the holding of general assemblies of all workers in enterprises (*Pravda*, 1 July 1987). By the end of 1987, more than 36,000 managers had been elected in industry and construction (*Pravda*, 24 January 1988). Newspaper accounts showed that nominations, and often also the elections, were controlled by the local party committee. The immediate effect of these elections was an extension of local party power over enterprises at the expense of branch ministries. However, the element of actual choice and public scrutiny is likely to gain importance, if glasnost and democratisation develop further.

On the surface, the many organisational changes appear muddled. However, at another level a picture of strife between contradictory principles emerges. Most of the central administration wants as little change as possible, and, if change is necessary, it prefers fakes. The dominant feature at a senior policy-making level has been a desire to rationalise, streamline and concentrate the administration. However, this trend has been complemented and countered by the trend to cut the administration down to size and prepare it for more market-oriented economic reform. Substantial cuts have been made in the central administration, but the present intermediate stage appears untenable. If the ministries are not effectively deprived of their detailed supervision of enterprises, they are likely to recover numerical strength. The cuts need to go further—on Kurashvili's or Hungarian lines—if they are to become effective and facilitate a real change in the economic system.

PLANNING

The Soviet discussion on planning has changed nature. The search for 'optimal planning' has virtually ceased. Centralised planning has lost its credibility as a rational economic solution among senior Soviet economists, but it survives as a dogma and vested interest. The fundamental doctrine persists: 'Centralised planning is ... an important advantage of a socialist economy' (Khachaturov, 1987, p. 80). Axiomatically, this is understood as planning in physical terms with centralised material balances and production tasks being directed from the top. However, after sixty years of planning, certain results could be requested. One outstanding claim is: 'The most important task of economic planning is the attainment of balance and proportionality' (Khachaturov, 1987, p. 80), but after having scrutinised the results of all five-year plans, the Novosibirsk economist B. P. Orlov (1987, p. 53) concluded that many plans had been poorly founded and unrealistic; numerous attempts to turn medium-term plans into the base of annual plans had failed; over the last fifteen years, there had been a rift between word and deed; and Gosplan had been too occupied with current tasks to investigate the causes. Vasili Selyunin has concluded: 'nearly sixty years of experience has failed to reveal any particular advantages of planning as a method of centralizing economic managment' (*Moscow News*, No. 18, 1988).

Nikolai Shmelev's breath-taking attack on the Soviet economic system in *Novy mir* in June 1987 broke most taboos on planning, calling its foundations 'economic romanticism': 'Today we have a shortage [economy], unbalanced on virtually all accounts and in many ways unmanageable, and to be completely honest, an economy which almost does not yield to planning, and which in any case does not accept scientific-technical progress' (Shmelev, 1987, p. 144). Shmelev noted the enormous price paid in fear of market relations, and exclaimed: 'Let us lose our ideological virginity' (*ibid.*, pp. 146–7). After this article, whose analysis Gorbachev approved of (*Pravda*, 22 June 1987), public attacks on planning became permissible—though still not advisable.

The eternal alternative to central planning is the market. A substantial number of Soviet economists are convinced market economists, but they are coy about expressing this view. At the beginning of 1985, the moderate party economist Rem A. Belousov complained: 'Some economists, probably not without influence from current monetaristic theories in the West, see in market relations, if not the only, at least the major, regulator of the economy, minimising the active role of the plan' (Belousov, 1985, p. 12). The conservative economic deputy general editor of *Pravda*, Dmitri Valovoi, even complained about reflections of market thinking at a meeting of the Presidium of the Council of Ministers: 'Frankly speaking, the issue is actually the liquidation of centralised management and planning. According to the opinion of supporters of that approach "the economy under socialism must be, like under capitalism, self-regulating". "No physical indicators!"' (*Pravda*, 30 May 1988).

The bravest of marketeers tend to present the market as the natural or normal state of affairs: 'The development of a normal market is the key to radical reform ... A normal market needs a natural price formation system ...' (the economists P. Medvedev and I. Nit in *Sots. ind.*, 28 April 1988). At the Party Conference, the delegate G. I Zagainov even attacked Yegor Ligachev for one of his anti-market statements: 'But the market as an effective feedback mechanism in the economy is an ancient innovation ... A stable development of the economy is only possible in the presence of social and economic feedback mechanisms, including the market' (*Pravda*, 2 July 1988).

In a forceful advocacy of the market, Aleksandr Yakovlev noted that 'money-commodity relations' (which even Ligachev accepted) could not exist without a market. Yakovlev criticised 'scholastic' disputes for having missed that 'the market has historically been formed as an objective and social reality' and went on to call the market a 'natural, self-regulating mechanism' (*Pravda*, 11 August 1988). This was an obvious reply to Yegor Ligachev, who had just argued that the market brought about chronic unemployment and social stratification (*Pravda*, 6 August 1988).

When fewer academic economists supported central planning in the press, Gosplan officials themselves had to defend the vested interests of their organisation. The First Deputy Chairman of Gosplan and its most senior academic economist (soon to become Academician), Stepan A. Sitaryan (1987, pp. 18–19), wrote in the spring of 1987:

Theoretical attempts to reduce the idea of a centralised foundation in the management of the socialist economy and to weaken the role of USSR Gosplan as its leading element are capable of causing irreparable damage ... one cannot forget that the principle of planned and proportional functioning of our economy as ... a unified economic complex, its purposeful development ... and, finally, the effective functioning ... of the national ownership cannot be assured without a centralised base in the management of the socialist economy.

These arguments had been rejected by empirical evidence, and Sitaryan is not a dogmatist. It is all too clear that the real issue was power.

Doubts about the meaningfulness of central planning lingered in the background, but the operative discussion was limited to issues like the extent of directive planning, the number of material balances, and the nature of planning. The Director of Gosplan's Economic Research Institute, Vadim Kirichenko (1986, p. 13), made a typical categorisation. In raw material extraction, a high degree of centralised planning in physical terms was to be maintained, as the main purpose was still to maximise gross production. In manufacturing, more contracts and self-financing would be applied, while consumer industry would be influenced by consumers as much as possible.

A more concrete concern was the number of material balances. According to Academician Nikolai Fedorenko (1984, pp. 7–8), Gosplan elaborated about 4,000 material balances, Gossnab 18,000, and the ministries 40–50,000. The number of balances increases lower down in the hierarchy as they are disaggregated.[13] Everyone agreed that the number had to be lowered. Deputy Chairman Gosplan, Leonard Vid, alleged that the number of material balances elaborated by Gosplan had been reduced to 2,117 in 1987 and that there would only be 415 in 1988 (*Pravda*, 18 August 1987), but personal inquiries clarify that the number of material balances was considerably higher in 1988. Vadim Kirichenko (1986, p. 15), who appears to be one of the last competent Soviet economists to believe in optimal planning, sought his inspiration in the GDR and Czechoslovakia and favoured a limited number of material balances—250–300 at the central level—to facilitate the utilisation of an econometric model, though this would imply 3,000–5,000 material balances at ministerial level. Curiously, even Nikolai Shmelev (1987, p. 151) suggested that Gosplan should plan in physical terms for 'not more than

250–300 kinds of strategic production (but perhaps considerably less)'.

In parallel, the number of plan indicators submitted by Gosplan was reduced from about 43,000 in 1986 to 22,000 in 1987, and the planned number for 1988 was 8,000 (interview with First Deputy Chairman of Gosplan Anatoli Reut in *Izvestiya* 17 August 1987). The Central Committee forced the Central Statistical Directorate to cut the statistics it requested by half (*Pravda*, 5 June 1986). However, the reductions in material balances and plan indicators prepared by Gosplan did not imply any qualitative change in the system of planning. Leonard Vid even stated that the lapsed material balances had been passed on to Gossnab (*Pravda*, 18 August 1987). These reductions only make sense if they are seen as the beginning of a transition to another system.

On paper, the Law on State Enterprises brought about essential changes in planning. Enterprises appeared to become independent in planning: 'An enterprise elaborates and confirms a five-year plan independently.' 'Annual plans are elaborated and confirmed by an enterprise independently on the basis of its five-year plan and concluded economic agreements ' (*Pravda*, 1 July 1987). These enterprise rights had not been inscribed in the published draft of the Law, underlining their controversial character. However, the Law was not unambiguous. In planning, enterprises were to consider 'control figures', 'state orders', 'long-term economic normatives' and quotas (*limity*).

The control figures would include production in value, profit (or revenues), currency revenues, scientific-technical progress, development of the social sphere, and, during a transition period, labour productivity and material intensity of production as well. This was a tall order. In the final version of the Law, it was inserted that the control figures 'are not of a directive character', but these words did not sound convincing. It was an obvious compromise of contradictory purposes. The long-term economic normatives were essentially tax-rates and financial regulations, which would be necessary in a reformed system. The quotas were rations of investment capital and centrally distributed material supplies, belonging entirely to the sphere of command economy.

The concept of state orders was a novelty, and the ensuing discussion focused on them. In the autumn of 1986, state orders suddenly emerged as a general theme in the economic debate. The article of 1964 by Academician V. Nemchinov, which Gorbachev quoted at the CC Plenum in June 1987, is referred to as a source of the present Soviet thinking about state orders. Nemchinov (1987, p. 25) advocated that 'the plan organs efficiently and rationally distribute ... profitable orders between enterprises ...'. His intention was to combine central allocation of plan targets with profit-steering of enterprises. The concept of state orders was introduced in Poland in the economic reform launched in 1982, where state orders were supposed to cover particularly important production. Since they were accompanied with better supplies, enterprises rushed for state orders, which minimised the marketisation of the economy. It was pretty obvious that the same would happen in the Soviet shortage economy. Gorbachev favoured competition, but the state orders would safeguard the interests of the state:

Enterprises must be put into such conditions that economic competition (*sorevnovanie*) develops between them for the best satisfaction of the consumers' demand. At the same time, the interests of the state are guaranteed by a system of state orders. But they shall have priority and favourable economic conditions; mutual responsibility is envisaged and as a rule [they] will be distributed on the basis of competition (*Pravda*, 26 June 1987).

It appeared as if this was both an operational compromise and a suitable means of transition. According to the Law on State Enteprises, the composition of the state orders was to be decided at three levels—Gosplan, the union branch ministries, and by the Republican Council of Ministers. In August 1987, Leonard Vid of Gosplan said that state orders would on average cover only 50–70 per cent of the production volume (*Pravda*, 18 August 1987). As early as November 1987, enterprise reports started appearing in the press: first, 'as before, the ministry plans, and the collective takes responsibility'. Second, 'state orders included all 100 per cent of the planned volume of production'. Third, plans were not consistent: 'The assortment plan for 1988 that has reached us exceeds the plan for volume of production in value by more than 15 per cent.' Fourth, supplies were as uncertain as before. Fifth, 'by mistake or misunderstanding, production for which there are no customers is included in the state order' (*Ek. gaz.*, No. 47, 1987, p. 7). Similar reports flooded the newspapers in December 1987 (e.g. *Lit. gaz.*, 16 December 1987; *Ek. gaz.*, Nos. 51 and 52, 1987).

In early 1988, it was plain: 'for the majority of enterprises and organisations [the production programme] for 1988 is virtually fully composed of state orders, which do not differ in any way from the ordinary plans, which were previously confirmed from above' (*Ek. gaz.*, No. 17, 1988, p. 2). Academician Leonid Abalkin summarised the situation:

Of all the clauses in the Law on Enterprises, in which the conception of state order was formulated, only one has been implemented—about its compulsory character; the others have not been implemented—the state order is spread to virtually all production, and not to the most important part; it is not allocated on the basis of competition; mutual responsibility of the sides has not been assured' (*Izvestiya*, 15 May 1988).

Apart from a certain reduction in paperwork nothing had happened. The command economy won the first round over the reform, and the display of bureaucratic techniques was impressive. Gosplan has been ordered to elaborate a statute on state orders, but it dragged its feet. It was criticised by the Prime Minister for its delays, but without a legal codification the status of state orders remained unclear (*Izvestiya*, 15 May 1988; cf *Pravda*, 30 May 1988). With three administrative tiers allowed to issue state orders, it was natural that every one of them added something.

When presenting the plan for 1988, the Chairman of Gosplan, Nikolai

Talyzin, simply neglected the reform (*Pravda*, 20 October 1987). The ministries were accused of having broadened the state orders to 100 per cent, contrary to the intentions of Gosplan, and the branch ministries had been given production tasks from Gosplan in the old manner. Nothing had changed in the relationship between Gosplan and the branch ministries (*Izvestiya*, 23 April 1988). Considering the severe shortages, it was natural for every body to demand as extensive state orders as possible, since they implied preferential treatment. The Soviet Union had not become a *Rechtsstaat* overnight, so it was not law but naked power that counted, and unlike enterprises, Gosplan and the branch ministries possessed a lot of power. The similar Polish experiences of state orders were hardly mentioned in the Soviet press, and were probably disregarded by leading Soviet economists as well. It would have been surprising if state orders had not proliferated as they did.

Still, the traditional Soviet system might have won a pyrrhic victory against the reformers. Glasnost gave voice to an extraordinary public reaction against Gosplan and the branch ministries for their failure to implement the reform. The reformers demanded more specific laws, leaving little leeway to authorities (e.g. G. Kiperman in *Sots. ind.*, 21 January 1988). On 5 February 1988, Nikolai Talyzin, who appears to have been unable to comprehend the reform, was replaced as Chairman of Gosplan by Yuri Maslyukov (*Pravda*, 7 February 1988). On the whole, enterprise directors obediently accepted the absence of change, but the gigantic Urals Machine-Building Association, Uralmash, in Sverdlovsk insisted on its newly-won legal right to adopt its own plan. After intense strife, Uralmash won its case against its ministry, but Uralmash's courage, and fortune, were boosted by the fact that Prime Minister Nikolai Ryzhkov had been its director general (*Izvestiya*, 23 April 1988). There were other enterprises that refused to accept directives contradicting the Law on State Enterprises (see *Moscow News*, Nos. 6 and 8, 1988). At the 19th Party Conference, Gorbachev cited their experiences, spelling out his verdict:

In a number of cases we are encountering direct attempts to distort the essence of the reform, and to fill new forms of management with old content. More often than not, ministries and departments deviate from the letter and spirit of the Law on Enterprises ... This is nothing but a result of arbitrariness by ministries in the absence of proper control, and also with the connivance of Gosplan and the permanent bureaux of the Council of Ministers of the USSR (*Pravda*, 29 June 1988).

The conservatives' disregard for their compromise with the reformers over planning suggested an extreme difficulty in the implementation of any compromise in a Soviet context. The lesson for the reformers was that they could not stop at half-measures but had to go further. Otherwise, nothing would change. A polarisation developed between reform economists and Gosplan. The reformist ambition was to reduce the share of state orders in GNP to 20–30 per cent in 1991 (primarily arms), corresponding to the US proportion of state procurement. Gosplan wanted to proceed much more slowly, with a reduction of the share of state orders to 65–75 per cent for 1989, and 50–65 per cent for 1990 (*Planovoe khozyaistvo*, No. 6, 1988, p. 126).

THE ALLOCATION OF SUPPLIES

The actual distribution—or rationing—of industrial inputs to producers is carried out by Gossnab (the State Committee for material and technical supplies). It is one of the conservative pillars of the Brezhnevian system, with a large monopolistic organisation throughout the country.[14] Gossnab acts in the shade of, and in collusion with, Gosplan, and may be seen as its auxiliary body, which elaborates material balances in greater detail. Lev Voronin, its Chairman since November 1985, was previously a First Deputy Chairman of Gosplan (where he worked together with Nikolai Ryzhkov, Nikolai Slyunkov and Yuri Maslyukov). Voronin is one of those officials who speak favourably of the market but appear unable to understand what it means in real life (see *Pravda*, 17 October 1988). Gossnab's highly centralised mode of allocation is often subject to criticism, because of its bureaucratic nature and poor services. It is significant that the word 'buy' has been replaced by words like 'organise' in the enterprise sphere (*Lit. gaz.*, 23 March 1988).

Reformists attack rationing as such, and point out the absurdity that Gossnab centrally issues supply authorisations for no less than one million different kinds of goods (Fedorenko, 1984, p. 8). Reformers advocate a 'socialist market': 'Economic independence for enterprises is unrealistic without a choice of suppliers and clients and without competition ... it is essential to guarantee equal rights for producers and consumers' (Nikolai Petrokov in *Izvestiya*, 15 March 1988).

In substance, the polarisation over the system of allocation is complete. However, the main ideological issue is plan versus market rather than rationing versus wholesale trade. Presumably, conservative communists find it more palatable to defend planning than rationing, and they avoid polemics over the supply system. The reformist catch-word is 'wholesale trade', but it presupposes financial demand constraints and market-clearing prices. However important allocation is, it has become a sideshow ideologically, politically and economically.

An attempt to establish wholesale trade was part of the 1965 reforms. But it fizzled out quietly when the reforms failed, though wholesale trade remained legally endorsed (Fasolyak and Barmina, 1985, p. 124). Local experiments with wholesale trade had been pursued in Estonia and Georgia. Reformists made favourable references to syndicates, large commercial wholesalers of the NEP period (K. Smirnov in *Sots. ind.*, 19 May 1985; A. Levikov in *Lit. gaz.*, 23 March 1988). In June 1985, Gorbachev (1985, p. 26) spoke up in favour of wholesale trade. This issue did not appear to be particularly controversial, because unlike other reform topics, it did not vanish from authoritative party media in the quiet autumn of 1985 (see *Pravda*, 3 October 1985).

At the 27th Party Congress, Gorbachev declared briefly: 'Wholesale trade with means of production must be developed' (*Pravda*, 26 February 1986). Soon afterwards, on 27 March 1986, the Politburo decided to experiment with wholesale trade in the 'non-productive' sphere and in one machine-building ministry (for Construction, Road and Municipal Machine-Building —*Minstroidormash; Pravda*, 28 March 1986; *Izvestiya*, 17 March 1986). The intention was that Gossnab should keep a certain ratio of previously planned supplies for the experiment branches, but enterprises in these branches no longer had to submit orders for every acquisition a year in advance. Now, they would be able to order and receive deliveries within a week or two.

The selection of Minstroidormash for the experiment appears misguided, since it was not involved in the experiment with self-financing. Furthermore, it required a great deal of scarce, specialised supplies. The outcome was all too predictable: 'In the beginning, Ministroidormash ... gathered materials above any moderation' (*Pravda*, 26 January 1988). Its budget constraint was soft, and many commodities were scarce, so why not hoard as much as possible? On top of everything, Minstroidormash did not even reach its production targets (*Lit. gaz.*, 23 March 1988). The disregard of economic consistency was so conspicuous that it looked like an attempt by conservatives to discredit wholesale trade. In the non-productive sphere, the experiment appeared surprisingly successful, causing a rapid fall in the demand for several kinds of construction materials (*Lit. gaz.*, 23 March 1988). The explanation was probably that these low-priority organisations had limited financial means, and thus quite hard budget constraints, and especially scarce commodities remained rationed (*Lit. gaz.*, 23 March 1988).

The Law on State Enterprises stated ambiguously that allocation should occur either in wholesale trade or in centralised order, without specifying any proportions. In addition, direct links and contracts between enterprises were praised (*Pravda*, 1 July 1987).[15] The ensuing decree on the supply system was one of the most contradictory and conservative. It set out that over 4–5 years 'a decisive transition' would take place from centralised allocation to wholesale trade with means of production, but the distribution of means of production 'of particularly great economic importance' would be subject to rationing (*O korennoi perestroike*, 1987, p. 111). Moreover, the material balances were supposed to become 'the main instrument of the organisation of material-technical supply' (*ibid.*, p. 114), which implied a reinforcement of the prevailing system.

According to Lev Voronin, the share of the total volume of production that would be distributed through wholesale trade would increase gradually: to 60 per cent in 1988–90, and to 75–80 per cent in 1990–2. In 1988, about 15 per cent of total production would be distributed through wholesale trade— compared with some 4 per cent in 1988 (*Pravda*, 23 September 1987). These plans were neither related to the development of self-financing nor to the extension of state orders (*Sots. ind.*, 17 March 1988). Moreover, sales and pricing were unconnected. Gossnab's powers were intact, and its warrants (*naryady*) remained a condition for the distribution of any supplies. Enterprises concluding their own decentralised agreements found: 'Gossnab of the USSR does not issue warrants for our metal and nobody explains the reason for its stubbornness' (letter to *Pravda*, 16 May 1988). As before, many enterprises could not utilise additional earnings, since there was no legal market where goods could be bought.

Gossnab's structure corresponds to the present, highly-centralised, monopolistic system of allocation. A transition from a vertical to a horizontal system of allocation would require a completely different kind of organisation, but the decree of 17 July 1987 implicitly favoured a further monopolisation through its criticism of inefficient departmental supply organisations which are 'duplicating' the work of Gossnab's organs (*O korennoi perestroike*, 1987, p. 110), although, admittedly, the same decree favours the establishment of departmental and republican supply bases outside the auspices of Gossnab (*ibid.*, p. 119). Gossnab is supposed to have switched to self-financing in 1988 (*Pravda*, 23 September 1987), but profit-orientation without any competition whatsoever does not inspire a behaviour beneficial to the national economy.

So far, Gossnab has successfully averted reformist threats by simulating change and promoting inconsistencies harmful to reform. Reformist criticism has not focused on the material supply system yet, but if the reform proceeds, it is likely to be perceived as a major impediment because of its centralised, authoritarian and monopolistic nature. How could these nasty bureaucrats, who are used to being flooded with demands, transform themselves into service-and-consumer-oriented salesmen? The whole infrastructure for trade and marketisation is missing.

PRICE AND FINANCE SYSTEM

For a long time, pricing has formed the central battleground for Soviet reformers and conservatives. Both sides have chosen this issue for an open fight. The reformers rightly see a reform of the price system as a condition for the success of economic reform, and they are confident their views are correct both in theory and practice. The conservatives, on the other hand, feel confident in their struggle over pricing, because of good support from ideology, the bureaucracy and the population at large. As a result of this intense struggle, it has been harder to compromise on pricing than on any other issue.

The price debate has raged primarily between the reform economists of TsEMI (Nikolai Fedorenko, Nikolai Petrakov and Yuri Borozdin) and Goskomtsen (former Chairman Nikolai Glushkov and Deputy Chairman Anatoli Komin), but few issues have engaged so many. Just before Gorbachev became General Secretary, the heads of the two camps, Fedorenko and Glushkov, pursued such bitter polemics over pricing (Fedorenko, 1984, and Glushkov, 1985b), that eventually both lost their jobs.[16]

Under the highly-centralised price system all state prices are regulated directly or through calculation rules, based on costs plus a profit mark-up. In the early 1980s, the major categories of prices were revised—industrial wholesale prices in 1982, agricultural purchase prices in 1983, and construction tariffs ('estimate prices') in 1984. Although many retail prices had been changed openly or tacitly, no general revision of retail prices had taken place since 1955. The price of bread has not changed since 1955, and the official state retail price of meat and dairy products since 1962.[17] Before any reform was conceived, Goskomtsen had planned a general price revision, in order to correct relative prices, taking effect in 1991.

A multitude of issues were disputed by conservatives and reformers. They agreed only to Marx's tenet that prices should be based on 'socially necessary costs'. But what did it mean? The reformers wanted to include all costs, while the conservatives preferred a narrow scope. Similarly, the reformers opposed subsidies, which the conservatives looked upon with complacency. The conservatives argued, on the basis of Marx, for average costs as a basis, while reformers preferred marginal costs in line with ordinary western price theory. Another principal question was the impact of market forces on prices. Reformers aspired to market-clearing prices, but an unfortunate corollary was that it was virtually essential to raise the general price level or undertake a currency reform. The conservative favoured centralised, fixed prices to facilitate planning, while the reformers called for decentralised, flexible pricing. Conversely, the conservatives wanted to reinforce price control, while reformers advocated its abolition. According to the reformers, foreign trade prices should be integrated into the domestic price system, which conservatives considered destabilising. The reformers desired some interrelation between all groups of prices, while the conservatives treated each price category separately. Both sides favoured, and opposed, some kinds of price discrimination, though they patently disagreed. These points of contention are typical of any discussion between dogmatic Marxist-Leninists and market-oriented economists. There was a great deal of unity within the kernels of each camp, but they reached out to very different groupings on particular issues, making the agenda an important determinant of the outcome.

More than on any other reform issue, a genuine public debate with strongly opposing views evolved, presumably influencing decision-making. As glasnost developed, so did a number of important disputes involving prices. The reformers, who had long used a muddled language, attempting not to violate Marxist-Leninist dogmas, became more comprehensible in their writing.

An emotional debate concerning the diversion of Siberian and Northern rivers involved the question of setting a price for water in agriculture.[18] Russian rural writers, who wanted to preserve Russian nature (notably Sergei Zalygin and Vasili Belov) were the driving force. They joined hands with reformist economists (Otto Lacis and Nikolai Petrakov), who favoured setting a price for water in order to achieve a more rational usage of natural resources. The Ministry of Water Economy and the Central Asians opposed this idea. The Ministry had a vested interest in the construction of such projects, and the Central Asians in the water.[19] The former camp had close links with the new men in the Kremlin, while the latter camp was Brezhnevian in every sense. What was most surprising was how long the latter camp managed to hold out.

In the autumn of 1986, the authoritative party journal *Kommunist* turned reformist, as the later Gorbachev aide Ivan Frolov was appointed its editor. Its first major debate under the new editor attracted great attention. It was spearheaded by an article by Academician Tatyana Zaslavskaya (1986), 'On the Human Factor and Social Justice', which was followed by outspoken articles by reform economists, such as Stanislav Shatalin (1986), Aleksandr Bim and Aleksandr Shokhin (1986), and Yuri Borozdin (1986).

All dealt more or less with price issues. The focus was on retail prices, and all favoured the abolition, or at least a sharp reduction, of subsidies for meat and milk, with compensation for the poorest. Bim and Shokhin (1986, p. 72) recommended the introduction of higher 'commercial' prices of high-quality foodstuffs together with the extension of rationing during a transition period. Zaslavskaya (1986, pp. 68–9) attacked privileges in access to goods and social utilities, proposing a 'unified consumer market in the country with equal access to all kinds of commodities for all groups of workers and equal purchasing power of the ruble'. She went on to attack the free distribution of social benefits and subsidised housing. At the time, polyclinics that people had to pay for were given a public boost as a complement to the free (but substandard) public healthcare (*Izvestiya*, 10 July 1986).

Another topic in this discussion, brought out primarily by Borozdin (1986), was to make pricing 'anti-cost'-oriented. He criticised the dominance of producers over consumers and focused on the need to overcome shortages and disequilibria in the consumer market. Shatalin (1986, p. 68) wanted a currency reform as well. Many other themes were ventured: various forms of social injustice and inequality, harmful monopoly effects, hidden inflation, alienation and demoralisation.

Some features in Zaslavskaya's programmatic article repelled many readers. *Kommunist* (1987, No. 3, pp. 97–108) reflected negative popular sentiments in letters from readers under the sub-title: 'Are We Losing What We have Gained?' The concerns appear representative: 'Free education, medical care, favourable prices of housing are among the most important achievements and advantages of socialism' (p. 106); 'the sale of [meat and dairy products] at their social price ... can lead to the lowering of the standard of living of workers and employees' (p. 107). 'The stability of retail prices of essential goods is our great achievement' (p. 108).

Regardless of positive comments on these and other issues, many perceived the reformist economists as anti-consumerists, intent on jeopardising the few achievements of socialism. This became all the more apparent in the popular newspaper debate on pricing, in which reformist journalists distanced themselves from ideas of raising prices (notably Anatoli Rubinov, *Lit. gaz.*, 19 September 1987, 17 February 1988). One reformist economist, L. Lopatnikov, regretted that out of 1,500 letters on retail prices to *Literaturnaya gazeta* (20 January 1988) in late 1987, only about ten were in favour of price increases, and all the others against (cf *Lit. gaz.*, 12 August, 30 September 1987). In the public's eye, the question of price reform had become a question of raising meat prices, and there was no reason to believe that price increases would bring about any improvements in supplies, given the political nature of distribution.

The reformist economists had been bogged down in the least desirable of all debates: over the deterioration of the standard of living. Furthermore, the dominant theme was subsidies and not market balance. It mattered little that Nikolai Petrakov pointed out that the wealthy paid an average of 2.9 rubles for a kg of meat, while others paid on average 4.2 rubles a kg (*Izvestiya*, 19 November 1987). To ordinary people, the primary issue was not social justice or market balance, but their own concrete standard of living. Academician Oleg Bogomolov suggested that the struggle against shortages was more important than the maintenance of an unchanged level of prices. He stated candidly: 'many economists suggest, that a regulated inflation, which is partly compensated through an increase in incomes of the population, is a lesser evil than artificially frozen prices and a distribution based on rationing cards' (*Lit. gaz.*, 16 September 1987).

Goskomtsen's leading officials said little and spoke more cautiously about price increases, while emphasising compensation (Pavlov, 1987; *Izvestiya*, 1 April 1988; Komin, 1988).[20] One conservative economist of Goskomtsen's research institute went as far as to warn that 'the safeguarding of political stability in our society' made it vital to keep retail prices at their present low level (Chubakov, 1987, p. 66), which may be seen as a reflection of Ligachev's repeated statements on political stability as the essence of social policy (*Pravda*, 28 February 1986, 6 August 1988). Conservatives complained about hidden inflation, resulting from insufficient centralisation of pricing and the paucity of price control (Kulagin, 1985; Deryabin, 1988; Deryabin and Salimzhanov, 1985, pp. 54–9, 84–92). The odd Stalinist raved about Stalin's price decreases after the war and demanded strict price control (Ochkin, 1987).

The Law on State Enterprises contained surprisingly little on pricing, but the ensuing decree 'On basic directions of the perestroika of the system of pricing...' dealt with most essential issues (*O korennoi perestroike*, 1987, pp. 150–64). New industrial wholesale prices as well as service and transport tariffs were to be introduced in 1990, and new estimate prices in construction and agricultural purchasing prices in 1991, but nothing was said about retail prices. A few principles were resolved more or less in line with reformist demands: raw material prices would be raised; land rent and charges for all resources, notably water, were to be introduced; the aim was to 'maximally reduce state subsidies', without necessarily abolishing them; prices were to be brought closer to the world market both in terms of level and structure.

For the rest, these guide-lines formed an impossible mishmash of contradictory principles. No stand was taken on average costs versus marginal costs. The decree stated that pricing should reflect both 'socially necessary costs' and 'consumer properties, quality and solvent demand', without clarifying the influence of costs and market forces, respectively, on prices. The most market-oriented formulation was: 'to overcome the tendency to price increases through the development of economic competition between enterprises, the abolition of shortages and all kinds of monopolies, and consumer pressure on producers', but the basic necessity to raise the price level was ignored. The decree almost precluded an increase in the level of retail prices: 'their change should not lead to a deterioration of the standard of living of the workers, but, on the contrary, to a rise of this level for certain categories of workers. . . .' On the one hand, 'the usage of basic actual costs as the main basis for the determination of prices' was condemned, but on the other hand no 'unfounded price increases' were to be permitted, and price control and punishments for the 'violation of state price discipline' were to be reinforced.

No resolution was reached on the degree of centralisation or flexibility: 'to ensure democratisation, an optimal combination of stability and flexibility in the setting of prices ... with broad utilisation of economic methods, at the same time as the centralised basis of the price-setting process is strengthened'. Three categories of prices were envisaged: centrally-set prices, negotiated prices, and independently-set prices. The range of each was not clarified. No relationship between different groups of domestic prices was suggested. Thus, almost all the contested issues remained open, and each failure to produce a consistent law was a victory for the conservatives. The problems had been identified, but each essential sentence appeared to be a combination of contradictory elements, indicating that neither side was prepared to give in.

Soon afterwards, the Chairman of Goskomtsen, Valentin Pavlov, published an authoritative article in *Pravda* (25 August 1987), adding that Goskomtsen should set the prices of 'basic kinds of fuels, raw materials, other kinds of basic production, and also of final production of the all-state plan'. Little was left for independent pricing. Moreover, Pavlov announced the creation of an all-union system of price control. This was an advance for the conservatives. *Pravda* carried detailed and positive articles on retail price increases in Poland and China, hinting at similar actions in the USSR (*Pravda*, 4 and 14 May 1988). At the 19th Party Conference, Gorbachev stated that the unresolved issue of price reform severely complicated the realisation of the economic reform. 'We cannot create normal economic relations without a price reform.' He declared that a reform of retail prices was being worked out, and promised that all proposals would be subject to an extensive discussion among the people, and that all state gains resulting from higher retail prices would be returned to the population as compensation (*Pravda*, 29 June 1988). The issue of balancing the market was set aside, rendering the rest of the price reform pretty ineffective. Meanwhile, the balance of retail markets deteriorated as a result of the campaign against alcohol.

The reformers had managed to put all their issues on the political agenda and may have won the intellectual debate, but they seem to have directed their writings at experts and political leaders, disregarding popular reactions. They had focused on hard decisions rather than benefits, though the two top economists, Academicians Abel Aganbegyan and Leonid Abalkin, were more cautious. In April 1988, Professor Nikolai Shmelev (1988, p. 171) suggested that a reform of retail prices should not aim at changing the market's macro-balance, which could be solved with financial measures instead. This reflected a reformist realisation that the popular fear of price increases was insurmountable.

Major financial goals were the establishment of a monetary balance and a convertible ruble within the country and the formation of a framework for a rational enterprise management and a rational direction of capital flows. The surplus of money on Soviet markets comprises two problems: an accumulated monetary overhang (a stock) and a surplus of current incomes over expenditures (a flow). A natural Soviet response to the monetary overhang would have been a currency reform, with exchange of the currency and confiscation of fortunes. A letter to *Pravda*, 1 February 1986, proposed such a reform. In those days, *Pravda*'s word was still authoritative and a frenzied purchasing spree grasped the country, but on 19 February 1986, *Pravda* published a denial by the Chairman of Gosbank. Similar public denials by the Minister of Finance, the Chairman of Goskomtsen and First Deputy Prime Minister Geidar Aliev ensued, underlining the public worry.

In the summer of 1987, an article by Ed Stevens in the *Sunday Times*, broadcast to the USSR by the BBC, gave a detailed outline of a currency reform, unleashing another surge of hoarding. Once again, after a couple of weeks (on 27 July 1987) a denial was issued on TV by the Minister of Finance. In the public debate, one reform economist—Shatalin (1986)—called for a currency reform. Petrakov (1987b) urged a return to the currency reform of 1922–4, with the introduction of a new hard convertible currency parallel to the existing soft ruble. Other reform economists from TsEMI (V. Ivanter, Yu. Leibkind and V. Perlamutrov, 1987, p. 42), on the contrary, argued that 'a denomination of money ... would undermine the confidence of the economy and the population in the monetary system'. In addition, Nikolai Shmelev (1988, p. 172) noted that the late Academician Aleksandr Anchishkin had estimated that only 20–30 billion rubles of the 260 billion rubles in private bank accounts had originated from illegal sources, so just to confiscate them should not be a consideration. A currency reform was an option, but a very controversial one.

Reformers have suggested a number of alternative financial solutions. The most obvious option would be a more active policy of savings banks (Petrakov, 1987a, p. 8). Nikolai Shmelev (1988, p. 170) has proposed that the Soviet Union should exploit its relatively low indebtedness in order to borrow 'several tens of billions of dollars' to buy western machinery and consumer goods to saturate the market. Shmelev also wanted to activate the assets of the population by selling bonds and shares in state-owned companies to individuals. He assumed that it would be possible to mobilise 'tens of billions of rubles', if the returns were sufficiently high—7-10 per cent a year (Shmelev, 1988, p. 169). Oleg Bogomolov has supported the idea of selling shares and bonds to workers, a policy that has been tried in Poland, Hungary and China. He has also suggested that workers could buy loss-making enterprises from the state and transform them into cooperatives (*Lit. gaz.*, 16 September 1987).

On the turn of 1987, the first joint stock companies with private ownership emerged. They were formed by employees of state enterprises, which needed more capital. Their formation had the character of a grassroots movement and was not preceded by any legislation (*Moscow News*, No. 11, 1988; *Pravda*, 30 May 1988). In fact, they were a kind of joint venture between the state and shareholders-employees. Boris Kurashvili suggested that workers of an enterprise be allowed to own up to 49 per cent of its assets (*Moscow News*, No. 23, 1988). Surprisingly little ideological resistance surfaced in the Soviet press.

In the enterprise sphere, there was a mismatch of resources. Enterprises had both excessive debts and stocks of inputs. Directors needed incentives to sell surplus stocks. One proposal was to raise the interest rate of credits (Petrakov, 1988a, pp. 8-10). The decree on banking of July 1987 envisaged a general introduction of interest rates on all bank deposits and differentiated interest rates (*O korennoi perestroike*, 1987, p. 173). At the end of 1987, the Council of Ministers gave ministries extensive rights to mobilise internal resources to offset payments in arrear (*Ek. gaz.*, No. 50, 1987, p. 4).

However, enterprises had to become concerned about costs—to have their budget constraints hardened. The Law on State Enterprises stipulated the possibility of enterprise closures. A few bankruptcies, which resulted in the liquidation of enterprises, were announced in 1986 and 1987.[21] The word 'bankruptcy' appeared in newspaper articles, but it was not used in legal texts; no law on bankruptcy appeared to be planned (although it was discussed); the poorly conceived decree on banking of July 1987 implied that credits to loss-making enterprises would continue almost automatically (*O korennoi perestroike*, 1987, p. 175). A general problem was that the profit level was considered too low to facilitate a strict financial policy. According to V. M. Ivanchenko's pessimistic estimation, in 1984, as few as 12 per cent of Soviet industrial and agricultural enterprises enjoyed sufficient profits to be really self-financing (*Ek. gaz.*, No. 32, 1986, p. 8). Besides, the losses were often caused by distorted prices.

The decree on the finance mechanism was one of the most well-conceived of the ten reform decrees of July 1987. It envisaged a system of 'long-term stable economic normatives and financial norms', prohibiting the confiscation of enterprise profits and the interference of ministries in the financial activities of enterprises (*O korennoi perestroike*, 1987, pp. 134, 136, 140). However, it did not stipulate that capital charges and tax rates would be unified, and soon it became clear that capital charges varied from 0 to 12 per cent of fixed and working capital, while profit taxes ranged from 0 to over 90 per cent (Bunich, 1987, p. 6; Shmelev, 1988, p. 166). These rates were set by branch ministries, and the Ministry of Finance did not see itself fit to impose more generalised charges and rates before 1991. The financial conditions of enterprises remained unstable, discouraging initiative. Still, the reform had provoked severe criticism of beneficial treatment of inefficient loss-making enterprises and stifling severity towards the most profitable (cf Bunich, 1987).

The question of how to direct capital towards efficient projects had barely arisen. Banks were the ideologically most acceptable channels. Reform economists favoured commercial credit (Bunich, 1987, p. 12). There was a realisation among Soviet economists that banks can only work in a market-oriented manner. One economist, L. Braginski, remarked: 'we do not need to invent anything, creating some kind of special construction of "our own"', and added that the experience of foreign banks was only superficially known in the USSR (*Izvestiya*, 27 July 1987). At a conference on Soviet bank reform in December 1986, G. Skorov from the USA and Canada Institute discussed whether the US system of setting interest rates could be utilised in the USSR (*Voprosy ekonomiki*, No. 8, 1987, p. 151). However, the decree on banking of July 1987 took only a short step by adding two new banks. There were altogether six banks: Gosbank, the bank for foreign economic relations (Vneshekonombank), and four branch-specialised banks—approximately as in the 1950s. The establishment of a capital market was still barely discussed, but commercial credits was a hot issue. A Deputy Chairman of Gosbank, I. Levchuk (1987, p. 15), noted that they would naturally lead to the appearance of notes of exchange, discount rates, decentralised credits and some sort of shares, which he seemed prepared to accept under certain conditions.

A fundamental monetary problem was that the ruble was not convertible domestically. Not only did enterprise funds and cash circulate in separate spheres, but the value of a ruble in cash also varied, depending on whether it lay in the hand of a member of nomenklatura with access to special supplies or in the hand of a citizen in a distant corner of the country without state supplies of essential foodstuffs. A similar differentiation existed among enterprises. Reform economists like Tatyana Zaslavskaya and Nikolai Petrakov concurred with popular resentment against the privileged élite. Petrakov (1987b, p. 220) proposed the transformation of hard currency shops into ruble shops with high-quality goods at higher prices, as in the GDR and Hungary. A decision to abolish hard currency shops for Soviet citizens from 1 July 1988 was taken (*Lit. gaz.*, 3 February 1988), but the domestic convertibility of the ruble remains a distant target.

While pricing is a minefield for the reformers, they have encountered little overt resistance on financial principles, because of the absence of a socialist financial theory. The problems have been of a more mundane nature. The branch ministries and the Ministry of Finance are used to thinking of balancing their own accounts. If they do not have money on one account, they seize funds wherever they can extract some. In the first round, the branch ministries came under fire, but the sudden change in the taxation of cooperatives in the spring of 1988 showed that the Ministry of Finance was not much better (see Chapter 6). Such has also been the lesson in Poland, where the Ministry of Finance has to a large extent replaced branch ministries as the tormentor of enterprises (see Fallenbuchl, 1988).

THE FOREIGN TRADE SYSTEM

In the reform process, foreign trade has not been treated as an element of the economic system, but as a branch of the economy. While Gorbachev has taken the lead on most reform issues, Prime Minister Nikolai Ryzhkov has directed the changes in the system of foreign trade. At the 27th Party Congress, Ryzhkov made clear that a foreign trade reform was under way (*Pravda*, 4 March 1986). The basic decision on this reform was made by the Politburo in mid-August 1986, in the wake of the Party Congress (*Pravda*, 16 August 1986). Thus, the reform of foreign trade was not coordinated with the reform package adopted one year later.

Soviet foreign trade is riddled by many problems. It is very small. The Soviet foreign trade expert Valeri Karavaev has spoken of the 'backward, one can say "colonial" structure of Soviet exports to the West, four fifths of which is composed of energy' (*Lit. gaz.*, 21 October 1987). At the same time, a great deal of imports have been wasted, notably expensive western equipment that has not been installed for years. The idea of import substitution, favouring import of machinery over finished goods is deeply entrenched also among reformers. The drastic fall in the value of Soviet exports to the OECD area by some 40 per cent from 1984 to 1986, because of plummeting energy prices, exposed the weakness of Soviet exports.

Prime Minister Ryzhkov's words on foreign trade at the 27th Party Congress clarified that the regime had a sincere intent to reform, but he said little about direction. A basic aim was to connect branch ministries and enterprises with foreign trade (*Pravda*, 4 March 1986). According to competent Soviet officials, another purpose was to encourage Soviet producers of manufactured goods to export. A third goal was to force Soviet producers to raise their technical level and quality. In addition, a more efficient allocation of imports and a reduction of red tape in foreign trade were intended, as well as more coordination above the Ministry of Foreign Trade and the State Committee for Foreign Economic Relations (GKES, responsible for exports of large projects and arms and assistance abroad). In systemic terms, the Soviet ambitions were humble. The changes outlined in the decree of 19 August 1986 (that became effective in 1987) amounted to standard East European changes implemented in the 1970s (Hanson, 1987b).[22]

Fundamental questions about the foreign trade system are: How far is it decentralised? Is the decentralisation supported by adequate changes in the regulation of foreign trade and currency? Is foreign investment allowed? The Soviet foreign trade reform brought about changes in all these regards.

The original decree on the 'perfection of the management of foreign-economic relations' of August 1986 appeared more rudimentary and more poorly elaborated than other reform decrees. Many basic issues were not even alluded to. One obvious reason was that the decree was issued before the reform had been reasonably conceptualised; another that the technical expertise of the Ministry of Foreign Trade and related bodies were excluded.

The treatment of the Ministry of Foreign Trade may be likened to a hostile take-over. There was an almost clean sweep at the top of the Ministry, with an outsider (Boris Aristov, Deputy Minister of Foreign Affairs) as new minister. While the changes in other central economic organs were revised by these bodies themselves, the reform in foreign trade was imposed from the outside. The original reform design was elaborated by a group of academic economists—primarily from Bogomolov's institute—headed by its deputy director Vladimir Shastitko, but it also included Ivan Ivanov—Deputy Director of the Institute of the World Economy and International Relations, later Deputy Chairman of the State Foreign Economic Commission. The project was greatly altered by the administration, but its hostility to the Ministry of Foreign Trade was preserved.

The Ministry lost its monopoly over foreign trade, and a new superministerial body, the State Foreign Economic Commission, was established to supervise it. The Ministry's staff was cut by 30 per cent (Kamentsev, 1987, p. 27). Finally in January 1988, it was amalgamated with the GKES into a new Ministry for Foreign Economic Relations, and the Chairman of the GKES, Konstantin Katushev, became its minister, while Aristov retired (*Pravda*, 17 January 1988). A second wave of personnel changes and cuts further reduced the former Ministry of Foreign Trade.

The Ministry might have been an easy target, since it has developed into a secluded caste, almost to the same extent as the Ministry for Foreign Affairs. The children of the higher nomenklatura filled the ministry (with Leonid Brezhnev's alcoholic son being the First Deputy Minister). Its corruption was obvious, with one Deputy Minister being sentenced to thirteen years in prison on corruption charges.[23] The Ministry was singled out for a fierce attack one year before other ministries and central economic bodies. Because they were subject to a simultaneous attack, these bodies had reasons to cooperate in their resistance, but by then the Ministry of Foreign Trade had fallen victim.

The prime issue, to break the monopoly power of the Ministry of Foreign Trade, was accomplished, but it was less clear to whom the foreign trade rights would be given. Initially, twenty-one branch ministries and sixty-seven large associations (enterprises) were named, but the number was somewhat extended during the year.[24] The decentralisation primarily concerned civilian manufactured goods, while the trade in raw materials and commodities remained centralised. In 1988, 213 associations had foreign trade rights.[25]

The process of decentralisation was long and messy. It was reasonably clear which ministries and enterprises were involved, but it took a long time to settle their claims. When both a branch ministry and some of its enterprises were given foreign trade rights, the branch ministry tried to monopolise the rights of its enterprises. Several of the associations with foreign trade rights were located in cities closed to foreigners (e.g. Gorki, Sverdlovsk and Chelyabinsk), compelling them to establish foreign trade firms in Moscow, where they became easy targets for their respective branch ministry. Regional authorities saw a role for themselves. Notably in Leningrad, they tried to coordinate and monopolise the foreign trade rights of enterprises in their area. Estonia was the first republic to establish a republican foreign trade enterprise. The organisations of the Ministry of Foreign Trade joined this bureaucratic scramble for power and money. It took charge, when essential issues were left unsolved. The natural winners were the powerful branch ministries. Vladimir Shastitiko noted: 'In the absence of certain safeguards, the "monopoly" of the Ministry of Foreign Trade may be supplanted by the "monopolies" of a number of ministries invested with powers to conduct external economic activities' (*Moscow News*, No. 30, 1987). In the future, the desires of republics for foreign trade rights may gain strength.

The lesson from Poland is that it is dangerous to give strong branch ministries foreign trade rights; the Yugoslav experience shows the dangers of republican foreign trade prerogatives, while Hungary and the GDR have proved the benefits of giving enterprises foreign trade rights. The Soviet authorities had not realised the importance of these distinctions. The result was a drawn-out struggle, that has harmed foreign trade and probably made more difficult the preconditions for future attempts at a foreign trade reform, since reformers now have to contend with the powerful branch ministries rather than the isolated Ministry of Foreign Trade.

In the decree of August 1986, the ideas of incentives in foreign trade were rudimentary. Enterprises were supposed to be encouraged to export by retaining a share of 30–50 per cent of their yield (*vyruchka*) from exports (*Lit. gaz.*, 8 July 1987). The concept of yield was not defined in Soviet law. In practice, it was replaced by export revenues. Moreover, in intra-CMEA trade there was no mechanism for using additional transferable rubles, so exporters to CMEA countries found themselves with substantial amounts of useless account money (*Ek. gaz.*, No. 31, 1987). The centralisation of foreign trade decisions prevailed. In November 1987, the majority of the enterprises with formal rights to act on foreign markets had not even opened currency accounts with Vneshekonombank, which was a precondition for foreign trade activities (*Ek. gaz.*, No. 49, 1987). For enterprises, the incentives to develop independent foreign trade had proved insufficient.

The Basic Provisions on Economic Reform, which were adopted at the CC Plenum in June 1987, contained one paragraph relating to foreign trade. It urged a gradual move towards the convertibility of the ruble, primarily within the framework of the CMEA (*Pravda*, 27 June 1987). The first attempt at a foreign trade reform had led to the establishment of differentiated so-called currency coefficients for various groups of commodities, allowing the calculations of a domestic ruble value of each item in foreign trade. Such a system had existed in Hungary before the reform in 1968. Ever more currency coefficients were established, as enterprises demanded more favourable coefficients for particular groups of goods. In the spring of 1987, there were 1,600,[26] but by 1988 their number had increased to 10,000 (Shmelev, 1988, p. 173). In the end, there was one individual currency coefficient for each significant trade commodity, and they varied widely from 0.3 to 6.0 (in relation to wholesale prices in domestic rubles) (*Ek. gaz.*, No. 47, 1987). One resulting demand was for a cut in the number of currency coefficients and for their differentiation to be diminished, moving towards the unification of the exchange rate. In the longer run, an orderly currency system requires both an orientation of the domestic price structure towards the world market and a devaluation of the ruble (*Ek. gaz.*, No. 40, 1987; Shmelev, 1988, p. 173).

In connection with its decision of a reform in foreign trade in August 1986, the USSR also changed its policy towards GATT, and is now intent on becoming a full member (Kamentsev, 1987, p. 34; see Åslund, 1988). In the wake of these decisions, Soviet authorities have started thinking of a new customs mechanism. Work is presently under way on a new 'modern' customs mechanism, apparently intended to facilitate a marketisation of foreign trade (*Izvestiya*, 18 March 1988). The Soviet attitude to the International Monetary Fund, and thus the World Bank, remains reserved. The new Soviet stand is that 'scientific contacts at expert level' with the Fund are desirable (Kamentsev, 1987, p. 34).

The CMEA (Council for Mutual Economic Assistance; Comecon) was a particular concern. Officially, intra-CMEA trade accounted for 61 per cent of Soviet foreign trade in 1986 (*Vneshtorg 1986*, p. 8), but this figure is exaggerated because intra-CMEA prices are highly inflated, and a large share of the goods traded are unsaleable on competitive markets. Intra-CMEA trade may be described as highly centralised barter, in which enormous bundles of goods are agreed bilaterally on a five-year basis, allowing little flexibility. This system is rigid and economically arbitrary.

The initial approach of the new Soviet leadership (incorporated in the new Complex Programme of the CMEA adopted in December 1985) was to urge more organisational integration with 'direct links' between couples of enterprises and joint ventures. By 1987, direct links had been established between about 700 Soviet enterprises and enterprises in Poland, the GDR, Czechoslovakia, Hungary and Bulgaria, but these connections were artificially imposed from above and gave little in return.

From November 1986, the Soviets started calling for a change in the price system and currency-financed relations (*Pravda*, 4 November 1986). In June 1987, the CC adopted the demand for convertibility (*Pravda*, 27 June 1987). Such an aim had been included in the CMEA Complex Programme of 1971, but now it had some meaning, since the Soviet leaders had become serious about domestic economic reform. Gradually, Soviet experts realised that the convertibility of the transferable ruble within the CMEA was not feasible for both technical and political reasons.

In the spring of 1988, the Soviets adopted a new approach, oriented towards decentralised trade between enterprises in different countries. The solution was bilateral clearing in domestic currencies at freely negotiated prices without the intermediary 'transferable ruble', with the professed intention that centralised contingencies would account for a dwindling share of the mutual trade. A first bilateral agreement of this type was concluded with Czechoslovakia in the spring of 1988 (*Pravda*, 22 April 1988). Similar bilateral concords are expected to be concluded with Poland and Hungary, while more conservative CMEA countries like Rumania and the GDR are reluctant. An approach of gradual decentralisation has been adopted.

In May 1983, when Andropov was General Secretary, the Soviet Union quietly adopted a brief decree allowing the establishment on Soviet soil of joint ventures with CMEA countries (VVS, No. 22, 1983). Nothing happened until October 1985, when contracts on the creation of two Soviet-Bulgarian joint ventures were concluded. The new CMEA Complex Programme of December 1985 urged the creation of mutual joint ventures in line with its orientation towards closer organisational integration. The legislation of August 1986 envisaged joint ventures also with capitalist countries, and on 13 January 1987 two decrees were adopted on the creation of joint ventures with CMEA countries and other countries, respectively.

The conditions offered foreign partners were neither favourable, nor well-conceived. The Soviet share of an enterprise must be at least 51 per cent; the president of the board and the managing director must be Soviet citizens; joint ventures must fall under ordinary Soviet jurisdiction, implying an obligation to obey thousands of unpublished legal acts, which the foreign partner had no right to see; at the same time, joint ventures would be isolated from the domestic market, being forced to purchase from, and sell to, Soviet enterprises through Soviet foreign trade organisations; 20 per cent of sums taken out of the country were taxed; a condition for the transfer of profits abroad was that joint ventures had earned hard currency. The most positive stipulations were that the profit tax amounted to only 30 per cent and joint ventures were not subject to state planning (*Pravda*, 27 January 1987). Besides, much was unregulated and open to negotiation, but the legal vacuum was a hazard in itself. The joint ventures with the CMEA differed through a strict bilateral 50/50 division of everything—capital, production and profits.

From the summer of 1986, western enterprises were urged to present proposals for joint ventures. By 1 July 1988, sixty-six joint ventures had been registered—most of them with western firms (*Pravda,* 24 July 1988). However, most of these undertakings are small; several are oriented towards western tourists; and many appear to be a tribute paid by faithful western business partners to a new Soviet whim. The Soviet economic reform will not become effective before 1991. Meanwhile a sizeable market-oriented enterprise cannot be expected to function normally. The actual present conditions for joint ventures are more reminiscent of Rumania than of Hungary or China. The push for joint ventures appears premature. It seems to have been unleashed by a great demand for hard currency in the wake of the traumatic shortfall in Soviet hard currency earnings in 1986, and a desire for the cachet of joint ventures.

Some Soviet economists, who have realised that joint ventures cannot function normally under present Soviet conditions, have proposed 'free economic zones' of the Chinese type. Many Soviet officials and senior economists have visited them, but even reformists have written little and ambiguously about them (See Fedor Burlatski in *Lit. gaz.*, 11 June 1986; *Izvestiya*, 19 January 1987). *Pravda* carried a full-fledged criticism of them as late as 4 January 1987. This is one of the most controversial features of the Chinese reform in Soviet eyes. In a private conversation, one senior Soviet reform economist discarded them, with allusion to Soviet nationality problems; the existence of special currencies in the Chinese zones; and that a vast majority of the foreign investment comes from Chinese living abroad. However, *Pravda*, published a positive report on tax-free trade zones in Bulgaria on 3 May 1988. Academician Oleg Bogomolov has advocated free economic zones in the Baltic states, at the Black Sea and in the Far East, and he has said that discussions on their establishment are under way among the Soviet leaders (*Financial Times*, 11 April 1988). This idea has gained strong local support in Estonia and Latvia, where it is combined with demands for republican self-financing. It would be surprising if the USSR would opt for free economic zones, considering the present nationality problems.

The initial effects of the foreign trade reform were disappointing. In September 1987, the Politburo amended the reform with a number of improvements. They aimed at simplifications and clarifications. A substantial boon was a tax relief of two years for new joint ventures. The introduction of joint stock companies for joint ventures with socialist enterprises was envisaged (Kamentsev, 1987, p. 30). Even so, the Soviet foreign trade system remains a not very reformed muddle. The absence of serious discussion of foreign trade for so long has left this complex branch of economic theory particularly neglected, but Soviet economists do realise that the convertibility of a currency requires wholesale trade in capital goods, balance on a domestic market and a unified realistic exchange rate (e.g. M. Lyubski in *Izvestiya*, 16 January 1988). Therefore, foreign trade is likely to be the last link in the economic system to be completely reformed, although it has been given a premature start. Meanwhile, Soviet economists have time to learn foreign trade theory.

THE ROLE OF THE PARTY IN THE ECONOMY

Whatever the formal rules, the Communist Party plays an immense role in the operation of the Soviet economy. Its limits are only set by the number of its functionaries and the limitations of its expertise. At the central level, the CC apparatus with about 2,700 officials cannot possibly control the central management apparatus of 108,000 officials. Technically complex ministries, particularly in machine-building, appear to be subject to the least party control. Ministries' common disregard for CC directives show the limits of CC power. Nikolai Shmelev (1988, p. 163) notes that 'among the people the conviction has matured, that the provinces are stronger than Moscow and that some central ministries are stronger than the CC of the CPSU.' Regional party organisations have the best opportunities to interfere in branches with no military connections, little technical complexity, and small production units—essentially agriculture, small-scale production of consumer goods and services (Nove, 1977, pp. 127–8).

The role of the party has been one of the most long-lasting taboos, and the discussion of this topic has tended to be obscure. The democratisation drive launched by Gorbachev at the CC Plenum in January 1987 would increase the popular pressure on all authorities, including the party. The issue was opened. As early as at the 27th Party Congress, Boris Yeltsin criticised the CC apparatus for duplicating Gosplan and the Council of Ministers, while having forgotten what real party work was. He called for a change in the structure of the CC apparatus, implying the abolition of its branch departments (*Pravda*, 27 February 1986). It was widely assumed that this idea enjoyed the tacit support of Gorbachev. Similar demands surfaced in the public debate before the CC Plenum in June 1987. An article in *Pravda* (17 June 1987) advocated that party committees should stop their detailed control over economic work, and change their organisational structure accordingly, though previous party interference had been justified as a balance to departmental distortions. However, at first, the reform expanded party powers. Regional party organisations took over economic powers that branch ministries had been deprived of. Effectively, the strengthening of the local authorities implied a reinforcement of the local party organisation's hold on the local economy. Elections of enterprise managers extended local party influence over big industrial enterprises, since the party organisations controlled the nominations (*Ek. gaz.*, No. 47, p. 4, No. 52, p. 12, 1987).

The reformers felt obliged to take on the party itself. In an article in *Kommunist* in November 1987, Academician Oleg Bogomolov reviewed experiences of reforms in other socialist countries. He observed:

Party committees have the last word in a majority of questions that have formally been the competence of state bodies. With such a practice, state bodies have been transformed into simple executives of commands 'from above'. Situations are still common, when party functionaries interfere in all details and give instructions for any reason, but do not take responsibility for mistakes, that have been committed because of their faults (Bogomolov, 1987, p. 100).

Bogomolov argued that the party apparatus should no longer duplicate the state apparatus, stopping its 'petty control of every step of the state apparatus'. Instead it should concentrate on raising its influence on ideas and politics and assuring that the party's strategic direction was implemented. Arguments of this kind appeared in letters published before the 19th Party Conference. *Pravda* (20 April 1988) reported that all branch departments of the Bulgarian Communist Party had been abolished. The reformist intention was to eliminate the operative role of the party in the economy.

All these ideas were included in Gorbachev's big speech at the 19th Party Conference on 28 June 1988. He devoted one section of his speech to 'The Demarcation of the Functions of Party and State Bodies'. Arguing that the Communist Party should fulfil its role as political vanguard, Gorbachev urged that the functions of the party, the soviets and the executive bodies should be precisely defined. The 'Central Committee and Politburo must act and function as organs of political leadership'. Small issues should not crowd the agendas of party committees at any level.

the CPSU implements its political line through communists working in the organs of state power and in all spheres of society's life. All party organisations must act strictly within the framework of the USSR Constitution and Soviet laws. Everything that the USSR Supreme Soviet and the USSR Council of Ministers must do, must be done precisely by them (*Pravda*, 29 June 1988).

Hence, Gorbachev called for an end to the practice of party committees issuing directives to state and economic bodies and social organisations. He explained the failure of implementing similar ideas in the past with the 'Logic of the command-administrative system'. The new role of the party required a new organisation of the party, with fewer staff and without the 'fragmentation' of the CC apparatus and subordinate party organs (*Pravda*, 29 June 1988). In a coup-like manner, Gorbachev managed to have a brief resolution adopted at the very end of the Party Conference, on the reorganisation of the party *apparat* and necessary changes in the party structure before the end of 1988 (*Pravda,* 2 July 1988).

On the basis of this resolution, Gorbachev carried out a virtual coup at the hasty and brief CC Plenum on 30 September 1988, halving the number of CC Departments and drastically reducing the staff of the CC apparatus.

Gorbachev envisages a party with a much more humble role in the economy than a traditional party of a Soviet type. At the 19th Party Conference, he undertook the first serious attempt to rein in the party since Khrushchev's abortive attempt in 1962. If any reader remains unconvinced that Gorbachev is serious about radical reform, this should be the final proof.

CONCLUSIONS

A review of the measures to reform the economic system that have been initiated since Gorbachev became General Secretary reveals an impressively broad front. Far-reaching transformations of all pillars of the system have been enacted in authoritative party and state documents.

Most measures were legislated in the summer of 1987, to be gradually implemented until 1991. Foreign trade was an exception, having been subject to reform legislation in the autumn of 1986. Another exception was the role of the party. As a highly sensitive political issue its resolution was delayed until the summer of 1988. Organisational changes were legislated over a longer stretch of time, although the decisions in the summer of 1987 had the greatest impact. There was an ambition to coordinate legislation on economic reform, but the legislative plan adopted in late August 1986 did not foresee such a policy (VVS, No. 37, 1986), and the reform measures were implemented in a haphazard, uncoordinated manner, bound to cause considerable hardships during a transition period of at least three years.

The absence of consistency in the timing of the implementation of various reform measures is best explained by the prevalence of strife and departmental barriers. In addition, the legislative capacity was severely restricted, with the Supreme Soviet only adopting two major economic laws a year. The political and legislative processes allowed little precision, timing or coordination. Besides, the reform did not appear very consistent in theory, because of a lack of theoretical conceptualisation.

The relative importance of these factors varies with the issue. The battle over economic reform proper may be perceived as three major echelons. In the first echelon, we find the two most contentious issues, pricing and planning. All conceivable parties are involved in the strife over pricing, which is a vital question topping the reform agenda. It cannot be postponed with less than a delay of the whole reform. More than in any other case, conservative communists and the central economic bodies enjoy popular support for their stand on pricing. The reformers had worked out comprehensive proposals for price reform long ago. Thus, the conceptualisation of reform was not a problem, but political controversy was rampant. Another contentious, system-dividing issue is plan versus market. It is a deeply ideological question, but in reality vested interests matter more, uniting the whole central state apparatus against the reformers.

Reorganisation and reform of the supply system may be considered a second echelon of the struggle over reform. For obvious reasons, organisational changes arouse strong sentiments among those concerned. This process has been protracted, but it is impressive that the political leadership has been able to impose such far-reaching changes on the immense Soviet bureaucracy. Presumably, the political leadership is less split on these changes, as almost all favour a streamlining of the state administration. However, after sheer rationalisation, the system-dividing disputes surface. In this case, the reformers can benefit from the popular dislike of the bureaucracy. So far, there has been little qualitative strife over the supply system, but as a second echelon behind Gosplan, Gossnab might come to the forefront as the struggle intensifies. It has all reasons, and excellent opportunities, to fight for its continued monopoly power over most supplies.

The reforms of foreign trade and the finance system comprise a third echelon in the strife. Both require a high degree of theoretical competence not yet apparent among Soviet economists. Fortunately, the design of these elements may be completed at a late stage of the reform. The foreign trade reform appeared premature in relation to other parts of the reform. The current battle over foreign trade is intense, but it is a struggle for power and money of no benefit to the reform process. Financing has not been a very contentious topic to date. Only reformers have a theory of finance, and it is the most technical aspect of the economic system, so the discussion is dominated by qualified economists. However, in the future, the Ministry of Finance is likely to offer considerable resistance to reform, as its arbitrary taxation powers will be contested.

Reformist offensives have been launched by Gorbachev, academic economists and journalists. The CC apparatus has offered them considerable support, while the role of the Council of Ministers has been ambiguous, and the rest of the central state administration resists virtually everything. The population entered the conflict when its standard of living was endangered, notably by price rises. Reformers have been disappointed with minimal support, and often hostility, from enterprise directors—their presumed allies. According to one generalisation, directors of large, successful enterprises, tend to be more interested in independence than directors of small or medium-sized, unprofitable factories, needing central support.

The central economic bodies do not openly oppose reform as long as they can win by other means, but when their section of the battle-front is threatened by a reformist break-through, they do not hesitate to fight for their cause, distorting or even contradicting political commands. So far, the Ministry of Foreign Trade is the only casualty among the central economic bodies. The idea cherished by Zaslavskaya (1984) and others—that the branch ministries are conservative, but the central economic bodies more progressive—has proved incorrect.[27] The branch ministries and the central economic bodies have acted in unison against reform.

The central economic bodies appear to be well integrated with one another. Senior policy-makers tend to circulate among them. Gosplan's strong man on systemic issues, First Deputy Chairman Stepan Sitaryan, comes from the Ministry of Finance, from where he brought a number of competent economists to Gosplan, notably the new head of the Gosplan department for economic reform issues. The Chairman of Gossnab, Lev Voronin, served as First Deputy Chairman of Gosplan until his new appointment in November 1985. The Chairman of Goskomtsen, Valentin Pavlov, was First Deputy Minister of Finance until August 1986. The Deputy Minister of Finance responsible for reform issues, Vyacheslav Senchagov, previously headed one of Gosplan's research institutues. And these are only a few examples. The integration of the personnel in the central economic bodies is so great that it is natural for them to maintain a high degree of agreement.

With their emphasis on personnel, the new leaders have seemed to embrace the common perception that the aged, conservative and incompetent leaders of the Brezhnev administration blocked innovations and effective actions. An extraordinary exchange of leading personnel has taken place. In October 1988, twelve out of the fourteen members of the Presidium of the Council of Ministers had been appointed since 1985. All the central economic bodies had new masters. In May 1988, Gorbachev proudly announced that 66 per cent of the ministers were new since March 1985 (*Pravda*, 11 May 1988). It is plain that the new ministers work longer hours, but no qualitative economic impact has been apparent. The exchange of leading personnel has proved ineffective.

The professional backgrounds of leading officials in the central economic bodies appear to be undergoing a rapid change. Engineers are giving way to economists, and the academic qualifications of the top administrators have risen. Of the recently-promoted people mentioned above, all apart from Voronin are doctors of economics. The new regulations require more economic knowledge. Economists have long dominated the Ministry of Finance, Goskomtsen and Gosbank. Now, they are making inroads in the engineer-dominated Gosplan, while the hegemony of engineers remains unchallenged at Gossnab. However, most of these economists come from institutes within the sphere of the Ministry of Finance, and there is no sign of any integration of academic economists into the central economic bodies. On the contrary, the more conservative economists from the Ministry of Finance appear to block the entry of more reformist academic economists. So far, there is suprisingly little ground for a belief that the substitution of economists for engineers on economic key posts will favour the cause of reform. The new officials fend loyally, and more skilfully than their predecessors, for the vested interests of their institutions. The simple truth is that interests are more important than competence or professional background, a point well elaborated by Academician Zaslavskaya (e.g. 1985).

One frequent question concerns the effects of the poverty of Soviet economic theory on the reform. So far, the damage appears surprisingly slight. On the current front lines—pricing and planning—reformers have a pretty good analysis and conceptualisation, and the paramount obstacle is political and institutional resistance. In the case of organisation and the supply system, the theoretical tenets are simple, but ignored by the legislators. The reasons might be that these ideas have not yet been spread sufficiently and that the dominance of the central economic bodies has been too great. A press campaign could amend the situation. In financing and foreign trade, the theoretical shortfalls are serious, which is openly acknowledged by the Soviets involved, but these questions might be seen as a third echelon of the economic reform, leaving Soviet economists time to learn. It takes time to develop a financial system from scratch. Despite all talk about a comprehensive reform, the understanding of the need for consistency appears limited, but that requires little more than reflection.

This survey of major reform measures suggests that the present economic reform is a very serious undertaking. Since already the initial compromises have gone so far, much more is in store, if the reformers get the upper hand in the leadership. On the other hand, a multitude of contentious issues and strifes have already erupted, indicating that the struggle is likely to be protracted. Even in the ideal case, basic reform issues cannot be resolved before 1991. As long as no firm decision on the introduction of a market-clearing price and finance system has been taken, the reform cannot be expected to provide better economic results. The inconsistencies in both the implementation and the principal legal acts are so great, that it will be necessary to go back to the drawing board, if the first attempts at economic reform succeed in breaking through the resistance. The lack of economic theory is a problem, but it is hardly irreparable. A rapid process of learning is taking place, while the initial struggles over economic reform go on.

NOTES

1. The best western discussions, to date, of this reform are Hewett (1988, pp. 322–60), Schroeder (1987) and Ericson (1988).
2. Aganbegyan mentioned this decree at a press conference on 26 June, but it was apparently not adopted together with the other decrees on 17 July, so some late impediment seems to have stopped it.
3. Gorbachev himself stated to Karoly Grosz that the Soviet reforms most of all resembled the Hungarian (*New York Times*, 10 July 1988).
4. Popov (1985a) is presented as the second edition of a book published in 1976, but virtually all the material in the book is new, so it might be a device to have the book more quickly published.
5. Among the most prominent economists, Abel Aganbegyan tended to write on resources, Aleksandr Anchishkin on resources and forecasting, Leonid Abalkin on political economy, Oleg Bogomolov on socialist economies, Tatyana Zaslavskaya on sociological research, Nikolai Petrakov on pricing and finance and Pavel Bunich on enterprise management. Nikolai Fedorenko stuck out his neck on reform issues.
6. The foremost Soviet expert on organisation used to be Academician Dzhermen M. Gvishiani, but his place has been taken over by Professor Boris Z. Milner, who recently moved from Gvishiani's institute to the Institute of Economics of the Academy of Sciences. They edited a book published in 1987, which appears to be a rather authoritative view of the organisational changes needed (Gvishiani and Milner, 1987). It is the main source of this section. Another good source is Gavriil Popov (1985a).
7. Hanson (1986a) and Hewett (1988, pp. 335–9) have given good accounts of superministries.
8. Personal information from a first-hand Soviet source.

9. For instance, 27 per cent in Estonia (where great reductions had taken place previously), 36 per cent in Belorussia, 60 per cent in Georgia, no change in Uzbekistan (oral information received during personal visits to representatives of these republican agro-industrial committees in the summer and autumn of 1986; for Belorussia see *Izvestiya*, 26 February 1987—this figure apparently includes the *oblast* level as well).

10. Personal information from an initiated, but not centrally placed, Soviet expert.

11. The following is compiled from *Izvestiya*, 8 and 10 April 1988; *Moscow News*, No. 13, 1988; FBIS, 4, 6 and 20 April, 3 and 10 May 1988.

12. Credible personal information from a first-hand Soviet source.

13. V.M. Ivanchenko set the numbers a bit lower, with Gosplan handling 3,000–3,500 material balances at the time (*Ek. gaz.*, No. 32, 1986), and Gossnab acknowledged only 15,000 material balances (Fasolyak and Barmina, 1985, p. 32). The exact numbers seem to vary from year to year.

14. Gossnab, which was resurrected in 1965, provides more than 240,000 enterprises and organisations with inputs. Even when it does not carry out the physical allocation, its authorisation is required. Within its field of responsibility, Gossnab claims control of 98 per cent of the commodity flows. The exempted product groups are consumer goods, agricultural goods and petroleum products. The allocation of consumer goods is handled by the Ministry of [Domestic] Trade, and Gosagroprom takes care of distribution within the agricultural sphere. Until its recent abolition, the State Committee for the Supply of Petroleum Products allocated such products (see Fasolyak and Barmina, 1985, pp. 31–4, 125–6).

15. Direct sales between enterprises do not pass through the stores of Gossnab, but its warrants, indicating commodity, quantity, supplier and receiver, are still needed, and Gossnab frequently interferes and breaks such contracts. In 1987, 3,250 of Gossnab's aggregated material balances were set aside for direct deliveries between enterprises. Most of these goods were bulk goods, produced and acquired by relatively few enterprises. Their share of total Gossnab supplies amounted to 30 per cent in 1986—to compare with 37 per cent in 1980 (*Ek. gaz.*, No. 40, 1987, p. 18).

16. Glushkov's fall is probably connected with his outspoken conservatism. Just before he fell, Glushkov declared in public: 'I am conservative by nature' (*Moscow News*, No. 21, 1986, p. 12)—strange words for a communist. Fedorenko lost out because of a number of factors, such as the poor state of economic science and many personal enemies (Åslund, 1987).

17. For a good description of the Soviet price system and outstanding pricing issues just before the reform, see Bornstein (1987), though he misses the existence of higher 'cooperative' retail prices that were proliferating at this time and lends unjustified credence to Soviet statistics; cf Glushkov (1985a).

18. In 1982, a price for water had been introduced in industry, while agriculture and households remained exempt.

19. On this extensive topic, see *Lit. gaz.*, 2 October, 18 December 1985, 15 January, 2 July 1986; Zalygin (1987); *Izvestiya*, 21 August 1986. The first camp was composed of a rather implausible alliance. Outstanding Russophile and environmentalist writers, such as Vasili Belov and Valentin Rasputin, defied the reformers on everything else, while Sergi Zalygin appears to combine a Russophile and liberal outlook.

20. When Pavlov replaced Glushkov as Chairman of Goskomtsen in August 1986, he

was perceived to be Ryzkhov's man and had a reputation as a competent economist specialising in finance and a moderate reformist. He had kept a high profile as First Deputy Minister of Finance and was well-considered among academic reform economists. Yet, after a year without public statements, he came out with a moderately conservative position (*Pravda*, 25 August 1987). Anatoli Komin is an old Goskomtsen hand and its leading economist. After Pavlov had become Chairman, Komin was promoted from Deputy Chairman to First Deputy Chairman. At the same time his public views suddenly switched from conservative, close to Glushkov's line, to moderate reformist. He made statements such as: 'prices are now the basic obstacle in the introduction of new management methods' (*Izvestiya*, 19 November 1987).

21. The probably first report of an outright bankruptcy was published in *Lit. gaz.*, 23 April 1986.

22. There are four basic decrees on the foreign trade reform. Two were adopted on 19 August 1986 (one on foreign trade in general and one on cooperation with socialist countries). Two decrees on joint ventures (one for CMEA members, and one for others) were adopted on 13 January 1987. All four were published in full in English in the monthly journal *Foreign Trade*, No. 5, 1987.

23. A Moscow joke in 1987 was that the Ministry for Foreign Trade had opened a new branch in the Butyrka prison.

24. To twenty-two ministries and seventy-seven associations carrying out about 20 per cent of Soviet foreign trade and exporting more than 65 per cent of machinery and equipment (Kamentsev, 1987, p. 26).

25. Statement by an official of the Soviet Ministry of Foreign Economic Relations at a *Financial Times* conference in Budapest on 22 June 1988.

26. Personal information from a reliable source.

27. This idea might have been a tactical device to avoid attacking central economic bodies directly at a time when it was dangerous, but others, notably Nikolai Fedorenko, did criticise the central economic bodies over a long period.

6. The new policy towards private enterprise and cooperatives

Whatever the prospective accomplishments of the reform in the state sector, many problems that had matured in the 1980s involved property relations. On the output side, shortages of consumer goods and services and declining quality appeared insurmountable problems. The benefits of small enterprises, with their flexibility, market-orientation, innovativeness and small administration were acknowledged for certain sectors. On the input side, large resources were poorly utilised, and few resources could be mobilised by traditional means. In order to approach a financial balance, large cash holdings and excessive savings of the population needed to be soaked up. An extensive underground sector had grown uncontrollable, arousing concerns about the aggravation of social injustice and criminality. At the same time, a lot of useful private work belonged to a legally grey zone, being persecuted by police.

The non-state economy has been both larger and more complex than official Soviet publications have suggested. However, the relatively large cooperative sectors in agriculture, trade and housing have barely differed from state enterprises in their functioning. Most of the private economy has been unregistered, as legal private enterprise has been minimised by government policies. In November 1986, there were only 97,000 registered private entrepreneurs.[1] Cooperatives have lost all independence and become almost as petrified as state enterprises, while the aggravation of shortages and a comparatively lax attitude to the underground economy stimulated its development.

The most prominent form of legal private enterprise is agricultural production pursued on private plots (cf Wädekin, 1973). In 1985, there were 35 million private plots with an average size of 0.25 hectares (Popov, 1985a, p. 280). For the mid-1980s, estimates of their share of total agricultural production varied from 25 per cent (Geli Shmelev in *Ek. gaz.,* No. 9, 1986) to 30 per cent (Vladimir A. Tikhonov in *Lit. gaz.,* 8 April 1987). Private housing remains important, including no less than 29.2 per cent of the housing area completed in 1985, and 40.7 per cent of the total housing area in use (*Narkhoz 1985*, pp. 421, 426).

A huge, essentially illegal, private sector provides a wide range of consumer services. An article in *Izvestiya* (18 August 1985) stated that the private, unregistered, consumer (*bytovye*) services[2] to the population amounted to 5–6 billion rubles a year, while employing 17–20 people. On the basis of official Soviet family budget surveys, Vladimir Treml (1987, p. 4.13) has estimated income from private services at 17.8 billion rubles for 1985. The real figures are likely to be much higher, but even according to official estimates, one third of the demand for consumer services was satisfied by the state sector, one third by the unregistered private sector, while one third was left unsatisfied (presumably, given going prices). Private services were estimated by Soviet specialists to account for 50 per cent of shoe repairs, 45 per cent of house repairs, 40 per cent of repairs to private cars and 30 per cent of repairs to household appliances in towns, and 80 per cent of consumer services in the countryside (*Izvestiya*, 18 August 1985; cf *Pravda*, 5 September 1987). In addition, private tutoring has been estimated to have amounted to 2 billion rubles in the mid-1980s (*Sotsiologicheskie issledovanie*, No. 2, 1987, p. 27). Still, state repression has left a large unsatisfied demand, and an untapped labour surplus. An inquiry in West Siberian towns found that 17 per cent of the workers there performed paid, additional work in their free time, while another 27 per cent would like to (*Izvestiya*, 24 November 1986).

A peculiar Soviet form of unofficial economy has been the so-called *shabashniki*, 'temporary construction brigades', informal teams of about 5–8 workers who take up seasonal employment in construction or agriculture. Several hundred thousand workers are involved.[3] *Shabashniki* migrate from areas with excess labour, notably Caucasus, to areas such as West Siberia with extreme labour shortages. Their legal status has been ambiguous. A decree regulates their work and remuneration, but even so *shabashniki* have frequently been sentenced to prison in connection with large earnings. In agriculture they lease land, and in construction they agree on a fixed price of a project. Consquently, they are well motivated to work extremely hard, and they earn at least three times more than ordinary construction workers, which has caused controversy.[4] The authorities have tried to limit both their freedom and incomes through a decree 'On the regulation of organisation and remuneration of the work of temporary construction brigades' of 15 May 1986, which was ensued by a new model statute. After that, *shabashniki* appear to have caused less concern (Kabalkin, 1987, p. 15).

Another peculiarity of Brezhnev's rule was the development of a neo-feudal society, particularly in the five Central Asian republics and Caucasus. Whole republics became criminal networks led by the first party secretary (Nuikin, 1988b; *Pravda*, 16 March, 28 December 1987, 23 January 1988). The cotton magnates in Uzbekistan are alleged to have stolen more than 4 billion rubles, of which they appropriated half for themselves (*Pravda*, 23 January 1988). A great deal of extortion, embezzlement and theft goes on in the socialist sector. Some of it may be labelled private work with the help of socialist property, while other activities are little more than theft (Grossman, 1977).

The second economy, including all kinds of private economic activities, is vast, but its exact size is an open question. In a pioneering interview study with Soviet émigrés, Gur Ofer and Aaron Vinokur (1980, p. 70), estimated that 10–12 per cent of total personal incomes come from private sources, but add only 3–4 per cent to GNP. However, their project was limited to the urban, European part of the Soviet Union, where the private sector is likely to be smallest, in the early 1970s. Another interview project for the late 1970s, with a broader definition of private income, including agriculture, and a wider geographical scope, was led by Gregory Grossman and Vladimir G. Treml. It has not yet presented its final results, but partial figures suggest private sources provide for 30–40 per cent of total personal incomes (Grossman, 1987, p. 219).[5]

The cooperative sector is large. In 1985, 26,200 collective farms, with 12.7 million workers, accounted for roughly half the socialist agricultural produce (*Narkhoz 1985*, p. 179; *Ek. gaz.*, No. 18, 1987). For 1985, the cooperative share of retail trade was estimated at 27.1 per cent, but this must be a severe understatement, as cooperative prices were assumed to be just 2 per cent higher than state prices, while they tended to be twice as high for foodstuffs (*Narkhoz 1985*, p. 462; *Lit. gaz.*, 16 December 1987). Cooperative housing accounted for about 8 per cent of all housing area built in 1985 (*Izvestiya*, 22 March 1986). Only 481 cooperative construction enterprises operated in 1985, to compare with 27,805 state enterprises (*Narkhoz 1985*, p. 374). Besides, there are several kinds of disparate cooperatives, such as garage-construction cooperatives, dacha-construction cooperatives, gardening cooperatives (with 12 million members), and even rabbit-raising cooperatives (with 1.5 million members; Popov, 1985a, pp. 279–80). Already before the new reform wave, cooperatives had emerged as the natural form of ownership for new kinds of economic undertaking.

On the other hand, it was evident that the state sector could not accomplish everything on its own. On the other hand, private enterprise existed on a large scale in any case, so why not legalise and civilise it? The Constitution of 1977 offered cooperatives and 'individual labour activity' a considerable scope, not reflected in operative law. The examples of private enterprise in the GDR, Hungary, China and Poland reported in the Soviet press, showed what private enterprise could achieve in a socialist state. The old dogmatism had proved infertile. A far-reaching revision of political economy prepared the ground for an extension and revitalisation of both cooperatives and private enterprises.[6] A vision of a cooperative movement appeared.

The new leaders wanted both forceful action against all illicit activities, and the promotion of a wide range of private and cooperative enterprises, thus marking the boundary between legal and illegal activities. Soon after Gorbachev had become General Secretary, legislation on private enterprise was initiated. Already in the spring of 1985, a commission was established on the elaboration of a law on individual labour activity, under the auspices of the Ministry of Justice.[7] A variety of administrative decrees aimed at promoting specific cooperative and private activities were issued intermittently, urging authorities to facilitate the development of these activities and provide material supplies.[8] These decrees indicated good will but had little impact.

At the 27th Party Congress, General Secretary Gorbachev clarified his intentions. On the one hand, an 'important function of a socialist state is the struggle against unearned income'. On the other hand, 'while cutting unearned incomes, we cannot allow any shadow to fall on those who receive additional earnings through honest work ... It is necessary to attentively examine proposals for the regulation of individual labour activity' (*Pravda*, 26 February 1986). Significantly, Gorbachev's call for a struggle against unearned incomes aroused 'prolonged applause', while his mentioning of individual labour activity merely attracted 'applause'. Both in Gorbachev's speech and in the overt reactions, the emphasis lay on measures against the underground economy.

The Politburo discussed both issues on 27 March 1986. Its bulletin bore witness to a linkage between them but stressed 'the reinforcement of the struggle against unearned incomes' that had been demanded by many workers. The struggle should be pursued 'actively and without compromises' in order to eliminate all means of 'illegal enrichment at the expense of the state and its citizens'. At the same time, the Politburo declared its intention to legislate 'a more accurate regulation of individual labour activity as envisaged in the Constitution' (*Pravda*, 28 March 1986).

However, the 'reinforced struggle against unearned incomes' was launched already on 28 May 1986, with the publication of three decrees and resolutions (*Izvestiya*, 28 May 1986), and this merciless campaign became a prominent feature of the Gorbachev era. The 'Law on Individual Labour Activity' was enacted much later—on 19 November 1986—and came into force on 1 May 1987 (*Pravda*, 21 November 1986). It was the first comprehensive law on private enterprises. Previously, little existed but a minor statute on handicrafts adopted in May 1976 (Kabalkin, 1987, pp. 13–14; *Lit. gaz.*, 3 September 1986).

In a parallel development, five decrees on various kinds of cooperatives were adopted by the Council of Ministers. Three of them were published on 12 February 1987 (one each in *Pravda*, *Izvestiya* and *Sots. ind.*). They were concerned with public catering, consumer services for the population, and the production of consumer goods, respectively. A decree on cooperatives for recycling waste had been adopted in the autumn of 1986 (*Izvestiya*, 20 October 1986), while a decree on bakery cooperatives appeared in early October 1987 (*Ek. gaz.*, No. 40, 1987). Each decree was accompanied by a model statute. Previously model statutes existed only for consumer cooperatives, *kolkhozy* and construction cooperatives (Yasmann, 1987), which functioned like state enterprises. However, the new cooperatives became real cooperatives, that is independent, self-managed and self-financing. As soon as a model statute was published, a sprinkle of cooperatives of that type started emerging.

In July 1986, Gorbachev envisaged a Law on *Socialist* Enterprise, implying a comprehensive treatment of state and cooperative property (*Pravda*, 2 August 1986; cf VVS, No. 37, 1986). However, on the turn of 1986 cooperatives were excluded from the scope of the law. The reformist endeavour to set state and cooperative enterprises on an equal legal footing had been blocked at the political summit. Instead, a 'Law on Cooperatives in the USSR' was promulgated by the Supreme Soviet on 26 May 1988 (*Pravda*, 8 June 1988). This law is by far the most liberal in the present reform wave, and it marks an ideological breakthrough of much greater significance than the Law of Individual Labour Activity.

THE STRUGGLE AGAINST UNEARNED INCOMES

In the summer of 1986, a battle against unearned incomes broke out. It assumed most features of a traditional Stalinist campaign, although punishments were incomparably milder. Besides, the press expressed scepticism at an early stage. It was probably the most effective economic measure undertaken in 1986, but its effects were negative.

The Soviet notion of 'unearned income' is spurious. In the commentary to the Civil Code of the RSFSR, it was noted: 'The concept of unearned income is not determined in the law, its presence is established by the court in each concrete case' (quote in *Izvestiya*, 6 July 1985). Similarly, a legal scholar, N. S. Malenin remarks: 'The term "*unearned income*" has entered legislation and legal literature, but there is no precise definition of this concept, and different indications are used' (Malenin, 1987, p. 57). Even so, this unclear notion is to be found in the USSR Constitution (Article 13) and in the RSFSR Criminal Code (Article 153). In general terms, it means personal gains exceeding the equivalent value of someone's work, but that would include pensions and social welfare (Malenin, 1987). In practice, any large, fast earnings may be persecuted as unearned income (Roucek, 1988, p. 47). Because of its diffuseness, this term suits the control agencies. They can act at will, since they decide what is unearned income.

The neo-Stalinist nature of this campaign came as a surprise to many, but its formation can be traced in official statements leading up to the struggle. At the 27th Party Congress, Gorbachev focused on 'unearned incomes from public property', that is direct theft from the state. He also mentioned bribetakers, but he underlined that no shade should fall on those 'who obtain additional earnings through honest work'; their endeavours should be facilitated (*Pravda*, 26 February 1986). The activities Gorbachev complained about would be equally unacceptable in a market economy. The ensuing Politburo bulletin went much further, calling for 'the eradication of unearned income, obtained through illegal activity, embezzlement, bribery, speculation ...' (*Pravda*, 28 March 1986). It introduced the key concept of 'speculation' which can mean any gainful private activity.

On 28 May 1986, *Izvestiya* published three legal documents 'On Measures to Reinforce the Struggle against Unearned Incomes'. They had been enacted by the CC, the Council of Ministers, and the Presidium of the Supreme Soviet, respectively. The lower we descend in this legal hierarchy, the sharper the edge is turned against the private sector.

The CC Decree was very general, but it specified illicit incomes. One group comprised 'embezzlement, speculation, bribery'. Another was the extortion of additional payments in public retail shops. A third group consisted of private activities which would be subject to reinforced control: the utilisation of housing (second-hand renting); internal passports in towns (to stop illegal migration); and *kolkhoz* markets (to 'stop the activity of speculative elements and middlemen'). A fourth focal point was the misuse of public transport for private gain. Furthermore, 'private-property psychology' should be combatted. A battery of police measures were commended, and all kinds of control agencies and social organisations were ordered to join the struggle. Unlike preceding political statements, this decree appears neo-Stalinist both in its aims and methods.

The decree of the Council of Ministers implied an escalation in comparison with the CC decree. It was directed against private sales on the *kolkhoz* market, contrary to Gorbachev's intention, calling for 'measures to improve the work of *kolkhoz* markets' which meant more control of the private traders to stop their speculation, and the promotion of state and cooperative traders. The punishments—fines of 50 to 100 rubles plus confiscation of merchandise —were to be meted out by policemen on the spot.

An edict issued by the Presidium of the Supreme Soviet entailed a further escalation against private enterprise. Its first half was devoted to punishments for illegal pursuit of individual labour activity and purchases of bread in public shops to feed animals, though punishments for bribery and embezzlement of public property were also specified.

Finally, in an interview in *Izvestiya* (31 May 1986), the Soviet General Prosecutor Aleksandr Rekunkov depicted the concrete nature of the campaign. He referred to complaints that

some owners [of private plots] grow agricultural products not for their own consumption, but for the market. In particular, hot-beds and green-houses were discussed, as well as flowers and sorghum, strawberries and cucumbers, because the sale of these cucumbers generate a larger income than work at a factory or *kolkhoz*.

Still, since this production was based on hard work during free hours, Rekunkov declared: 'naked prohibitions are hardly expedient'. He regretted 'obviously exaggerated prices' on *kolkhoz* markets. The General Prosecutor saw the solution in more control, although he acknowledged the poor qualifications of the controllers: 'It is ridiculous: the controllers and auditors cannot count to one hundred.' It should have been obvious that these substandard officials indulged in lawless persecution. To activate them meant to boost lawlessness.[9]

The whole exercise had already come full circle. Gorbachev had focused on crimes committed in the state sector, but the spotlight had been diverted to *kolkhoz* markets and individual labour activity, although the pronounced official policy was to stimulate citizens to grow vegetables and flowers on their private plots and sell their surplus at market prices. In particular, Rekunkov stood for a different policy to that of Gorbachev. The transformation of the policy on unearned income took place at the highest political and legislative level. We should seek the main villain in the Politburo, and the outstanding protagonist of the struggle against unearned income was of course Ligachev. Moreover, when this legislation was drawn up, in the spring of 1986, Gorbachev apparently suffered a political set-back, not speaking for a couple of weeks in connection with the Chernobyl catastrophe. The implemented policy on unearned income appealed to ideological dogmatism, the vested interests of the control agencies, and the jealousy of certain citizens.

A massive administrative campaign began. The main executives were the police, local authorities, the prosecutors and social organisations directed by the local party organisations. In a traditional manner, the authorities demanded regular success reports. A local prosecutor's aide reported: 'Every month we have to present a report to the *oblast* prosecutor's office about how we struggle with unearned incomes. How many cases have been uncovered, how many controls and raids have been undertaken, and investigations given to the court ... And what do you write in the report, if there is nothing?' (*Pravda*, 4 March 1987). It was self-evident that the campaign would be directed against ordinary citizens. For the controllers, they had the double advantages of being many, so that quantititative targets for the number of controls and punishments could be met, and powerless so that they could not take revenge. Major economic crimes could hardly be revealed so quickly, and the campaign was carried out by the ordinary administrative hierarchy, which had no reason to reveal its own corruption.

The negative effects of the campaign were evident from the outset, since deliveries to *kolkhoz* markets became a major target. As early as 14 July 1986, even *Pravda* highlighted the situation on the *kolkhoz* markets in a few places under the headline 'Is the Cucumber Guilty?'. In Perm, the price of tomatoes had instantly risen from 1.5–2 rubles a kg to 6 rubles, because kolkhoz peasants from Uzbekistan, who had come in large numbers to sell vegetables in Perm, had been deterred from going by Uzbek militia. In Krasnoyarsk, market booths were empty, as private producers in the neighbourhood had been forbidden to sell outside their *raion*. In Ivanovo, expected market supplies of southern fruit did not arrive, because police had intercepted them on the road. Although private production was legal, fruit and vegetables seized by the police were invariably confiscated and destroyed without legal recourse. 'High prices on the market upset many readers.' One of *Pravda's* informants noted: 'any unjustified limitations or problems reduce deliveries. The spontaneity of the market [then] raises prices.' Another informant noted: 'Low "ceilings" of prices in a number of *oblasti* have led to the impoverishment of the market.' This was only the start.

The transport of private produce to *kolkhoz* markets was another major target. There was virtually no private goods transport, and legal public transport was rarely available (*Izvestiya*, 14 July 1986). Consequently, 'until recently up to 80 per cent of the production appearing on the market was delivered by a "*levak*", a driver of a state car for payment in "live" rubles' (*Pravda*, 14 July 1986). With increased repression against illegal transport, the price of illegal transport doubled 'for the risk' (*Izvestiya*, 2 February 1987). To secure transport and a place at a suitable *kolkhoz* market were cumbersome procedures, and there were few alternatives. Public trade had little capacity to purchase, arousing queues; it did not provide transport; it frequently turned down goods offered, and it maintained artifically low prices (*Lit. gaz.*, 12 August 1988); but private middlemen had been singled out as a prime target by Rekunkov (*Izvestiya*, 31 May 1986).

A third target was the private renting of rooms or beds, boosted by the extraordinary shortage of housing (Sukharev, 1986, pp. 106–7). The self-evident result of this augmented control was a sharp decline in the private housing supplied. 'Flat landlords ... started to turn down their clients on a mass scale' (*Izvestiya*, 2 March 1987). In major tourist areas, such as the Crimea, Odessa and Krasnodar, private landlords simply stopped letting rooms and beds for the summer 1986, bringing havoc to tourism.

The article 'The Criminal Tomato' by Igor Gamayunov in *Literaturnaya gazeta* (12 August 1987) is possibly the most perturbing account of the lawless persecution engendered by the struggle against unearned incomes. Gamayunov reported how hundreds of greenhouses for tomatoes had been demolished in two *raiony* in Volgograd *oblast*. Their destruction had been directed by a local 'commission for the struggle against negative phenomena', which was composed of local authorities, prosecutors and militia. They ordered convicted hoodlums and students to destroy private hot-houses. On the roads, police controls seized and destroyed tomatoes transported out of the *raion*. Fines of 50 rubles per person and occasion were exacted. The local cooperative purchasing office refused to buy a lot of the tomatoes offered. The tomato-growers were labelled 'speculators' and accused of 'a parasitic life style' in the local newspapers. The local authorities received numerous anonymous letters about tomato-growers, who did nothing illegal. Several accusations concerned legal acts such as heating hot-houses. A decision to proscribe sales outside the *raion* had even been falsified. The outcome was lawlessness, economic decline and demoralisation.

In particular, Gamayunov wondered: 'why has the "struggle" essentially been concentrated on pensioners?' The answer he received was: 'so that the youth do not even think of leaving public production ... In other words, a preventive, prophylactic action.' It seems more likely that pensioners were singled out, because they were powerless. Similarly, numerous local bans were introduced in various parts of the country. For example, flower sales were prohibited in Leningrad, and many people saw their private plots reduced as a punishment for the 'improper utilisation of subsidiary plots' (Nuikin, 1988a). Gamayunov limited his criticism to local authorities, but their ideas corresponded to those of Rekunkov. All worried about excessive private earnings and labour being diverted from the public sector. Furthermore, the smashing of hot-houses appears to have become a common occurrence in various parts of the country, suggesting central orders. Ensuing judgements by Soviet reformers have been appropriately hard:

Under the banner of struggle for social justice, against unearned income, the most rabid leftism and bungling appear ... How can one comprehend the signs in the summer of 1986 of a new *pogrom* against [private] hot-houses, gardens, personally-tended farms? Was not the anti-state character of this campaign ... immediately visible? (Shmelev, 1987, p. 147).

We launched on a broad front a campaign to utilise all our frozen reserves and to develop independence, initiative, and enterprise, and suddenly, at the height of the march—we got the Decree on the Struggle against Unearned Incomes, which pulled society far back in the solution of these tasks. The country was swamped by an avalanche of persecution against people who tried not to sit down at the dominoes table after the plant whistle had blown but to work a little bit more at their own responsibility and risk (Nuikin, 1988a).

In parallel, serious measures were taken to uncover regional party mafias, but this operation against organised crime was separate from the campaign against unearned incomes. The purge was most extensive in Uzbekistan, where it started in 1983 and involved CC Secretaries and the Prime Minister of the republic (*Pravda*, 23 January 1988). All over the country, tens of thousands of people were sentenced for embezzlement of public property (Rekunkov in *Ek. gaz.*, No. 52, 1987).

On 23 December 1987, the Collegium of the Prosecutor's Office of the USSR evaluated the struggle against unearned incomes in trade and catering. It concluded: 'Theft and bribery; poor managment; and over–reporting, extortion, and concealment of goods are as widespread in the industry as before. Large-scale thefts in particular are increasing. The number of officials whose guilt of crimes of self-interest has been established is not decreasing' (FBIS, 4 January 1988). Rekunkov noticed: 'In a row of regions of the country, the size of the so-called "shadow economy" grows' (*Ek. gaz.*, No. 52, 1987). It had undoubtedly been boosted by the parallel campaign against drinking, but the campaign against unearned income had failed to limit the second economy, while the harm done to private enterprise was beyond doubt.

The whole campaign had been directed against ordinary, relatively law-abiding citizens. The struggle had not been called off, but it seemed to have faded out in the second half of 1987. Regardless of scant statistics on private activities, it was obvious that private agriculture suffered a severe setback. The number of privately-owned cows fell by 4 per cent from 1 January 1985 to 1 January 1987 (*Narkhoz 1984*, p. 27; *Narkhoz 1986*, p. 253). According to official estimates, during the first eleven months of 1987, total sales on *kolkhoz* markets fell by 4 per cent in comparison with the same period in 1986, and prices rose by 6 per cent (*Planovoe khozyaistvo*, No. 3, 1988, p. 125). The effects in 1986 must have been much worse. People had been deterred from getting involved in individual labour activities that were supposed to be encouraged by the next major law. It was a big blow to the whole reform endeavour.

The struggle against unearned incomes appears to have gone against Gorbachev's whole policy. Ligachev, on the contrary, seems to have touched upon this battle in every major speech from the summer of 1986, and he included 'speculators' among the targets of his highly moralistic criticism (e.g. *Pravda*, 10 July, 7 November 1986). In November 1986, Ligachev made a passing mentioning of 'Stopping excesses', but in fact he re–emphasised the severity of the struggle (*Pravda*, 7 November 1986). This campaign embodied Ligachev's urge for socialist morality, and his dislike for private enterprise and marketeering, while nurturing the power of the party and police agencies, though Gorbachev did not object in public. Presumably, he considered the political cost of such an objection too high.

THE LAW ON INDIVIDUAL LABOUR ACTIVITY[10]

The ideological status of property is of fundamental importance in a communist state. The Soviet Constitution of 1977 spells out the conditions in Articles 10–13 (*Konstitutsiya*, pp. 7–8). Both state and cooperative property are considered socialist, but state ownership 'is the principal form of socialist ownership' (Article 11). Individual labour activity is considered ideologically inferior, and no real revision has taken place on this point. Private enterprise remains a word of abuse. References to the necessity to 'overcome private-property' tendencies persist (e.g. V. Tolstykh in *Pravda*, 20 March 1987). NEP-men are still condemned even by radical reformers (Anatoli Butenko in *Moscow News*, No. 1, 1987). The restrictions are solidified by Article 17 in the Constitution:

Individual labour activity in the sphere of handicrafts, agriculture and consumer services for the population, as well as other types of activity, based exclusively on the personal labour of citizens and members of their families, is permitted in the USSR in accordance with the law. The state regulates individual labour activity, assuring that it is used in the interests of society (*Konstitutsiya*, p. 9).

These restrictions have been incorporated into the Law on Individual Labour Activity. While hired labour in allowed in the GDR, Poland, Hungary and China, it remains strictly forbidden in the USSR: 'Individual labour activity can be carried out with the participation of cohabitating members of the family (spouse, parents and other relatives and dependants, who have reached sixteen years of age).'

An additional restriction imposed by the new law is that individual work is only exceptionally accepted as a full occupation, but permitted for employees in the socialist sector during their free time, housewives, disabled, pensioners and students, though also for 'other citizens not occupied in social production' (*Pravda*, 21 November 1986).

Moreover, Article 13 in the Constitution restricts private capital: 'Earned income constitutes the foundation of personal property', exposing entrepreneurs to the risk of being accused of enjoying unearned income. Furthermore, 'Personal property may include household articles, articles of personal consumption and convenience, articles needed for auxiliary household farming operations, a house and earned savings' (*Konstitutsiya*, p. 8).

The law says nothing about social rights. If someone works privately on the side, he will obtain social provisions at his main job, but work exclusively in the private sector might imply the deprivation of social benefits. On 6 July 1987, *Pravda* published a telling letter. An ambivalent party member asked *Pravda* and its readers, whether a party member could allow himself to indulge in individual labour activity. In a balanced reasoning, he arrived at the conclusion that it was probably not possible. It had almost become decent to be an entrepreneur, but not quite.

The preamble of the Law on Individual Labour Activity distinguishes three purposes: 'to satisfy the society's needs for commodities and services more fully'; 'to increase the occupation of citizens in socially useful activity'; and 'to offer them opportunities to gain additional incomes in correspondence with the value of their work'. Private enterprise was only supposed to act where the socialist sector had failed entirely, that is to complement and not to compete with the socialist sector, neither for inputs nor on output markets. Moreover, private enterprise is supposed to serve the population and hardly to supply the socialist sector. Private enterprise was perceived as a necessary evil. No permanence was promised. It seemed pretty risky to become an entrepreneur.

A private entrepreneur needs a licence from the local authorities. Applicants have to wait a long time for a reply, and many applications are turned down. According to a participant in such a commission, a standard complaint raised by the militia is that it will be impossible to find legal inputs.[11] If an applicant is rejected, he can complain to regional authorities, and if legal rules have been violated, an applicant can sue the local authorities in a local court (Kabalkin, 1987, p. 18), but given the prevalence of bureaucratic rule, these rights are likely to have little impact. Licensing has become a major bottleneck, and since the Law on Individual Labour Activity states that the validity of a permit 'must not exceed five years', no stability was intended. With few exceptions, the self-employed do not have to prove their professional competence, and no attempt has been made to create a guild system. Still, the entry into the private sector has been severely restricted. Only clever operators seem to manage to overcome the bureaucratic hurdles, and they can feel assured of a monopolistic position on the market, however small their undertaking.

A wide-ranging discussion on what activities were to be allowed comprised most of the preparatory work for the Law on Individual Labour Activity. Lists of permitted and forbidden private professions fill up half the law. Twenty-nine broad branches were explicitly allowed for individual enterprise (see Roucek, 1988, pp. 57-9). They cover most traditional handicrafts, consumer services, a few social services and artistic handicrafts. Some of the twelve prohibited activities are obviously criminal (production of narcotics and arms); others involve political censorship (prohibition against all kinds of printing and photo-copying, teaching on topics not included in the school curriculum and the showing of films); but several seem to have been forbidden because they would generate undesirably large incomes (the production of chemical products, perfumes, and jewellery of precious stones and metals, as well as certain medical specialities); finally, potentially immoral undertakings, such as games and saunas, were outlawed.

On the whole, surprisingly many fields were opened to private entrepreneurs, and each section of the Law contains a statement like: 'Other kinds of handicrafts are allowed, if their occupation is not forbidden in the legislation of the USSR and Union Republics.' This was an innovation in Soviet legislation, whose standard view had been that everything that is not explicitly allowed is forbidden. However, in practice this statement does not seem to have played any role. Although it is not stated in the law, local authorities were instructed to establish a list of the 'most purposeful' individual activities (*Pravda*, 22 December 1987; *Izvestiya*, 27 February 1987), and licences were hardly issued for other activities. Virtually all the handicrafts and services mentioned are oriented towards the needs of the population, though the law does not explicitly prohibit private sales to the socialist sector. Engineering, which comprises large private branches in Poland and the GDR, is all but ignored, as if the legislators could not agree on whether to accept it or not. Still, there is no requirement of physical labour or technical backwardness. An impressively large range of private activities had suddenly become legal.

Surprising as it may sound, the word planning is not mentioned in the Law on Individual Labour Activity. A tiny rudiment persists in the local authorities' selection of 'needed' private activities. Presumably, it was realised that private enterprises would be pretty unwieldy, since the Soviet economy is not very orderly.

In a chronic shortage economy, the acquisition of supplies is the greatest problem of an independent enterprise. The Law merely states that Gossnab, its local organs and the local authorities are supposed to assure individual entrepreneurs of necessary material resources. An instruction issued by Gossnab extended the rights of entrepreneurs to purchase inputs from all kinds of trade outlets, though at retail prices, which are higher than wholesale prices for industrial goods (*Ek. gaz.*, No. 18, 1987). This is a rare case in which a central economic organ has issued an instruction that is more market-oriented than an ambiguous law, but Gossnab had obviously an interest in eluding any duty to supply private firms with resources. Shortages prevail and are aggravated by the absence of (legal) private goods transport. Therefore, it is difficult to conceive of any Soviet enterprise that can manage without purchases from the black market. The public discussion suggests that the pervasiveness of illegal supplies in the economy, and the mechanism behind it, has not been properly comprehended. Another major bottleneck is work premises, which local authorities are admonished to provide, but their incentives and capacity to do so are scant.

The Law on Individual Labour Activity is original in its complete bypassing of pricing. Privately, a leading reform economist called this a great victory, assuming that prices would be set by supply and demand. However, recommendations for the application of the law, adopted in February 1987, stated that negotiated prices of sales to enterprises and institutions should not be higher than corresponding prices in state retail trade (*Ek. gaz.*, No. 16, 1987). This recommendation has been generalised also for sales to the population, but it has not been reinforced (*Pravda*, 1 February 1988).

When the policy towards the private sector has changed in Eastern Europe, fiscal legislation has always come last, since it is technically the most complex regulator. The same is true of the present Soviet changes. When interviewed in the autumn of 1985, experts working on the draft Law on Individual Labour Activity said they had no idea what the tax system would look like. It was a question for the future. The law contains a brief outline of taxation. Two kinds of taxation were envisaged. For certain activities, a fixed lump-sum-tax-cum-licence has been established. For the rest, a progressive income tax applies, and the state requires a personal declaration of private incomes.

Tax-rates were set by republican authorities. The tax rules for the RSFSR appeared just before the Law on Individual Labour Activity came into force on 1 May 1987. The annual lump sum taxes varied from 100 to 560 rubles, depending on the branch. The highest one applied to private taxis (*Izvestiya*, 23 April 1987). According to the 1943 edict on taxation, there were three different progressive tax-scales for individual entrepreneurs with maximal marginal rates ranging from 65 to 81 per cent (Cherepakhin, 1987, p. 52). A new unified and milder progressive tax-scale with a maximal marginal tax of 65 per cent was introduced for all entrepreneurs. For a moderately high private income the tax would hover around 20 per cent (*Pravda*, 24 and 25 April 1987).[12] Income tax implied a duty to deliver an official income declaration. Since bribes and other additional costs for illegal supplies cannot be declared, assessed income is likely to contain considerable illicit costs. The lump sums demanded for licences for individual work were considered excessive for most minor entrepreneurs, who found little reason to get registered.

It may sound strange in a society characterised by control, but there were few controllers dealing with private enterprise because of its sudden reappearance. The police departments for the struggle against economic crime and the local finance departments did their utmost to fill the void, but demands soon arose for the establishment of greater price and finance control bodies.

Although many principles of the Law on Individual Labour Activity are quite liberal, and the official attitude positive, the ideological perception of individual enterprise has not been revised. Private enterprise is only allowed as a part-time family business. It is both difficult and expensive to enter the legal private sector. Licensing and high taxes have rendered private enterprise exclusive. The law impresses with the insight that many conditions cannot possibly be regulated in the disorderly Soviet shortage economy. The limitation of enterprise size was at least one guarantee that the earnings of private monopolists would not be unlimited.

THE LAW ON COOPERATIVES

The Law on Cooperatives, adopted on 26 May 1988, is by far the most liberal piece of legislation that the new Soviet regime has produced (see Hanson, 1988). It represents a consistent market-oriented thinking and caters for real cooperatives, owned by working members, self-managing, self-financing and profit-and-market-oriented. The law illustrates how much easier it is for Soviet communists to accept the market than private ownership. Rather than promoting private enterprise, reformers have tried to widen the scope of cooperatives as far as possible.

Cooperatives as an ideological issue have been maturing for long. In 1982, an acrimonious discussion on contradictions under socialism was initiated by Professor Anatoli Butenko of Bogomolov's Institute. Its thrust was that formal nationalisation should not be confused with social ownership: 'practical steps towards the real appropriation by the workers of the nationalised means of production are necessary' (Butenko, 1987, p. 143). This appears to be the same view that the Polish revisionist émigré Wlodzimierz Brus (1975) has long maintained. In December 1984, Gorbachev supported Butenko's stand in substance and demanded the 'perfection of the forms of socialist ownership' (Gorbachev, 1987a, p. 81; see Butenko, 1987).

At the 27th Party Congress, Gorbachev spoke concretely of some development of cooperatives, but his words were cautious. Cooperative property 'had not exhausted its possibilities in socialist production ... where there is need, it is necessary to support the formation and development of cooperative enterprises and organisations by all means' (*Pravda*, 26 February 1986). Consecutive decrees opened narrow branches to small cooperatives in line with Gorbachev's pronouncement (on recycling, public catering, production of consumer goods, consumer services and bakeries, respectively; SP, Nos. 10 and 11, 1987; *Ek. gaz.* No. 40, 1987).

However, at the CC Plenum in January 1987, Gorbachev ventured a new course, complaining that state ownership had often been 'devoured by departmentalism and localism' and even turned into a source of illicit income, while the attitude to cooperative property had been 'incorrect', since it had been treated as 'second-rate' and without prospects (*Pravda*, 28 January

1987). Aleksandr Yakovlev took up this ideological thread: 'In practice, the making of state ownership dogmatically absolute has turned into the primacy of administrative management and the extension of omnipotent bureaucratic rule' (*Pravda*, 18 April 1987). The issue was no longer only whether to tolerate the development of cooperatives but how to exploit cooperatives for the improvement of social ownership. A first sign of what was to come was a statement by Academician Leonid Abalkin in an interview with *The Financial Times* (27 November 1986, by Patrick Cockburn). Abalkin predicted that in ten years' time new cooperatives would account for 10–12 per cent of the national income and the private sector for another 4 per cent.

The experiences of the first new cooperatives were widely publicised. A lively discussion with a mixture of ideological and pragmatic viewpoints developed both in the popular and academic press.[13] At the same time, the liberalisation of the debate generated ideological support for cooperatives. These two processes reinforced each other, preparing the ground for a much more liberal perception of cooperatives. In addition, the Law on Individual Labour Activity had set a liberal precedent that had to be overtaken. The draft Law on Cooperatives, published on 8 March 1988 (*Pravda*) was impressively liberal, and the final version went even further on a few vital points. The law was elaborated by a special Politburo Commission reportedly headed by Prime Minister Ryzhkov, who presented the Law with a long speech to the Supreme Soviet (*Pravda*, 25 May 1988). A large number of economists participated in the work on this law.[14]

Ryzhkov enumerated six functions, which only cooperatives could perform: to react to market cycles, to improve agriculture, to provide consumer services, to trade, to promote scientific-technical development and to lend dynamism to the renewal in general (*Pravda*, 25 May 1988). In 1987, Academician Leonid Abalkin had set out three tasks for cooperatives in more general terms: first, to saturate the market's demand for commodities and services of high quality; second, to mobilise additional labour; and third, 'cooperatives stimulate the abolition of bureaucratic limitations in the state organisation of production in the service sphere' (VE, No. 11, 1987, p. 142). Thus, cooperatives were supposed both to compete among themselves and to shake life in the state sector, promoting its deregulation. 'Socialist competition (*konkurrentsiya*)' was commended by Ryzhkov (*Pravda*, 25 May 1988). Nor were cooperatives supposed to be backward. Gorbachev declared with all lucidity: 'We need highly-efficient and technically well-equipped cooperatives, which are capable of providing commodities and services of the highest quality and competing with domestic and foreign enterprises' (*Pravda*, 24 March 1988).

The reformers' ambition was to assure cooperatives of the same rights as state enterprises. Under the Law on Cooperatives, a cooperative is a juridical person, with independence, self-management and self-financing. It is full owner of its property, and its property rights are guaranteed by the state, though it cannot own land. Members can work full-time in a cooperative and enjoy the same social rights as state employees. Competition on the market between state and cooperative enterprises is encouraged. Still, the law states that property has a 'leading role'. The permanence of cooperatives is a crucial question, but the law fails to provide a clear commitment. Rather than promising cooperatives a permanent role, the law states what sounds like a poor compromise: 'Socialist cooperation forms a permanently developing, progressive form of socially-useful activity.' The ultimate approval of cooperatives was issued by *Pravda*, when its editorial enjoined communists to join cooperatives (3 May 1988).

Another crucial issue is whether a permit or sponsorship is needed. The Law on Cooperatives states categorically: 'A cooperative is organised at the desire of citizens, exclusively on a voluntary basis. The creation of a cooperative is not conditional upon any special permission whatsoever by Soviet, economic or other bodies.' The only formal requirement is that a cooperative must register its statutes with the local authorities, but they are compelled to take a decision within a month, and they are entitled to refuse registration only if a cooperative would contravene Soviet law. This liberalism was possibly a reaction to the problems the new cooperatives had encountered. In practice, they had needed a socialist institution as sponsor, which severely restricted their formation (*Sovetskaya Rossiya*, 24 July 1987). Premises had been another crucial condition for registration (VE, No. 11, 1987, p. 144). Local authorities had also refused to register cooperatives whose orientation they disliked (*Izvestiya*, 17 January 1988). Every tenth cooperative had been refused registration, while many more had been delayed (*Izvestiya*, 22 December 1987).

The Law on Cooperatives could hardly be more liberal on membership. It requires a minimum of three members and sets no ceiling. A family of three adults can open a cooperative and work full-time there. Hired labour is not allowed in cooperatives, but this appears a mere ideological formality, as they may employ an unlimited number of non-members on a contract basis. The law explicitly permits cooperatives to engage in any kind of activity, that is not forbidden by law.

The conditions of the functioning of cooperatives are consistently market-oriented on paper, and mostly in clear terms. An outstanding issue before the adoption of the Law on Cooperatives was whether *kolkhozy* would be subject to compulsory state orders. Ryzhkov argued that state orders should be 'strictly voluntary' also for them (*Pravda*, 25 May 1988), which was the verdict embodied into the law. It states plainly that cooperatives are to plan their production and finances independently, and plans are to be confirmed by the general assembly of all members of each cooperative. Still, cooperatives are presumed to compete for state orders and to 'utilise long-term economic normatives set by the state'. An ominous 'normative' is 'the price level of production'. The Law on Cooperatives opens all domestic sources of legal supplies to cooperatives: state and cooperative enterprises and organisations, *kolkhoz* markets, purchases from the population as well as state and cooperative retail trade, but the hitherto vital centralised supplies seemed to be reserved for the execution of state orders. Cooperatives have greater rights to acquire supplies on the market than state enterprises—in principle, an important victory for the marketeers. However, given the severe shortages, access to legal supplies are likely to condition the development of cooperatives.

Even pricing has been liberalised and marketised in the law. Regardless of a cautious wording, prices are supposed to be set independently on the market. The exception is cooperatives that receive cheap state supplies to carry out state orders. An unpropitious phrase in the draft law was that 'a cooperative should not allow economically unjustified high prices', but it was excluded in the final version. Yet, regulation of prices by state bodies is not explicitly forbidden and is bound to take place.

The law contains a number of amazing liberal stipulations, such as permission to cooperatives to sell shares or bonds, to choose banks, to set up banks, to form associations and to pursue foreign trade. The question is what loopholes the authorities will find, or how they otherwise will try to block the implementation of the Law on Cooperatives. The Ministry of Finance showed the way already in March 1988, when it all of a sudden raised the income taxes of members of cooperatives.

The new cooperatives had benefited from low tax-rates. For instance, the rates for bakery cooperatives were 2–3 per cent of the gross revenues during the first year, 3–5 per cent during the second year and 10 per cent for ensuing years (*Ek. gaz.*, No. 40, 1987). In addition, members of cooperatives paid the ordinary income tax for wage-earners with a maximum rate of 13 per cent (Tur, 1986, p. 20). The low tax rates for cooperatives, together with their sizeable potential and monopolistic positions, made it virtually certain that some members of cooperatives would earn fortunes in no time. Such *nouveaux riches* are hardly welcome in any society, and particularly not in a communist state that has just started a liberalisation, but Leonid Abalkin has stated that it 'was done deliberately to enliven and develop that sphere' (on Soviet TV, FBIS, 1 April 1988, p. 55).

There was no consistency between the taxation of cooperatives and individual labour. The most glaring example was that 'cooperative' taxis paid a lump sum of 30 rubles a year, while 'individual' taxis paid 560 rubles a year, although this was the only real difference between them. The official reaction was to abuse the cooperative drivers as swindlers and withdraw their permissions (*Sovetskaya Rossiya*, 28 November 1987). The Law on Cooperatives says a minimum about taxes, vaguely envisaging a fixed tax-rate, differentiated by branch, for a cooperative's income or profit over five years, while the personal incomes of its members would be subject to a mild progressive tax.

On 14 March 1988, the Ministry of Finance issued an edict of new income taxes for members of cooperatives, while the taxation of cooperatives' revenues remained unchanged. A highly progressive personal income tax was introduced. For a monthly income of up to 500 rubles (2.5 times the average wage), the tax remained as low as for state employees, but then the progression took over, peaking at a marginal tax of 90 per cent from 1,500 rubles a month. Presumably, it would be optimal for successful cooperatives to take out a gross income per member of about 1,500 rubles per month, yielding a net income of 880 rubles. Thus, personal incomes would be limited, while cooperatives would be encouraged to accumulate funds. In order to placate local authorities, taxes from cooperatives and individual enterprises were to be paid to them (though public finances remained highly centralised under the state budget). An unfortunate change was the delegation of the setting of lump-sum taxes for private entrepreneurs from republican to local authorities, with the justification that they were more familiar with local conditions (*Izvestiya*, 20 March 1988). This was an invitation to both bribery and arbitrary bureaucratic rule, and complaints about extortion by local officials have already surfaced (Shmelev, 1988, p. 162).

ACRIMONIOUS PUBLIC REACTIONS OVER COOPERATIVES

The new cooperatives and individual labour activity, which were discussed in the same context, were backed up by an impressive media campaign, starting at the end of 1986. A multitude of articles and notices, primarily in the popular press, described how a cooperative or a group of private firms had been established, and their first results were praised. This propaganda of success was accompanied with complaints against local authorities and other state organs for impeding the development of these new firms.

The new enterprises did not develop all that fast. At the end of 1987, just over 300,000 people were engaged in individual labour (*Pravda*, 22 December 1987), and about 150,000 worked (*Pravda*, 24 January 1988) in 13,921 cooperatives of the new type—just 0.3 per cent of the labour force (*Ek. gaz.*, No. 12, 1988). The new sector was praised for offering better services of higher quality. Previously non-existent up-market commodities and services started appearing on the market. 'The goods and services market has generally become richer in choice' (*Sots. ind.*, 12 March 1988).

The economic efficiency of cooperatives was invariably impressive: 'the labour productivity of workers in cooperatives is 3, 5, and even 10 times higher than in ordinary production' (*Izvestiya*, 27 February 1988), and the resulting earnings were splendid. An analysis by the economist Pavel Bunich verifies that the new cooperatives functioned like independent, self-managing and profit-oriented enterprises. As they were so small, they behaved like small private firms. Members of cooperatives worked more efficiently than state employees, because they enjoyed better incentives, with their incomes depending directly on their performance. Cooperatives were much freer than state enterprises to renew output and change prices, and as they were 'not hampered by cumbersome paper work, they don't have to wade through all sorts of instructions, nor conduct endless conferences'. 'As soon as they sense a market somewhere, they rush to that place and start work' (*Moscow News*, No. 10, 1988).

From the outset, accusations were amassed against various authorities for impeding the development of cooperatives and individual labour activity. Gorbachev complained: 'Very slowly and generally unwillingly are co-operatives created at large industrial enterprises' (*Pravda*, 24 March 1988). Local authorities were often 'prejudiced against the whole idea of the creation of cooperatives'. According to a CC resolution, they were slow in providing premises, supplies and transport, and they violated set deadlines for the regi-stration of cooperatives (*Pravda*, 25 November 1987). Gorbachev stated that several local authorities preserved 'all kinds of hindrances and introduce illegal prohibitions and limitations' (*Pravda*, 24 March 1988). A poll showed that only 26 per cent of the employees of local authorities thought that the cooperative sector would develop (*Izvestiya*, 22 December 1987).

On 3 May 1988, *Pravda* began its editorial noting that 'no other novel idea of perestroika arouses such perplexity and confusion in some heads as the idea of cooperatives.' The impressive economic results of the cooperatives did not mitigate a massive popular reaction against cooperatives and private enterprise, emerging in the summer of 1987 (*Sovetskaya Rossiya*, 24 July 1987; cf *Pravda*, 14 September 1987).

In November 1987, the reaction had gone so far that a CC resolution was adopted criticising many features of cooperatives, while still calling for a positive attitude towards cooperatives (*Pravda*, 25 November 1987). This occurred soon after the ousting of Boris Yeltsin, when orthodox ideologists were on the offensive, but even the reformist newspaper *Izvestiya* admitted that most of the letters it received were critical of cooperatives and individual labour activity. 'Letters are full of indignation, anger and insulting remarks about "private operators" and serious accusations against those "who allowed all this to happen"' (*Izvestiya*, 27 February 1988). 'Yes, today cooperatives pose a multitude of complex and sometimes unexpected problems' (*Izvestiya*, 17 January 1988). Soviet citizens harboured many grudges, targeting incom-patibility with the principles of socialism, excessive earnings and the ensuing stratification of society (*Izvestiya*, 27 February 1988). Officials pursued a somewhat different criticism. Their main concern was that the non-state sector had started to offer a small but unacceptable competition with state enterprises. These two discussions were quite different in character, but they reinforced each other. A key expression was 'serious distortions' in the development of cooperatives (*Pravda*, 1 December 1987). The foremost objects of criticism were cooperative restaurants.

To judge from newspaper accounts, ordinary Soviet critics of cooperatives were primarily concerned with the high incomes of some members. As early as 21 March 1987, a headline in *Komsomolskaya pravda* read 'They will become millionaires!' Characteristic statements cited from letters to news-papers were: 'What do we need newfound millionaires for?' 'What do you think I a *sovkhoz* tractor driver earning 2–3 rubles a day during repairs feel like, when I read that somewhere an operator who makes bra fasteners makes 100 rubles a day?' 'Not even government members earn that much!' (*Izvestiya*, 27 Februry 1988). In a cooperaive in Donbass, the members earned 5,000 rubles a month, producing 'plastic clip-on ear-rings, bracelets, and haberdashery articles. These are low-grade products intended for immature teenage tastes' (*Sots. ind.*, 12 March 1988). In another cooperative, average incomes of 12,500 rubles a month per member were cited (*Izvestiya*, 7 January 1988). These net incomes amounted to 60 times the average Soviet wage, and the official Soviet top salaries stopped at 1,200 rubles a month. The earnings of registered private entrepreneurs were comparatively modest.

Another regret was high cooperative prices. The idea of free pricing appeared both incomprehensible and illegitimate to many Soviet citizens, but the cooperatives exploited the principle with natural talent, going for goods assuring them of sizeable profits. In catering, prices tended to be 4–6 times higher than in state establishments (*Izvestiya*, 17 January 1988). The liberal argument was that cooperatives would lower their prices as shortages were overcome. Already in early 1988, a cooperative in Armenia was selling slippers at a lower price than the state (Pavel Bunich in *Moscow News*, No. 10, 1988). Yet, the average cooperative prices were probably 3–4 times above the state level, reflecting the degree of shortage: 'some cooperatives are turning into monopoly producers, much more so than state enterprises. They dictate conditions, inflate prices, and obtain undeserved profits.' (*Izvestiya*, 27 February 1988).

While the overt quality of cooperative produce was widely praised as better than in the state sector, it was not considered good enough. Commodities were said to prove substandard despite an attractive exterior. As cooperatives rarely used trademarks, there was no recourse (*Moscow News*, No. 10, 1988; *Sots. ind.*, 12 March 1988). Many popular grievances about cooperatives were dressed in traditional dogmatic language: 'The family contract in rural areas, and the cooperatives in cities will lead to a revival of the bourgeoisie.' (*Izvestiya*, 27 February 1988).

All this was what one would expect. A few bold entrepreneurs skimmed the market and did very well indeed because shortages were immense; competition and taxes were minimal; most regulations were unclear; and no one knew how long the feast would last. The most conspicuous profits arose in cooperatives, as they were larger and less constrained than individual labour activity, and cooperative restaurants were most conspicuous of all. They targeted an up-market stratum of foreigners and black marketeers, not endearing them to the ordinary population.

Various authorities and state enterprises raised as many complaints about cooperatives as they could: in some ways, cooperatives had developed differently from what had been anticipated; several 'disproportions' in the development of cooperatives had appeared; cooperatives were seen as unduly favoured in comparison with the more regulated state enterprises; demands for more restrictive rules followed suit; criminal activities were cited; some of the strictures were simply directed against anything that was not done in the old way.

A major complaint was that good workers departed from the state sector: 'In a number of places, a stream of qualified specialists from the state sector to cooperatives is noticed, which cannot avoid complicating the work for certain enterprises and organisations.' A state enterprise failed to reach its plan targets, because of the departure of some of its best staff to a cooperative (*Pravda*, 1 December 1987). 'The cooperatives will damage the state sector, because they will siphon off efficient and energetic cadres and good specialists and introduce mercenary motives into the moral atmosphere' (*Izvestiya*, 27 February 1988). Of the total number of members of cooperatives in late 1987, only 13 per cent were pensioners, 8 per cent housewives, and 3 per cent were students, while as many as 65 per cent worked in cooperatives as a secondary occupation (*Pravda*, 1 December 1987). '80 per cent of cooperative personnel are men' (*Moscow News*, No. 13, 1988). However, the hazards of establishing a cooperative were great, compelling a selection of the strongest. Intentions and reality did not match.

The economic efficiency of cooperatives could hardly be questioned. Instead, conservative critics underlined how small the total impact of the cooperatives were. They contributed merely 0.04 per cent of all services and commodities sold to the population towards the end of 1987 (*Pravda*, 1 December 1987). Their regional disproportions caused concern: 'They developed extremely unevenly over the territory of the country and particularly slowly in the countryside' (*Pravda*, 25 November 1987). As everyone had expected, they flourished in the Caucasus and the Baltic republics (*Pravda*, 1 December 1987), while little happened in large parts of the RSFSR and Central Asia. The amount of services provided per inhabitant by cooperatives was twenty times larger in Estonia than in Central Asia and Azerbaijan (Gorbachev in *Pravda*, 24 March 1988). On 3 May 1988, *Pravda* reported that there were 5,000 private taxis in Lithuania compared with only 2,100 state taxis.

Similar complaints were presented about the branch structure of the cooperative movement: 'are these the cooperatives that the town and its inhabitants need?' (*Izvestiya*, 17 January 1988). The legislation did not specify whether cooperatives could sell to the state sector, and some cooperatives tried to tap that attractive market, but local bureaucrats refused them registration, with the justification: 'cooperatives must be created only to provide the population with services and to produce consumer goods' (*Izvestiya*, 17 January 1988). On the contrary, Gorbachev argued: 'It is necessary to develop more boldly tight, mutually advantageous economic relations between state enterprises and cooperatives', envisaging also mixed state-cooperative enterprises (*Pravda*, 24 March 1988).

The initial political intention had been that new cooperatives should complement the existing public sector. However, 'In public catering, for instance, the major part of cooperatives are created on the basis of unprofitable enterprises of state trade and the consumer cooperation.' In the RSFSR, no less than 80 per cent of new cooperatives were formed in such a manner. As a result, total capacity barely expanded (*Pravda*, 1 December 1987). But the real issue was that local authorities and state enterprises wanted both to rid themselves of loss-makers and avoid competition.

Shortages made the development of cooperatives conditional upon the availability of jealously-guarded supplies: 'The profile of many cooperatives in catering is determined by available foodstuffs, without consideration of the demands of the population.' Allegedly, 'a large share of their produce originated from supplies purchased in state trade' (*Pravda*, 1 December 1987), but that was perfectly legal. At the beginning of 1988, complaints about illegal supplies started appearing: 'numerous transgressions and mysteries concerning sources of supply' occurred as well as financial violations of the law in cooperatives (*Sots. ind.*, 12 March 1988); 'about 50 per cent of the instruments on which musicians of stage groups play have been purchased by them through unofficial channels!' (*Pravda*, 29 March 1988). What else could they do, when no decent instruments were on sale? Similarly, photographers working for a state firm became upset by the appearance of licensed individual photographers, who 'have Japanese equipment, their own means of transportation and better opportunities to acquire the necessary materials and keep all the profits' (*Sots. ind.*, 12 March 1988).

A variety of complaints of economic criminality and immorality followed. Ex-convicts started emerging in catering cooperatives (*Pravda*, 1 December 1987). The large and often well-organised black economy exploited the opportunities that cooperatives opened, both to generate income and launder black money, and this process could be noticed by anyone. Democratic procedures were said to have been abandoned in some cooperatives, suggesting that they were run as private enterprises, as might have been the case (*Pravda*, 25 November 1987).

It also happened that a state enterprise sponsoring a cooperative simply confiscated its assets for no legal reason whatsoever, in line with the Soviet practice of superior state bodies redistributing assets to their own liking (*Sovetskaya Rossiya*, 24 July 1987). No stable legal standards existed, and the outrageous shortages compelled entrepreneurs and cooperatives to acquire supplies illegally. But the transitionary legislation was based on the faulty assumption that private enterprise and cooperatives could exist legally within a command-and-shortage economy.

A number of opinion polls of varying quality outlined the public view of cooperatives. Mostly, they were based on self-selected audiences writing or phoning to newspapers, implying a pre-eminence of the most involved. An opinion poll carried out in Moscow by the Sociological Studies Institute of the Academy of Sciences, presumably at the end of 1987, implied that 65 per cent of the Muscovites asked approved of cooperatives, while 17 per cent disapproved, and 17 per cent presented no view (FBIS, 19 January 1988, p.

66). A less reliable poll undertaken by *Izvestiya* (22 December 1987) showed 83 per cent of the population supporting cooperatives. The high positive figure should be looked upon with scepticism, while the overt resistance was significant.

The attitudes to cooperatives varied extraordinarily between generations, as a poll based on letters to *Sovetskaya Rossiya* (24 July 1987) shows (see Table 6.1).[15] The most prominent difference was that the young (under 45) with no memories of Stalin and the oldest (with memories from NEP) favoured cooperatives, while most pensioners and war veterans (61–75 years of age) remained unreformed Stalinists. The middle-aged Khrushchev generation (46–60) were confused and undecided. Pensioners were admonished to engage in work in cooperatives, but many of them rejected cooperatives as morally repugnant (*Izvestiya*, 22 December 1987). According to another poll, people who viewed cooperatives most positively were in the age groups 26–30 and 41–50. The first needed more incomes for the support of newly-founded families, and the second needed to support their children's families (*Moscow News*, No. 13, 1988). Pensioners play an important role in commissions of local authorities that can block the issuance of a licence to an entrepreneur or the registration of a cooperative.

Although we have no poll accounting for regional differentiation, we dare assume that the popular attitude to cooperatives is likely to be most positive in the Caucasus and the Baltic republics, while great Russians, especially in Siberia, the Urals and the North, must be the most negative. For instance, '53 per cent of the Leningrad audience, and 31 per cent of that in Tallinn have reservations about cooperatives and individual enterprise' (*Moscow News*, No. 13, 1988). The high negative figure even for Tallinn indicates the strength of the popular resistance (though many Russians live there).

Table 6.1:   Attitudes to cooperatives

(share in per cent of age group)

Age Group	–45	46–60	61–75	76+
For cooperatives	87.2	10.1	7.8	69.1
Against cooperatives	10.5	11.4	81.1	8.2
Undecided	2.3	78.6	11.1	22.7

Source: Sovetskaya Rossiya, 24 July 1987.

In that poll, white-collar workers were more positive towards cooperatives than blue-collar workers, and men were more positive than women (*ibid.*). Employees of local authorities and control agencies were as dogmatic as pensioners (*Izvestiya*, 22 December 1987). First-hand experience of cooperatives as a customer had increased the number of positive replies fivefold in Tallinn and twice in Leningrad (*Moscow News*, No. 13, 1988). A letter by a pensioner published in *Pravda* (21 December 1987) outlined three groups hostile to individual labour activity: 'people who are afraid that their neighbour will earn more than they and get rich; those who do not like to work and do not let others do it ... and those who do not like to work and only "push" ideas, phrases, views, but not deeds'.

The vocal promotion by the political leadership of cooperatives and individual labour activity rendered calls for prohibition extreme. Instead, friends and foes alike demanded swift changes in the regulation of cooperatives, though in opposite directions. The reformers seem to have adopted a two-track approach. On the one hand, they conceded to the urgent demand for a progressive income tax for members of cooperatives (see Gorbachev in *Pravda*, 8 March 1988). A prior poll had shown that 71 per cent of *Izvestiya* readers supported such a proposal, and only 11 per cent opposed it (*Izvestiya*, 22 December 1987). Still, the new tax-rates were widely regarded as too high, and the Minister of Finance defended his decision in vain at the Supreme Soviet in late May 1988. The Ministry appeared to have acted with great haste and independence. The Supreme Soviet demanded a milder tax. On the other hand, the reformers in the leadership ensured the successful adoption of the liberal Law on Cooperatives.

However, there was also a third, conservative track. Numerous authorities, and even a CC resolution, demanded tighter control over cooperatives and individual labour activity. Notably, 41 per cent of polled local officials and 68 per cent of law-enforcement officials called for harsher controls (*Izvestiya*, 22 December 1987). 'Who Will Control the Cooperatives?' read a telling headline in *Sovetskaya Rossiya* (28 November 1987). These officials desired a stricter direction in licensing and more (arbitrary) local regulation (*Pravda*, 25 November 1987; *Izvestiya*, 17 January 1988). As a reformist and a lawyer, Gorbachev strode against these ideas, advocating the Law on Cooperatives as the creation of 'a legal defence mechanism for cooperative democracy, to form economic, organisational and legal grounds for the activity of all kinds of cooperative enterprises and organisations, to regulate their rights and duties, [their] interaction with state and economic organs' (*Pravda*, 24 March 1988). Still, it has been decided to expand the price and finance control services, although the reformers have managed to put a lid on the people's control organisation.

PROSPECTS FOR CO-EXISTENCE BETWEEN VARIOUS FORMS OF PROPERTY

Two contradictory trends have characterised the new Soviet policy towards the non-state sector. The 'Reinforced Struggle against Unearned Incomes' represents the first one. It caused a great deal of damage to the private sector, as its main targets became *kolkhoz* makets, private plots and illegal transport in state vehicles. It was a truly neo-Stalinist campaign, characterised by lawless repression by local authorities ordered from above. This campaign appears to have fizzled out during the second half of 1987, but its negative effects on business confidence will linger on. The same tendency is apparent in the current attempts to strengthen control over cooperatives and individual labour.

The second trend has been to revive cooperatives and individual enterprise. The novelties in policy towards cooperatives and private enterprise are so many and qualitatively important that nothing of the kind has occurred since NEP drew to a close in 1928, but lasting communist dogmas stigmatise private enterprise. Instead, reformers have tried to do the utmost for cooperatives. The Law on Cooperatives could hardly be more market-oriented, and in this regard the USSR hardly lags behind any other communist country. However, the new non-state sectors have developed slowly, and it is doubtful whether a quick acceleration is possible, given the bureaucratic, popular and ideological resistance against cooperatives and private enterprise.

In a parallel development, a grey zone has emerged between state and non-state property, caused by reformist efforts to expand economic pluralism. In the boldest experiments with enterprise management, the distinction between cooperatives and self-managing units of state enterprises has virtually ceased; the difference between individual labour and individual leasehold is equally blurred; it is formally within the state sector that joint stock companies are being created; to this comes hybrid ownership, notably joint ventures; and the economic reform aims at the establishment of a 'socialist market', facilitating the co–existence of different enterprises.

For a country that has had virtually no legal, independent enterprises before, the rules for individual labour activity, and particularly for cooperatives, are surprisingly liberal. Furthermore, the major legislative act —the Law on Cooperatives—is quite consistent, in spite of the public controversy over cooperatives. However, the law is conceived for an economy with a functioning market. As long as such a market has not developed, cooperatives and private enterprises—as well as self-financing state entities— will persist in a legal limbo, since they have to rely on illegal supplies and may become subject to arbitrary persecution. The attitude of the reformers appear to have been storming: to try to introduce a market economy as fast as possible, while disregarding problems of transition. It is possible that this approach will be successful, but it appears to presuppose far-reaching and fast political changes.

The outstanding conditions of the establishment of a cooperative are that it is difficult to enter the market (because of problems to find premises and deal with local authorities) and to acquire supplies legally, while it is easy to sell, boost profits and expand a business after it has been set up. In practice, the Soviets have settled for the promotion of a relatively small number of medium-sized cooperatives that will inevitably engender large monopolistic incomes that are divided among a small number of new rich. The abolition of licensing for cooperatives is hardly sufficient to solve this problem. Hungary originally opted for an alternative approach, centring on the development of a broad, second economy of unlicensed individual work, which quickly gave a large contribution to the market and spread incomes reasonably evenly.

The two-pronged Soviet approach is not entirely a reflection of a struggle between reformers and conservatives. Many reformers wanted to persecute economic crime more harshly in the hope that a clear line could be drawn between the legal and illegal sectors. The most conspicuous example was Academician Tatyana Zaslavskaya, who stated that incomes of entrepreneurs 'should be kept under control so as not to allow them to turn into a petty-bourgeois stratum, into NEP men with their bent for "high life". In my opinion, the workers in the individual enterprise sector can have an income per unit of work two-three, maybe four times higher than the level attained in social production' (*Moscow News*, No. 9, 1987; cf *Izvestiya*, 18 April 1986). No regulated market economy is able to control incomes to such an extent, and in a chronic shortage economy extensive economic crimes with social stratification are inevitable. The unleashing of arbitrary police persecution of the pervasive illegalities in the economy has resulted in increased legal risks for all kinds of economic activities. Thus, the authorities have deterred many from entering the non-state sector, and removed the economy even further from market balance.

Little thought has been devoted to material supplies, and the authorities do not appear to understand that no enterprise—state, cooperative or private —can function under Soviet conditions of extreme shortage without paying bribes for supplies. It is necessary to improve the financial macro-balance and harden the budget constraints of state enterprises, but that is not enough. The authorities must realise that it takes time to develop a market and cure the economy from its state of legal degeneration. In the meantime, no detailed regulation of the non-state economy can be effective.

It is evident, both from the well-conceived laws and Soviet publications, that Soviet specialists had studied the regulation of cooperatives and private enterprise in other countries, notably in the GDR, Hungary and China, in this order, but also in Poland and Czechoslovakia. Even cooperatives in Sweden and Japan were discussed in this context. The GDR was the obvious success which was highlighted in the Soviet press.[16] The study of successes offered models for the Soviet legislation. However, it did not alert the Soviets to pitfalls. The public reaction against cooperatives and their speculative features obviously surprised the reformers. For instance, Otto Lacis (1987a, p. 82) cautioned that excessive, monopolistic earnings were possible under illegal, disorderly conditions, as if he believed that the market would soon eradicate them.

The present situation in the Soviet non-state sector is most reminiscent of Poland in 1957 (cf Åslund, 1985a, pp. 57–63). In both cases, a sudden and far-reaching liberalisation had taken place, and a relatively small number of clever operators-monopolists quickly skimmed the unbalanced market, arousing an outcry from bureaucrats, ideologists and the public. However, no responsible Soviet appears to have been aware of the situation in Poland in 1957, so the outcome surprised. With the extension of glasnost, negative information from Eastern Europe has begun to appear without necessarily implying any condemnation. On 23 February 1988, *Izvestiya* published most of an article from the Polish weekly *Polityka* (No. 1, 1988) on how a new stratum of conspicuously rich had arisen in Poland, without passing any judgement. *Pravda* (28 March 1988) even published a notice with Hungarian liberal criticism against the limited social rights of individual entrepreneurs in the new Soviet legislation.

As in no other field, the attitudes to cooperatives were characterised by a complete polarisation. In the case of the Law on Cooperatives, the reformers had not gone for a compromise but bided their time in order to achieve a complete legislative victory. Whether it will be followed by a successful implementation depends on how far econmic, political and legal reform as a whole goes. Every link has to be in its place, if the social chain shall grow strong enough to carry cooperatives and individual enterprise. It is a question of all or nothing—a functioning market economy with a large cooperative sector or a preserved command economy with petrified state property. The Law on Cooperatives shows how far the present political leadership can go.

NOTES

1. Statement by Ivan Galdki, Chairman of Goskomtrud, at a press conference in Moscow in November 1986.
2. This concept of services is very narrow and includes primarily 'material' services sold to the population.
3. The knowledgeable journalist Aleksandr Borin states that in districts with great shortage of labour, not less than 300,000 seasonal workers arrive (each year) (*Lit. gaz.*, 15 July 1987).
4. *Izvestiya*, 14 April, 15 June, 29 July 1985, 27 Feburary 1987; *Lit. gaz.*, 15 July 1987; Murphy (1985).
5. The contribution of private incomes to total personal income for the different regional samples varies from 20.6 per cent in Eastern RSFSR (which is not very eastern is this definition) and 64.1 per cent for ethnic Armenians in Armenia. The overall figure for the RSFSR and the Baltic republics—where the second economy is least developed—is 29.6 per cent.
6. Otto Lacis (1987a) offers an extensive survey of problems leading to demands for a comprehensive law on individual labour activity.
7. Three research institutes, the Institute of State and Law and the Institute of Economics under the Academy of Sciences and the Institute of Jurisprudence under the Ministry of Justice, undertook the preparatory work. (Personal information from three scholars with inside knowledge.)
8. Topics of such decrees have been construction services for gardening cooperatives (*Sots. ind.*, 14 April 1985); sales of construction materials to individual house-builders (*Izvestiya*, 18 July 1985); the development of consumer cooperation (*Izvestiya*, 1 February 1986); the development of gardening cooperatives

(*Izvestiya*, 6 June 1986); the improvement of *kolkhoz* markets (*Izvestiya*, 1 April 1987); the development of citizens' personal subsidiary farms (*Pravda*, 25 September 1987); and the development of individual house construction (*Pravda*, 21 February 1988).

9. It may be added that Rekunkov himself, the highest legal official in the USSR who has worked as a prosecutor all his life, has only taken a correspondence course in law and has no single year of full-time law studies in his *curriculum vitae* (*Deputaty*, 1984, p. 370).

10. The general framework of analysis and references to Eastern Europe originate from Åslund (1984, 1985ab).

11. Personal information from Moscow.

12. For a registered entrepreneur, private earnings of less than 840 rubles a year (70 rubles a month) remain exempt from tax. State employees are only entitled to earn 300 rubles a year privately without paying tax (Tur, 1986, p. 19; *Izvestiya*, 23 April 1987).

13. See especially *Voprosy ekonomiki*, No. 11, 1987, pp. 142–58, for a representative discussion with a multitude of arguments. The reported meeting was typically chaired by Academician Leonid Abalkin and Lev Nikiforov was the main speaker. Both belong to the Institute of Economics (cf *Voprosy ekonomiki*, No. 3, 1988, pp. 42–60).

14. Argricultural economists, notably Academician Vladimir Tikhonov (at the time at the Institute of Economics) played a major role. Lev Nikiforov and the Institute of Economics had some coordinating role. The Institute of State and Law lent legal and ideological expertise. The role of Bogomolov's Institute, with its expertise on other socialist countries, is not known to this author.

15. Leonid Khotin drew my attention to this source.

16. See Levikov (1986), *Sots. ind.*, 24 August 1986, and *Pravda*, 26 February 1987.

7. Evaluation of the new reform wave

The emerging Gorbachev era can be assessed from many perspectives. The new Soviet expression 'post-April' (with references to the April 1985 CC Plenum) shows that it is presented as a new epoch. An unparalleled number of important decisions have already been adopted. The turnover of leading personnel has been larger than at any time after 1937. The freedom and depth of the discussion have never been greater since the 1920s.

At the same time, it is vital to notice what has not changed. At the 19th Party Conference, Academician Leonid Abalkin soberly sized up the situation: 'a radical breakthrough in the economy has not occurred and [the economy] has not departed from its state of stagnation' (*Pravda*, 30 June 1988). The economic growth rate has not recovered, but fallen. On consumer markets, shortages have grown worse as a result of the ardent campaign against alcohol and a lax financial policy. No significant qualitative improvements have occurred as yet. Economic efficiency, product quality and technical progress remain dismal (cf Abalkin in *Pravda*, 30 June 1988).

The 'command-administrative system' created by Stalin remains in place, but it functions ever worse. A multitude of significant economic changes have been legislated, but many features of the economic reform are still ambiguous. Certain measures, that have suited the inclinations of the bureaucracy, have been implemented with vigour, notably the campaigns against unearned income and alcohol, but reform measures threatening the power of strong state bodies have been muted at best and sometimes even nullified. According to the official timetable, the reform will not gain such coherence that we may expect significant economic improvements before 1991.

SOVIET LESSONS FROM THE INITIAL REFORM ATTEMPTS

It might appear disappointing that about five years of reform attempts pass without economic amelioration, but this period might prove both inevitable and valuable. It will teach the Soviet leadership, their advisers and the Soviet people a number of important lessons. Influential groups have already learnt five lessons.

First, the lingering conservative Brezhnevian model has become thoroughly discredited. Too many shortcomings of the Soviet economy have been exposed, and at long last been contrasted with other economies. Domestic Soviet criticism has also taken on a systemic nature. In particular, the excellent articles by Nikolai Shmelev (1987, 1988) and Vasili Selyunin (1988) have presented a liberal view of the Soviet economic system to broad segments of the population. Phrases frequently spoken are: 'This system does not go any further.' 'We are in a dead end.' There is a common yearning for a 'normal' society, essentially a euphemism for a modern, democratic, western society—a far cry from traditional Soviet claims to originality and superiority.

Secondly, several measures that we may call neo-Stalinist (campaigns against alcoholism and unearned income, massive personnel changes) have been implemented with such frenzy and poor results, that they have been discredited among a large number of Soviet citizens. At the same time, the economic history of Stalinism is being revised into a moderate achievement at extraordinary cost. The neo-Stalinist view, that the system is good but poorly run, must have become less convincing to people outside the circle of fanatic neo-Stalinists.

Thirdly, a streamlining of the Soviet system on GDR lines has also been discredited. Most of this programme of technocratic modernisation (production associations, a new investment policy, new wage tariffs, more shiftwork, and quality control) has been attempted under Lev Zaikov's aegis, but it has made little headway. Some measures could be implemented in Leningrad or Belorussia, but they appeared to be rejected by the system in other parts of the country. The Soviet leadership has largely failed to impose efficiency from above. The apparent reason is that the Soviet administration is much more difficult to steer than the GDR administration. Soviet officials fend much more for their own vested interest with less concern for the national interest. GDR measures simply do not appear applicable.

Fourthly, the experiments with enterprise management (like the experiences of the reforms of 1965) have led influential Soviet economists to conclude that it is not feasible to reform enterprises alone. They have resolved that it is necessary to undertake a comprehensive reform, involving all superior bodies, the economic system ('the economic mechanism'), and the political system (VE, No. 2, 1988, pp. 55–79).

A fifth lesson could be drawn from an abortive event. Numerous observers have deduced from the Chinese and Hungarian reforms that a reform would be most effective in agriculture, services, small-scale production and trade —that is in small-scale, consumer-oriented activities. One frequent suggestion is that Gorbachev has made a mistake by not promoting family agriculture (e.g. Goldman, 1987). However, Gorbachev has repeatedly pushed for agricultural reform with family farms—at the 27th Party Congress in February 1986, in a speech in August 1987, and at big CC meetings on leasehold in agriculture in May and October 1988. The principal problem has been that he has failed to win sufficient support from the rest of the leadership. The political resistance has been overwhelming. Fundamental agricultural reform would deprive a large share of the party apparatus of the reason for its existence. The conclusion is that not even agricultural reform seems to be possible in the USSR without political reform. Unlike China and Hungary, the Soviet Union appears unable to reform any branch of its economy without both ideological revision and political reform.

All these experiences have influenced Soviet policy-makers' thinking on economic reform. Another source of inspiration has been previous Soviet reforms. From the New Economic Policy in the 1920s, reformers have drawn a range of permissible socialist alternatives blessed by Lenin. The economic reforms of 1965 were rarely mentioned in the early 1980s. In 1985, they became a positive reference for reformists, while conservatives tended to criticise them as inflationary. By 1987, however, the reforms of 1965 were turned by reformers into examples of failed half-measures, illustrating the necessity of going further.

A conference of Soviet economists in Moscow in June 1987, chaired by Academician Leonid Abalkin, addressed what conclusions that could be drawn from previous reform attempts for the present perestroika. The most immediate inferences were drawn from the reforms of 1965 (VE, No. 2, 1988, pp. 55–79; cf Hanson, 1988). A major conclusion was that no fundamental economic reform was possible without *political democratisation*.[1] On the one hand, ordinary employees had to be activated. On the other hand, the power of the bureaucracy had to be broken. N. Shukhov of TsEMI cited some workers:

Between the Central Committee of our party and the working class stands an inert, sticky social-economic grouping; ... 'a party-administrative stratum', which is afraid of any changes, any social-economic transformations in our society. This bureaucratic 'stratum' is the main hindrance on the road towards a consistent democratisation of our society, and it is necessary to pursue an uncompromising struggle with it (VE, No. 2, 1988, p. 62).

Soviet reform economists see far-reaching democratisation as the only way of breaking the harmful power of the bureaucracy over the economy—a lesson well learnt by reform economists in Eastern Europe. It is symptomatic that it was Leonid Abalkin—one of the top economists—who raised the fundamental political question at the 19th Party Conference, would a 'democratic organisation of social life' be possible with a one-party system (*Pravda*, 30 June 1988).

The other principal conclusion was that the reform had to be comprehensive, involving all aspects of management and the economic mechanism. It had to be carried out consistently. One mistake of 1965 had been that only enterprises had been reformed. Now all superior bodies and all elements of the economic system should be reformed for the sake of consistency. Another shortfall of 1965 had been that marketisation had not developed far enough. Finally, the reforms of 1965 had been introduced so slowly that they had fizzled out. This time, a faster implementation was demanded (VE, No. 2, 1988, pp. 72-9). In short, reformist economists learnt that *the reform had to go further and faster*.

Many parallels have been correctly drawn between the Soviet and Chinese reform (e.g. Kaser 1987). However, there are important differences between the two countries causing necessary disparities in their development. In China, the cultural revolution and the ensuing backlash discredited ideological excesses in a way that has never happened in the USSR, where basic dogmas remain major impediments, which must be broken before reform can proceed. One could argue that perestroika started in political economy with the revisions of ideology suggested by Anatoli Butenko (1982) and Yevgeni Ambartsumov.

Another disparity is that the Soviet Union has built up a stronger, and more centralised, party and state apparatus than China, offering a more effective resistance. In the Soviet Union, it appears vital to break this institutional resistance in order to make any headway for reform.

A third important disparity concerns the relative level of economic development. The main Soviet production problems are wastage, inefficiency, technical development and quality, while China has a greater need for longer production volumes—a problem that is much easier to solve quickly. The predominance of industry in the Soviet economy also implies a political dominance of industry, which may explain why the new Soviet leadership undertook an ill-fated initial attempt to boost machine-building before other branches. Only at the 19th Party Conference did the leadership accept that consumer industries would be given priority. In China, with four fifths of the labour force occupied in agriculture, and much greater poverty, it was more obvious where to begin. Soviet agriculture is large-scale and mechanised, while Chinese farm work is manual. For purely practical reasons, it is not easy to reorganise the centralised Soviet agriculture. Nor is it easy to accept that large resources would become immobilised or privatised. The longer communist legacy in the USSR and Stalin's long terror have also contributed to distortions in, and a petrification of, Soviet society.

For all these reasons, it might be necessary to start with a revision of history and ideology and democratisation in the Soviet Union in order to reform the economy. However, as Vasili Selyunin (1988) has argued, there is no reason to believe that the Russians would be unable to adapt to a liberal economy. This has been a common thought both in the West and among Russophiles, but similar ideas have been commonplace among other peoples at the stage preceding modernisation.

IN SEARCH OF A NEW ECONOMIC MODEL

These conclusions are well-reflected in Gorbachev's two key demands: radical economic reform and democratisation. The ideological limits have been stretched ever further by Gorbachev and Yakovlev, together with a multitude of reformist intellectuals. The bottom-line is that the Soviet Union will not depart from socialism. Concrete minimum requirements are the prohibition of private ownership of means of production and hired labour; the maintenance of constitutional social rights, notably full employment; and the preservation of central planning. However, to a considerable extent these restrictions have already been circumvented. Joint stock companies with substantial private ownership have been established; cooperatives may function like private companies; the distinction between contract labour in cooperatives and hired labour appears more ideological than real; the new Soviet openness shows that most social rights have been grossly transgressed and that a hidden unemployment, in the millions, already exists; planning can mean many things and be reduced to a matter of little significance. While Gorbachevian reformers perceive few ideological restrictions, the party *apparat* has accepted few of the novelties, which are only partially reflected in the revised Party Programme of 1986.

These premises offer Soviet reformers a broad spectrum of alternative models. Gorbachev's people have turned their back on all Soviet models after 1929, but it is still unclear what model they will choose. A large number of fundamental systemic issues, such as the principles of price formation, have not been settled politically. The standard reformist position is that the new economic model should be a specifically Soviet model, but based on elements from other economic models. It should combine a considerable marketisation with a strong regulating role maintained for the state. The emphasis on comprehensiveness and consistency has grown over time, and the thinking is becoming less eclectic, After the reform decisions of June 1987, senior Soviet economists have travelled abroad on an unprecedented scale in search of reform ideas. Soviet newspapers have started devoting more attention to alternative economic solutions, not only in the communist world. The top economists appear to concentrate their attention on about half a dozen countries: Hungary, China, the USA, the United Kingdom, Japan and Sweden.

Among the socialist countries, only Hungary and China appear to be favoured. Socialist economies are studied thoroughly by Bogomolov's Institute. Most elements of the Hungarian model are scrutinised and appreciated. The Soviet reforms legislated in the summer of 1987 appear to be inspired more by the Hungarian reforms than by anything else; however, Soviet reformers are well aware of the shortcomings of the Hungarian economy. In particular, they notice that its investment policy remains highly politicised; technical progress in large-scale industry has been scant; the growth rate has been unsatisfactory, inflation excessive , and the foreign debt daunting. Leading reform economists, such as Aganbegyan and Abalkin, appear to have concluded that the Hungarian reform has not gone far enough.[2]

The influences from China have been more limited. A group of Soviet intellectuals, including Oleg Bogomolov and Fedor Burlatski (*Lit. gaz.,* 11 June 1986), are enthusiastic about certain elements: family agriculture, small-scale private enterprise, and free economic zones for foreign capital. So far, the arguments for free economic zones have not won the support of the Soviet leadership. Their detractors point out that free economic zones have not been all that successful; they have caused severe regional imbalances, which would be much more dangerous in the Soviet Union with its nationality problems; the vast majority of foreign capital in the free economic zones is invested by Chinese abroad, and the USSR would not benefit from such an effect.

The present Soviet disinterest in the GDR is spectacular, denying many early western assumptions that Gorbachev would favour the GDR model (e.g. Goldman, 1987, p. 261; Hanson, 1987, pp. 111–12). Exceptions have been the regulation of private enterprise in the GDR, and the organisation of *Kombinate*, which are reminiscent of Soviet NPOs. Yugoslavia and Poland are presently perceived as failures of reform in both the East and the West. They attract very limited Soviet attention. Soviet reformists prefer to dwell on successful socialist attempts at economic reform, as their main task is still to defeat adversaries of reform. Besides, criticism of anything in another socialist country by the Soviet media has long had ominous implications pertaining to foreign policy. In the future, Soviet economists need to have an open discussion on the failures of socialist economic reforms, if they want to avoid the same pitfalls themselves. Our discussion of the new Soviet policy on individual labour illustrates how the Soviet leaders could have avoided a hazard, if their advisers had been acquainted with the Polish situation in 1957.

Soviet economists are approaching capitalist economies with a new curiosity and open-mindedness, wanting to learn how capitalism actually functions. They are prepared to adopt western elements that are not too ideologically tainted. In 1988, the USA was the focal point for trips by senior Soviet economists. In their appearance in the USA in early 1988, both Aganbegyan and Abalkin mentioned the US share of state procurement in the GNP (about 24 per cent) as an indication of how large Soviet state orders ought to be in the future. Since real federalism and local taxation have entered the USSR agenda, a delegation of senior Soviet economists studied these topics in the USA in the spring of 1988. The United Kingdom has been another centre of attention. The Soviets have been impressed by Prime Minister Margaret Thatcher's ability to carry out reform despite strong bureaucratic and popular resistance. Many Soviet economists have travelled to Japan. Akin to many a Westerner, they observe the society with awe, but fail to draw relevant conclusions for their own society.

Most West European countries have attracted surprisingly little attention.

An exception has been Sweden. Within a year of the CC Plenum in June 1987, both Aganbegyan and Abalkin visited Sweden twice. The second time, they travelled with a delegation of senior economic officials both from the Central Committee and state authorities with the explicit purpose of studying the Swedish economic model. Sweden appears to be a natural object of study as it is the most socialistic of the free market economies. It could also be considered the most socialistic economy that functions well. Abalkin has stated that it is the Swedish combination of economic growth and social equity that has attracted Soviet interest. The Soviet economists particularly studied cooperatives, family farms and labour market policies (*Svenska Dagbladet* and *Dagens Nyheter*, 11 June 1988; cf *Lit. gaz.*, 24 August 1988). For the first time since the October revolution, Soviet theoreticians are seriously looking at the achievements of social democracy (Vadim Medvedev in *Pravda*, 5 October 1988). In the autumn of 1988, the Soviet Union appears to be a country in an open-ended search for a new economic model, though many ingrained prejudices persist.

GORBACHEV'S MODE OF POLICY-MAKING

The reform wave is conditioned by the nature of the policy-making process. During Gorbachev's three-and-a-half years in power, a distinct Gorbachevian way of policy-making has become evident. If we clarify his tactics, we can better understand what has already happened and anticipate future events. The essence of Gorbachev's political manoeuvring may be summarised in the following points.

Gorbachev remains one of the most radical reformers in the Soviet leadership. His ideological speech in December 1984 revealed his radicalism, and there does not appear to be any good reason to dispute it.

The General Secretary has pushed a broad agenda of both economic and political reform, but he tends to single out one or a few major issues at a time. Like any clever embattled politician, he does not reveal more of his political agenda than is good for him. As long as Gorbachev belongs to the most radical wing of the leadership, we cannot establish how far towards marketisation and democratisation he wants to go.

Gorbachev appears to thrive on decision-making. Rather than accepting a stalemate, he forms a sufficiently broad alliance to be able to promote some kind of action, even if it barely complies with his own purposes.

The longer Gorbachev has stayed in power, the more he has revealed of his own political programme. This might appear a natural consequence of his consolidation of power, but the political risks he has taken in pushing ahead are remarkable.

About a month before a principal party meeting, radical ideas have been brought to the fore, initially as rumours, and later, as glasnost has gained momentum, in publications. Gorbachev's men seem to test various thoughts in this manner, sizing up the reactions before choosing concrete proposals.

After each Gorbachev offensive, a backlash of varying strength and duration appears inevitable. Reminiscent of Khrushchev's time, a pattern of waves for and against reform has evolved (see Tatu, 1967). The oligarchic nature of Soviet politics could explain these waves. Whenever anyone becomes too strong, others join forces against him. Later, when someone else looks too powerful, he becomes the object of new coalitions. Such politicking goes on all the time, warranting swift changes.

Issues selected for major party meetings have been: a new investment strategy for the CC conference in June 1985; agricultural reform for the 27th Party Congress in February 1986; democratisation for the CC Plenum in January 1987; economic reform for the CC Plenum in June 1987; political reform for the 19th Party Conference in June 1988. Each of these meetings has marked a peak of a Gorbechev offensive. Although Gorbachev undoubtedly has considered these tasks important, it would be a mistake to conclude that they top his agenda, because he does not set the political agenda independently, as evidenced by the long aborted CC Plenum on agricultural reform.

The current legislation spree has exposed the limited capacity of the Soviet legislative machinery. Major laws can only be adopted by the Supreme Soviet, which has met for just a couple of days twice a year. It has not been able to adopt more than a couple of laws on each occasion. Another bottleneck in the legislative process is that every big law is elaborated by a commission headed by one of the three top economic officials—Prime Minister Nikolai Ryzhkov, CC Secretary for Economic Affairs Nikolai Slyunkov and Chairman of Gosplan Yuri Maslyukov. Naturally, these men are extremely hard-worked, but they appear to put a lot of time and effort into reform issues. Similarly, the top economists, particularly Aganbegyan and Abalkin, appear to be involved in all big reform acts. They must be overworked as well. These legislative bottlenecks imply that it will take years of reform legislation to be drawn up and that it cannot be very coordinated.

The control over the reform exercised by the like-minded grouping Ryzhkov, Slyunkov and Maslyukov has meant that they set a limit for how far reform may develop. The procedures for designing reforms ensures that academic reformers, conservative state functionaries, as well as moderately reformist functionaries in the chancery of the Council of Ministers, and the *apparat* of the Central Committee have a say. The self-evident outcome is that all reform laws are compromises. The overall conclusion is that Gorbachev pushes energetically for reform, but does not control its design. The Soviet Union is actually governed by a truly collective leadership. Therefore it is not very accurate to talk about 'Gorbachev's economic reforms'.

OBSTACLES TO OVERCOME

The present reasons for economic reform in the Soviet Union are probably stronger than at any time since the 1920s, but the obstacles to economic reform remain formidable. They are both of economic and political nature. We shall try to focus on the most crucial ones. Most of them must be overcome, if the reform is to succeed, so their removal may be regarded as a necessary condition for a successful reform, since an economic system must be reasonably consistent to perform well. The dictum 'no chain is stronger than its weakest link' applies here. The most vital conditions are that enterprises become independent and that marketisation prevails in their mutual relations.

The paramount obstacle is *top-level political resistance*. Most studies of the Soviet economy treat politics as extraneous, but one outstanding problem has been that there has not been a reformist majority in the Soviet leadership, as we have discussed in Chapter 2. Four members of the Politburo—one third— (Gorbachev, Yakovlev, Shevardnadze and Medvedev) appear to be convinced radical reformers. Two other members of the Politburo (Ryzhkov and Slyunkov) might be considered moderate reformers, accepting many, but far from all, the ideas of the radical reformers. That leaves us with six reformers out of twelve full members of the Politburo, though the important offices of Gorbachev, Ryzhkov, Slyunkov and Maslyukov give them particular powers in the economic field. Until Gorbachev's coup on 30 September 1988, the pivotal vote between the reformers and the conservatives appears to have belonged to Lev Zaikov, whom we have called a technocratic moderniser, while Vorotnikov's stand is obscure. Ligachev forms his own reactionary group, presumably with the support of Chebrikov, while Shcherbitski and Nikonov may be considered conservative.[3]

It is difficult to believe that a sensible reform could be both legislated and implemented without a clear reformist majority in the Politburo. Therefore, Gorbachev has been compelled to try to oust several reactionaries and conservatives from the Politburo—a tall political order. He almost attained a turning-point at the CC Plenum in September 1988. In a typical conspiratorial Soviet manner, Gorbachev launched a surprise attack, when his competitor Yegor Ligachev was on leave. Two Politburo members (Gromyko and Solomenstev) and two candidate members (Dolgikh and Demichev) from the enemy camp were retired, while Gorbachev's associates Medvedev and Lukyanov advanced to member and candidate member, respectively.

Gorbachev's most prominent adversaries, Ligachev and Chebrikov, were not ousted but moved. Ligachev was demoted somewhat from Second Secretary to CC Secretary for agriculture, while Chebrikov was formally promoted from Chairman of the KGB to CC Secretary for legal affairs. However, both appear vulnerable in their new posts. They have the choice of pursuing their own or Gorbachev's policies. In the former case, they can be accused of deviating from the party line; in the latter case, they are prone to alienate their own constituencies. In both cases, Gorbachev gains arguments for their eventual retirement. In addition, Ligachev and Nikonov appear to tend towards the same area of responsibility, making them natural competitors. Even so, Gorbachev's opponents still occupy central positions, and he will need to do away with such formidable foes as Ligachev and Chebrikov before he is able to promote consistent reform policies in the leadership.

Political resistance is not limited to the top. A second, much-debated hindrance to reform is the *bureaucracy*. A large share of the administration has a vested interest in nullifying any attempt at reform. The first reformist task is to cut bureaucracy down to size numerically from the top down. Massive cuts embracing about 40 per cent of the central and republican administration are supposed to have been implemented in 1988. However, as a regional party leader (V.I. Kalashnikov) said at the 19th Party Conference: 'a mechanical reduction in the *apparat* of ministries without changing [their] functions changes little, preserves *diktat*, petty tutelage, and bureaucratic methods of guidance' (*Pravda*, 30 June 1988).

Staff cuts can be quick, but it will take at least a few years for the state and party administration to find their new roles. Since production is controlled from above, severe disruption in the work of most enterprises appears inevitable in the course of a general reorganisation. If officials did nothing, it would be enough to create chaos. Enterprises can do little without receiving a variety of authorisations, especially for the acquisition of supplies. One important element in the breakdown in Polish production in 1980–2 was the massive personnel changes in the administration, minimising the issuing of directives by the administration, while enterprises were not allowed to act without authorisation from above. Such a calamity may be avoided, but it is a real danger. The harmful influence of state bodies can hardly be kept within tolerable limits if enterprises are not declared formally independent from their branch ministries. It is not enough to redefine the functions of the administration, effective checks must be established, so that state and party functionaries do not overstep their competence. The only convincing means Gorbachev and Soviet reformers appear to see is democratisation, and such a political innovation cannot be implemented swiftly.

A third obstacle is *popular resistance* which may have great impact, if it results in substantial *labour unrest*. The most plausible catalyst of large-scale strikes is price increases on basic foodstuffs, but the introduction of a market-clearing price system is a necessary condition for a successful market-oriented economic reform. Otherwise markets will not function; hoarding will prevail; costs will be disregarded; and profits will neither motivate nor have much meaning.

The crucial problem is that the very price level will have to be raised significantly in order to establish macro-balance on consumer markets, and any price increase encounters considerable popular resistance. The best-known example is the strikes in Novocherkassk in June 1962 which ended in a blood bath. Their cause was increased meat prices. Similarly, strikes broke out in the Donbass coalfields in the Ukraine in August 1986, when Donetsk was deprived of the most privileged supply status and meat prices were tacitly raised as sales were transferred from 'state' shops to 'cooperative' shops with higher prices.⁴ A conservative economist attached to Goskomtsen has presented 'the safeguarding of political stability of our society' as a major reason to keep retails prices at their present low level (Chubakov, 1987, p. 66). On no other social issues do the Soviet leaders tread as cautiously as on pricing. The most plausible explanation is that they fear massive labour unrest, but the regime must be able to make prices profitable to the market if the economic reform is to work. The longer they wait, the longer they will delay the reform. However, a price reform must be accompanied by a financial reform in order to be effective.

Popular discontent is spearheaded by inflationary pressures, which are a fourth major hazard and appear characteristic of a partially reformed socialist economy. In particular, the Yugoslav and Polish cases suggest that such an economy tends to suffer from chronic inflation. Janos Kornai (1980) offered a theoretical explanation with his concept 'a soft budget constraint', implying excessive state subsidies to large state enterprises. A socialist economy may be described as a negotiation economy, in which actual economic results play a rather limited role.⁵ Enterprises and the state need to be mutually independent, if demoralising and wasteful subsidies are to disappear.

The positive effects of a hard budget constraint on efficiency would be manifold. No enterprise would be able to build up large losses, so wasteful subsidies would disappear and major loss-makers would be forced into bankruptcy. Such examples would encourage other enterprise directors to push for more efficiency. Qualitative and technological improvements would be the natural means of defence. If economic results really matter, directors are likely to be selected on economic criteria regardless of selection procedure. Industry would be alerted to the need for restructuring. Inflationary pressures would ease, as credit, and thus money supply, dried up, forcing managers to resist economically unjustified wage demands. This list of potential effects might appear wishful. The heart of the problem is that a hard budget constraint cannot be imposed by decree. Can the authorities in a socialist state accept widespread bankruptcy with ensuing unemployment? Institutional checks on state and party power are needed.

It is not always easy to distinguish a genuine enterprise failure from a short-term crisis. Nor is it easy to assess where new capital should be directed. A fifth impediment to economic reform therefore is *the absence of any form of market for capital and equity*. How can investment be rationally allocated under socialism? A stock exchange and competitive commercial banks appear difficult to avoid. It matters less who owns shares than that there is an active assessment of the value of various forms of capital by many mutually independent traders. Only then will it be possible to evaluate which enterprises deserve to be saved and which should go down.

National unrest is a sixth hazard that is so great that it may determine the course of the economic reform. The traditional Soviet response to national obstinacy has been repression by troops from other parts of the country.

Considering the explosive nature of long neglected Soviet nationality problems, as evidenced in Alma-Ata, Azerbaijan, Armenia and the Baltics, the temptation to clamp down rather than to try to manage national conflicts and reach viable compromises must be great. Such repression would imply centralisation and have a negative impact on economic reform as well.

The international situation looks uncommonly conducive to economic reform. The most apparent seventh threat to reform might lie in *unrest in the most reformist East European countries*, notably Hungary and Poland. On the one hand, repression is too limited in these countries to be perceived as an insurmountable threat; on the other hand, their economies are not providing satisfactory results, and political opposition is tolerated rather than coopted. This is particularly true of Poland, while Hungary might be moving towards a more satisfactory economic and political system (Garton Ash, 1988). Grave disturbances in these countries would obviously discredit Soviet reform attempts as well, and the traditional Soviet response has been repression, with domestic repercussions in the USSR as well. The effects of unrest in less-reformist East European countries are more difficult to predict. Otherwise, the risk of negative effects from abroad appears slight. The illusion of the 1970s with large-scale imports of western machinery on the basis of credit can hardly be repeated, as such means are not likely to boost the economy sufficiently these days. There is no leftwing challenge worth worrying about around the world.

An eighth hurdle is *the CMEA trade system*, which is an immensely complex system of barter trade. As for other foreign trade, a system of marketisation appears to be necessary and that is what the USSR now demands, though the extraordinarily bureaucratic CMEA is not very conducive to change, and its red tape has arisen as an East European defence against the overwhelming Soviet domination. A unified exchange rate and an orderly system of customs tariffs are among the improvements required.

The paucity of Soviet statistics is a ninth obstacle to economic reform. As long as official statistics do not indicate that the economy is even approaching a crisis, reform does not seem to be necessary—even to many western observers. Moreover, with the present unreliability of Soviet statistics, a more conservative Soviet leadership can always call off attempts at reform by declaring that they have been successfully implemented.

Apart from these existing obstacles, a number of potential concerns may hamper the progress of reform. An integral part of the economic reform is *self-management*. It is motivated on many grounds: enterprises must gain independence from their branch ministries, and in the absence of concrete owners, the workers' collective is the natural alternative master; because of a dearth of 'socialist' ideas, the concept of economic democracy with an increased role for workers' councils evolved at the right time; self-management can be supported by quotes by Lenin; it is seen as a means to overcome alienation. The world possesses one outstanding example of self-management, namely that of Yugoslavia, although the present Yugoslav situation is characterised by very high inflation (around 250 per cent a year), sizeable unemployment, an overwhelming foreign debt, and extraordinary regional differences. All these problems can be linked with the self-management model, as for instance Wlodzimierz Brus (1975) has argued.

To our mind, real self-management of large state enterprises is a dangerous trap for economic reformists' endeavours. The Yugoslav model offers a relevant illustration of this, and it is not correct to dismiss the Yugoslav experience on the grounds of, admittedly, important national peculiarities. Workers employed in a large state enterprise have an interest in maximising the profits per worker, and hence the state capital per worker, within their enterprise. Therefore, they are not interested in hiring more workers. The maximisation of profits per worker leads to less employment per capital than capitalist profit-maximisation, and far less than under the traditional Soviet model with its weak demand constraints. Thus, unemployment is in theory more likely under self-management than under capitalism.

Moreover, self-management strengthens the political muscles of producers, while the sensible present Soviet desire is to increase the power of consumers. In particular, the leverage of large state enterprises over state bodies is likely to be reinforced. The natural outcome would be continued large subsidies to the largest enterprises, and further distortions of investment. On the basis of their monopoly power and state subsidies, large enterprises would be able to raise wages. The outcome would be reinforced inflationary pressures, as we see in Yugoslavia, and they may be easily articulated as demands for foreign credits, aggravating foreign indebtedness for no good economic reason.

If the workers of an enterprise elect their director, they might prefer a director demanding little from them but much from the state. Such a director is not likely to go for restructuring and technological innovations. If workers influence the wage structure collectively, they tend to level incomes within their enterprise, while attempting to maximise the wage level within their enterprise in comparison with other enterprises. In Yugoslavia, the result has been excessive wage-levelling within enterprises and considerable differences between enterprises and regions. The idea of equal pay for equal work has been abandoned.

One great advantage of self-management is that it caters for market functioning, but it would be a grave mistake to believe that anything is better than the old command system. From an economic point of view, it is better to democratise politics than the economy. Self-management is likely to strengthen the independence of an enterprise from the state, but instead the state will probably become a hostage of the largest state enterprises. Mutual independence is needed. Regionalisation of economic management, another idea that some Soviet reformists toy with, might be approximately as detrimental as self-management if enterprises do not become independent. Enterprises are hardly likely to be better run if they become subject to local politics rather than union politics. The experience of Khrushchev's *sovnarkhozy* was not encouraging. *'Yugoslavisation'*, both in terms of self-management and a lack of regional integration, appears to be a very real danger for the Soviet Union because of the design of the present reform attempts.

CRITERIA FOR SUCCESSFUL REFORM

One question often posed is how the success of a reform in process can be judged. The issue at stake is not short-term economic performance, but to what extent qualitative changes of the economic system are introduced. Therefore, the prime success indicators for the economic reform are institutional and not quantitative. Even in the best of circumstances, the effects in macro-economic measurements are not likely to become convincing until the early 1990s. Our list of obstacles suggests a corresponding list of criteria of success for the implementation of economic reform. These standards are institutional and political.

Little is likely to succeed before most of the apparent opponents of radical economic reform and democratisation have been demoted from the Politburo. The top antagonists appear to be Ligachev, Chebrikov, Nikonov, Shcherbitski and to some degree Zaikov—almost half the Politburo.

Reductions in the power of the bureaucracy can be registered in many ways. A curtailment of the number of government agencies and their staff is a first indication, though it is important to check that the abolished bureaucracy is not recreated in other institutions or at other adminstrative levels. More important but difficult to establish is the reduction in actual powers of the bureaucracy. Noteworthy signs are the number of material balances, the number of plan indicators, the share of production included in state orders, the nature of state orders, and the extent to which enterprises openly disregard illicit ministerial commands. The ultimate success of reform would be the abolition of all direct interference in current enterprise affairs by superior state bodies.

The key issue in pricing is whether it is market-clearing or not. Such a transformation is fairly easy to detect, since it would imply the disappearance of shortages. If the price reform becomes muddled, its efficacy may be judged by the degree of market balance it brings about. It is easy to figure out whether most pricing is decentralised to enterprises and whether pricing is flexible. Labour unrest could indicate a variety of things; that strikes are reported; that workers dare to strike; that they are becoming organised; that they are upset about deteriorating conditions (in food supplies, prices or wages); or that actual wage-negotiations have started. Therefore, labour unrest in itself is neither a sign of success nor of failure.

The hardness of the budget constraint of enterprises would be reflected in the number of bankruptcies, workers laid off, and loss-making enterprises. If more financial statistics were published, a variety of quantitative measurements could be exploited. However, the amount of subsidies is not all that informative. It is the conditions of subsidising—and not the amount of subsidies—that determine the hardness of the budget constraint. The establishment of a capital market or a stock exchange would be an evident institutional change, as would a reform of the CMEA trade system. An accompanying change should be the imposition of a unified, market-oriented exchange rate (while convertibility is a distant target; many countries in the world have almost market-determined exchange rates, while their currencies are not convertible).

One of the least interesting indicators is the number of joint ventures established in the USSR, since their economic significance is likely to remain limited, while their symbolic, political value is great to the regime. The existence of western joint ventures in Rumania tells us nothing about economic reform in that country, while it says a lot about Rumanian foreign policy in the 1970s.

It might be difficult to judge whether statistics have improved or not. In the late 1970s, the Polish statistical authorities published ever more statistics and eloquent explanations, but crucial data were withheld, and a great many statistics were of poor quality.

What do current aggregate statistics tell us about the reform process? Our basic point is that a reform is a long-term undertaking, while current statistics focus on a year or an even shorter time. Moreover, if a reform is really implemented, we would expect a certain disruption, and thus a stagnant or declining real growth rate. However, a decreasing growth rate can also signify continued petrification of the economic system or simply disruption without a move towards a more market-oriented system. A high official growth rate is a bad sign, while a low number tells us little.

Looking at different sectors of the economy, a high official growth in the production of civilian machine-building is ominous, since most of its output is so obsolete and substandard that continued production would indicate disregard for economic effects. In addition, a higher number would show that the evaluation of industrial output has not become more realistic. On the other hand, a precipitate fall in industrial production would cause bottlenecks and disturbances in production. Consequently, serious economic reform would initially lead to a low growth rate or a small decline in industrial production; but low growth could equally be the result of continued stagnation. Agricultural statistics are so dubious and inaccurate that it is difficult to say what they mean. The same is true for statistics on sales of foodstuffs. Any change must be assessed after scrutinising alterations in the quality of statistics. However, an increase in the production of foodstuffs—as well as of services—could be the first indications that reform is gaining momentum. A growth in the number of family farms, individual entrepreneurs and new cooperatives are certainly positive developments. A swift expansion of the non-state economy indicates that enterprise has become possible and provides economic preconditions for further reform.

Another early result of successful attempts at reform would be savings in inputs. However, one caveat is that such savings are measured in relation to aggregate output, and the latter measurement is utterly abitrary. Another caveat is that such achievements can be accomplished without systemic reform, as the GDR has proven in the 1980s. Investment statistics might be more informative. The relevant indicator is the development of the amount of unfinished investment.

A much more important sign would be if the Soviet Union would be able to upgrade the structure of its exports to the West. However, Poland managed to attain such a success on a limited scale in the 1970s because of an increase in imports, bought on credit, from the West (Poznanski, 1988). Therefore, all qualitative improvements of Soviet exports must be assessed in the light of the development of Soviet terms-of-trade and foreign indebtedness.

The essence of this discussion of the indicators of successful reform is that a long-term undertaking cannot be properly assessed by short-term statistics; quantitative data hardly tell us anything without a simultaneous evaluation of qualitative changes; hence, we ought to take a cold-headed attitude to current statistics and concentrate on institutional factors. One exception is that we need to consider how much the patience of ordinary Soviets is taxed. It is in the consumer sphere that short-term improvements are possible and should occur. If people do not perceive any upswing in their personal life, they are not likely to lend their support to perestroika, and then no effective counter-weight to the bureaucracy will emerge.

The first three years of Gorbachev's rule may be considered a period of learning and conceptualisation. Therefore, it is still early to apply our criteria. If we do, the positive developments are both few and minor. However, it would have been surprising if any significant achievements could have taken place in such a short time, since both the leadership and the people were taken by surprise by Gorbachev in 1985. Still, it is troubling that one of the most evident developments has been aggravated market imbalances.

PROSPECTS FOR CONTINUED REFORM

So far, we can envisage three probable periods in the process of economic reform. A first period of learning and conceptualisation, 1985–7, has passed. The second period of implementation of the first reform measures and improvement of the design, 1988–90, has started. The focus of the 19th Party Conference was the political system, and purely political issues need to be settled before the economic reform can take a more comprehensive and consistent form. The CC Plenum on 30 September 1988 appears to have brought the leadership struggle closer to a solution, but further political strife is still likely and will distort the reform efforts under way. In any case, economic reform strategy cannot become effective until 1991. In the meantime, economic performance is likely to be poor. Both economic malaise and the long stalemate in the leadership have favoured a polarisation of the Soviet debate over politics and economics. Three scenarios appear as the main options for the 1990s. We shall discuss them in order of probability.

The first scenario is *radicalised economic reform with far-reaching democratisation*. As Soviet reformist economists are waking up from their imposed lethargy, they are becoming ever more radical, because they realise that the state of the economy was worse than they had imagined and that half-measures do not offer any results. Therefore, they want to go further towards a market economy and independent forms of ownership than they themselves had anticipated. The impressive resistance from the party and state bureaucracies is convincing them that little can be achieved without a considerable democratisation, which does not need to go all the way towards western democracy. There may be many fruitful intermediate stages in a democratisation process. This scenario embraces several very different alternatives, ranging from little more than the Hungarian reforms, via 'Yugoslavisation' towards the Swedish economic model. The main arguments for this scenario are: the General Secretary himself appears to opt for it; the economic situation is so bad that radical solutions are required; there is no apparent alternative that can offer sustainable economic growth. A precondition for this scenario is the political survival of Gorbachev. I would consider this scenario a real possibility, but it presupposes a large number of conscientiously undertaken measures, so it would take a long time to mature.

The second scenario is a *reactionary* or neo-Stalinist attempt to improve the Soviet system by a bit more repression, harder discipline and greater centralisation than under Brezhnev. We have argued that the last few years offer good evidence that such an option is not likely to have any positive effect worth mentioning, but probably the advocates of this line do not care much about empiricism. This might be seen as a Ligachev or military option. It would be the most obvious Soviet choice if Gorbachev is ousted.

Our third scenario is *Brezhnevite*: to muddle through along the old lines without much more repression and without major economic or political reforms. This is the natural *modus vivendi* of the nomenklatura as Mikhail Voslensky (1980) convincingly has argued. However, the economic and moral decay of the Brezhnev system is perceived as so serious by many in the present Soviet leadership that it is difficult to believe in a conscious return to that option. As public openness evolves, more and more Soviet citizens are likely to turn their backs on this alternative. If it emerges as the winner, the cause will probably be a political stalemate rather than a conscious choice. Were we instead to take the CIA view of the Soviet economy seriously, the Brezhnevite scenario would be more plausible, as the CIA assesses that the Soviet economy is in such a good shape that it would not be necessary for the nomenklatura to suffer the hardships of democratisation or neo-Stalinism. The worse we consider the state of the Soviet economy, the more likely either of the two first scenarios becomes.

In all these scenarios, relative Soviet military might is likely to dwindle in the medium and long term, but only radicalised economic reform is likely to be accompanied by a decisive cut in military expenditure in absolute terms. However, military adventurism could occur under any scenario. Even under the most favourable assumptions, the reform process is likely to be long and difficult with a few more years of economic stagnation. If the Soviet economy recovers strength, it is likely to be subject to such strong democratic and consumer constraints that the USSR will spend a much smaller share of its national income on defence than today. Under these assumptions, outsiders have every reason to wish the Soviet leaders good luck in their attempts at economic reform. The world is likely to be a safer place if the Soviet reforms succeed.

A GDR streamlining of the Soviet economy appears to be out of the question. The technocrats favouring marketisation and a strong role for Gosplan are likely to choose sides. At long last the Soviet system, as created by Stalin, really appears exhausted. If it is maintained in its impotent Brezhnevian form, it can only bring decline. What we are seeing is a society in a severe bind, but it is trying to avert its apparent fate and recover as a great power. It remains to be seen whether this attempt will succeed, but it appears far more serious than any other Soviet attempt at reform since the 1920s. Moreover, this is likely to be the last chance Soviet communism gets to reform. The next Soviet generation appears to be too disillusioned with socialism to bother about reforming it—a state that Poland and Hungary have already reached. Whatever turn Soviet events will take in the next few years, they are likely to belong to the most important developments of this century.

NOTES

1. This was expressed similarly by several speakers. S. Dzarasov stated: 'The experience of the past teaches [us] that the fate of economic reforms depends on the development of political democracy... ' (VE, No. 2, 1988, p. 60). B. Rakitski of TsEMI agreed: 'Democratisation in society is the key, decisive factor in the perestroika of management of the economy' (ibid., p. 61). The conference concluded: 'deep transformations in the management of the economy cannot be realised without corresponding changes in the political system and in the social and spiritual spheres' (ibid., p. 79).
2. My interpretation of somewhat diplomatic statements by Aganbegyan and Abalkin at the Wilson Center, Washington, DC, on 25 February and 14 March, respectively, 1988.
3. According to oral information leaked by a prominent Gorbachev loyalist, a vote of confidence for Gorbachev took place in the Politburo in late March 1988, concerning the Nina Andreeva letter in Sovetskaya Rossiya on 13 March 1988 (considered a conservative manifesto). Reportedly, the result was eight votes for Gorbachev (Gorbachev, Yakovlev, Shevardnadze, Ryzhkov, Slyunkov, Zaikov, Vorotnikov and Nikonov) and five against (Ligachev, Chebrikov, Solomentsev,

Gromyko and Shcherbitski). This anti-reformist opposition group was more or less confirmed by Ligachev at the Party Conference, when on 1 July 1988 he pointed out that Gorbachev was elected General Secretary in March 1985 'thanks to ... Chebrikov, Solomentsev, Gromyko'. Ligachev also implied that he had supported Gorbachev then (*Pravda*, 2 July 1988). Shcherbitski is known to have supported Viktor Grishin in that election for General Secretary (and was in the USA at the time).

4. Reliable personal information from two independent Soviet sources. The Soviet émigré Lyudmila Alekseeva (1986) has investigated seventy-five strikes in the Soviet Union from 1956 onwards. She found that the causes fall into two major groups: shortage of food and reductions of wages in one way or another (Alekseeva, 1986, p. 86). It would seem that improved food supplies because of a drastic deregulation and quasi-privatisation of agriculture would be an expedient means to render price increases more palatable.

5. Many market economies may also be considered negotiation economies, obviously corrupt ones, but there are also countries that favour an influential role of the state in the economy.

Appendix 1: The Soviet leadership[1]

Full Politburo Members	Major Posts
M. S. Gorbachev (1931)	General Secretary; Chairman of the Presidium of the USSR Supreme Soviet
Ye. K. Ligachev (1920)	CC Secretary for Agriculture
N. I. Ryzhkov (1929)	Prime Minister
L. N. Zaikov (1923)	CC Secretary; First Party Secretary of Moscow City
A. N. Yakovlev (1923)	CC Secretary for International Affairs
N. N. Slyunkov (1929)	CC Secretary for Economic and Social Affairs
V. A. Medvedev (1929)	CC Secretary for Ideology
V. M. Chebrikov (1923)	CC Secretary for Legal Affairs
V. P. Nikonov (1929)	CC Secretary for Agriculture
E. A. Shevardnadze (1928)	Minister for Foreign Affairs
V. V. Shcherbitski (1918)	First Party Secretary of the Ukraine
V. I. Vorotnikov (1926)	Chairman of the Presidium of the RSFSR Supreme Soviet

Candidate Members	
G. P. Razumovski (1936)	CC Secretary for Personnel
Yu. D. Maslyukov (1937)	Chairman of Gosplan, First Deputy Prime Minister
D. T. Yasov (1923)	Minister of Defence; Army General
A. V. Vlasov (1932)	Prime Minister of the RSFSR
A. I. Lukyanov (1930)	First Deputy Chairman of the USSR Supreme Soviet
Yu. F. Solovyev (1925)	First Party Secretary of Leningrad *oblast*
A. P. Biryukova (1929)	Deputy Prime Minister; Chairman of the Bureau for Social Development
N. V. Talyzin (1929)	Deputy Prime Minister; Permanent Representative to the CMEA

CC Secretary outside   *Field of Responsibility*
the Politburo

O. D. Baklanov (1932)   Military-industrial complex

1. In October 1988 in approximate political ranking, which differs from the official
    ranking, especially by putting CC Secretaries higher in relation to state
    functionaries. However, several politicians are of approximately the same
    ranking, in particular the many CC Secretaries (cf Rahr, 1988; *Deputaty*, 1984;
    Pravda, 1 and 2 October 1988).

Appendix 2: Brief biographies of selected leading politicians

BAKLANOV, Oleg D. Born in 1932; Ukrainian; graduated as an engineer; worked at enterprises in the armaments industry, 1950–76; Deputy and First Deputy Minister of General Machine-Building, 1976–83; USSR Minister of General Machine-Building, 1983–8; CC Secretary for the military-industrial complex since February 1988.

BIRYUKOVA, Aleksandra P. Born in 1929; Russian; graduated as a textile engineer in Moscow; senior trade union official, 1968–85; CC Secretary for light and consumer industries, March 1986-September 1988; candidate member of the Politburo since September 1988; Chairman of the Bureau for Social Development and Deputy Chairman of the Council of Ministers since October 1988.

CHEBRIKOV, Viktor M. Born in 1923; Russian; graduated as an engineer in Dnepropetrovsk in the Ukraine; served in the Red Army during World War II; party official, 1951–67, advancing to second secretary of Dnepropetrovsk *oblast* party committee; transferred to the USSR KGB in 1967; Deputy Chairman and later First Deputy Chairman of the USSR KGB, 1968–82; Chairman of the USSR KGB, December 1982–October 1988; full member of the Politburo since April 1985; CC Secretary and Chairman of the CC Commission on Legal Affairs since September 1988.

DOLGIKH, Vladimir I. Born in 1924; Russian; graduated as an engineer in Irkutsk; served in the Red Army, 1941–3; worked at metallurgic enterprises, 1949–69; First Secretary of Krasnoyarsk *krai*, 1969–72; CC Secretary for heavy industry, 1972–September 1988; candidate member of the Politburo, May 1982–September 1988.

GORBACHEV, Mikhail S. Born in 1931; Russian; graduated as a lawyer at Moscow University in 1955 and as an agronomist in Stavropol in 1967; Komsomol official in Stavropol *krai*, 1955–62; party official in Stavropol *krai*, 1962–78; First Secretary of Stavropol *krai* party committee, 1970–8; CC Secretary for Agriculture, 1978–85; candidate member of the Politburo, 1979–80; full member of the Politburo since 1980; General Secretary of the CC of the CPSU since 11 March 1985; Chairman of the USSR Supreme Soviet since October 1988.

GROMYKO, Andrei A. Born in 1909; Russian; Doctor of Economics; worked as an economic scholar in Moscow, 1932–9; transferred to foreign service in 1939; Ambassador to the USA, 1943–6; Deputy Minister for Foreign Affairs and Permanent Representative to the UN, 1946–9; First Deputy Minister for Foreign Affairs, 1949–52 and 1953–7; Ambassador to the United Kingdom, 1952–3; Minister for Foreign Affairs, 1957–85; full member of the Politburo, 1973–September 1988; Chairman of the Presidium of the USSR Supreme Soviet, July 1985–October 1988.

LIGACHEV, Yegor K. Born in 1920; Russian; graduated as an engineer at Moscow Aviation Institute; worked as an engineer, 1943–4; Komsomol official in Novosibirsk, 1944–9; party and state official in Novosibirsk *oblast*, 1949–61; worked in the CC apparatus, 1961–5; First Secretary of Tomsk *oblast* party committee, 1965–83; CC Secretary since December 1983 (second secretary, April 1985–September 1988, Chairman of the CC Commission on agriculture since September 1988); full member of the Politburo since April 1985.

LUKYANOV, Anatoli I. Born in 1930; Russian; graduated as a lawyer at Moscow University, 1953; Doctor of Law; held a variety of posts as a legal expert at the USSR Council of Ministers, the Presidium of the Supreme Soviet and the CC apparatus; first deputy head of the CC General Department, 1983–5; head of the CC General Department, November 1985–March 1986; CC Secretary for administrative bodies, March 1986–September 1988; candidate member of the Politburo since September 1988; First Deputy Chairman of the Presidium of the Supreme Soviet since October 1988.

MASLYUKOV, Yuri D. Born in 1937; Russian; graduated as an engineer in Leningrad; worked as an engineer, 1962–74; worked in the Ministry of Defence Industry, advancing to Deputy Minister, 1974–82; First Deputy Chairman of USSR Gosplan, 1982–November 1985; Chairman of the Military-Industrial Commission (VPK) and Deputy Chairman of the USSR Council of Ministers, November 1985–February 1988; Chairman of USSR Gosplan and First Deputy Chairman of the USSR Council of Ministers since February 1988; candidate member of the Politburo since February 1988.

MEDVEDEV, Vadim A. Born in 1929; Russian; Doctor of Economics; Professor; corresponding member of the Academy of Sciences; worked as an academic political economist in Leningrad until 1968, when he became a party official; deputy head of the CC Propaganda Department, 1970–8; Rector of the CC Academy of Social Sciences, 1978–83; head of the CC Science and Education Department, 1983–6; CC Secretary for liaison with socialist countries, March 1986–September 1988; CC Secretary and Chairman of the CC Commission on ideology since September 1988; full member of the Politburo since September 1988.

NIKONOV, Viktor P. Born in 1929; Russian; agronomist; worked as an agronomist, 1950–8; party official in Krasnoyarsk *krai*, 1958–61; second secretary of the Tatar *oblast* party committee, 1961–7; First Secretary of the Mari *oblast* party committee, 1967–79; Deputy USSR Minister of Agriculture, 1979–83; RSFSR Minister of Agriculture, 1983–5; CC Secretary for Agriculture since April 1985; full member of the Politburo since June 1987.

RAZUMOVSKI, Georgi P. Born in 1936; Russian; graduated as an agronomist in Kuban (Krasnodar *krai*); worked as an agronomist, 1958–9; Komsomol official, 1959–61; party official in Krasnodar *krai*, 1961–71; worked in the CC apparatus, 1971–3; Chairman of the Krasnodar *krai* state executive committee, 1973–81; head of the agro-industrial department of the USSR Council of Ministers, 1981–3; First Secretary of Krasnodar *krai* party committee, 1983–5; head of CC Department for Party Organisational Work since April 1985; CC Secretary for party organisational work since March 1986; Chairman of the CC Commission on party organisational work since September 1988; candidate member of the Politburo since February 1988.

RYZHKOV, Nikolai I. Born in 1929; Russian; graduated as an engineer in Sverdlovsk; worked as an engineer at the Ural Machine-Building Association (Uralmash), 1950–75, as general director, 1970–5; First Deputy Minister of Heavy and Transport Machine-Building, 1975–9; First Deputy Chairman of USSR Gosplan, 1979–82; CC Secretary for Economic Affairs, November 1982–October 1985; full member of the Politburo since April 1985; Chairman of the USSR Council of Ministers since September 1985.

SHCHERBITSKI, Vladimir V. Born in 1918; Ukrainian; graduated as an engineer in Dnepropetrovsk; served in the Red Army, 1941–5; worked as an engineer until 1948, when he became a party official in Dnepropetrovsk *oblast*; First Secretary of Dnepropetrovsk *oblast* party committee, 1955–7 and 1963–5; Secretary of the CC of the Ukranian CP, 1957–61; Chairman of the Ukrainian Council of Ministers, 1961–3 and 1965–72; full member of the Politburo since 1971; First Secretary of the Ukrainian CP since 1972.

SHEVARDNADZE, Eduard A. Born in 1928; Georgian; graduated as a teacher in Georgia; Komsomol official in Georgia, 1946–61; party official, 1961–4; Georgian Minister of Interior, 1965–72; First Secretary of the Georgian CP, 1972–July 1985; candidate member of the Politburo, 1978–85; full member of the Politburo since July 1985; USSR Minister for Foreign Affairs since July 1985.

SLYUNKOV, Nikolai N. Born in 1929; Belorussian; graduated as an engineer in Minsk; worked as an engineer and a trade union official at the Minsk Tractor Factory, 1950–60; director of various enterprises in Minsk, 1960–72; First Secretary of Minsk city party committee, 1972–4; Deputy Chairman of USSR Gosplan, 1974–83; First Secretary of the Belorussian CP, 1983–7; CC Secretary for Economic Affairs since January 1987; Chairman of the CC Commission on economic and social affairs since September 1988; full member of the Politburo since June 1987.

SOLOMENTSEV, Mikhail S. Born in 1913; Russian; graduated as an engineer in Leningrad; worked at various enterprises; party and state official in Chelyabinsk *oblast*, 1954–9; senior party official in Kazakhstan, 1959–64; First Secretary of Rostov *oblast* party committee, 1964–6; CC Secretary, 1966–71; Chairman of the RSFSR Council of Ministers, 1971–83; Chairman of the Party Control Committee, June 1983–September 1988; full member of the Politburo, December 1983–September 1988.

SOLOVYEV, Yuri F. Born in 1925; Russian; graduated as an engineer in Leningrad; served in the Red Army, 1943–4; worked at enterprises in Leningrad until 1973; party official in Leningrad *oblast*, 1974–8; First Secretary of Leningrad city party committee, 1978–84; USSR Minister of Industrial Construction, 1984–5; First Secretary of Leningrad *oblast* party committee since July 1985; candidate member of the Politburo since March 1986.

TALYZIN, Nikolai V. Born in 1929; Russian; graduated as an engineer in Moscow; Doctor of Technology; Professor; worked at a research institute, 1955–65; Deputy and First Deputy Minister of Communications, 1965–75; Minister of Communications, 1975–80; Chairman of USSR Gosplan, October 1985–February 1988; First Deputy Chairman of the USSR Council of Ministers, October 1985–October 1988; candidate member of the Politburo since October 1985; Deputy Chairman of the USSR Council of Ministers and USSR Permanent Representative to the CMEA, 1980–5 and since October 1988.

VOROTNIKOV, Vitali I. Born in 1926; Russian; graduated as an engineer in Kuibyshev; worked at a factory producing military machinery until 1960; party official and state official in Kuibyshev *oblast*, 1960–71; First Secretary of Voronezh *oblast* party committee; First Deputy Chairman of the RSFSR Council of Ministers, 1975–9; Ambassador to Cuba, 1979–82; First Secretary of Krasnodar *oblast* party committee, 1982–3; Chairman of the RSFSR Council of Ministers, 1983–October 1988; Chairman of the Presidium of the RSFSR Supreme Soviet since October 1988; full member of the Politburo since December 1983.

YAKOVLEV, Aleksandr N. Born in 1923; Russian; Doctor of History; Professor; corresponding member of the Academy of Sciences; served in the Red Army, 1941–3; party official in Yaroslavl *oblast*, 1946–53; official of the CC apparatus, 1953–73; first deputy head of the CC Propaganda Department, 1965–73; Ambassador to Canada, 1973–83; Director of the Institute of World Economy and International Relations (IMEMO), 1983–5; head of CC Propaganda Department, 1985–6; CC Secretary since March 1986; Chairman of the CC Commission on foreign affairs since September 1988; candidate member of the Politburo, January–June 1987; full member of the Politburo since June 1987.

ZAIKOV, Lev N. Born in 1923; Russian; graduated as an engineer in Leningrad; worked in branches of the armaments industry in Leningrad, 1940–76; Chairman of the executive committee of Leningrad city, 1976–83; First Secretary of Leningrad *oblast* party committee, 1983–5; CC Secretary since July 1985; full member of the Politburo since March 1986; First Secretary of Moscow city party committee since November 1987.

Bibliography

Abalkin, Leonid I. (ed.), *Politicheskaya ekonomiya sotsialisma—teoreti-cheskaya osnova ekonomicheskoi politiki KPSS* (Mysl, Moscow, 1986).
——, 'Ekonomicheskie protivorechiya sotsializma', *Voprosy ekonomiki*, 58, 5: 3–13 (May 1987a).
——, 'Opriayas na uroki proshlogo', *Kommunist*, 64, 16: 9–17 (November 1987b).
——,*Novy tip ekonomicheskogo myshleniya* (Ekonomika, Moscow, 1987c).
Aganbegyan, Abel G., 'Na novom etape ekonomicheskogo stroitelstva', *EKO*, 16, 8: 3–24 (August 1985a).
——, 'Strategiya uskoreniya sotsialno-ekonomicheskoga razvitiya', *Problemy mira i sotsializma*, 9: 13–18 (September 1985b).
—— (ed.), *Reforma upravleniya ekonomikoi: problemy i poisk* (Ekonomika, Moscow, 1987a).
——, 'Programma korennoi Perestroiki', *EKO*, 18, 11: 3–19 (November 1987b).
——, *The Economic Challenge of Perestroika* (Indiana University Press, Bloomington and Indianapolis, 1988).
Alekseeva, Lyudmila, 'Zabastovki v SSSR (poslestalinski period)', *SSSR vnutrennie protivorechiya*, No. 15 (1986) pp. 80–145.
Amann, Roland, 'Towards a New Economic Order: The Writings of B. P. Kurashvili', *Detente* (Winter 1987) pp. 8–10.
Andropov, Yuri V., *Izbrannye rechi i statyi* (Politizdat, Moscow, 1984).
Åslund, Anders, 'The Functioning of Private Enterprise in Poland', *Soviet Studies*, 36, 3: 427–44 (1984).
——, *Private Enterprise in Eastern Europe: The Non-Agricultural Private Sector in Poland and the GDR, 1945–83* (Macmillan, London, 1985a).
——, 'Yellow Light for Private Enterprise in Poland?', *Osteuropa Wirtschaft*, 30, 1: 21–9 (1985b).
——, 'Gorbachev's Economic Advisors', *Soviet Economy*, 3, 3: 246–69 (1987).
——, 'The New Soviet Policy towards International Economic Organisations', *The World Today*, 44, 2: 27–30 (February 1988).
——, 'How small Is the Soviet National Income?', 1989 (forthcoming).
Asselain, Jean-Charles, *Planning and Profits in Socialist Economies* (Routledge & Kegan Paul, London, 1984).
Bauer, Tamas, 'The Contradictory Position of the Enterprise under the New

Hungarian Economic Mechanism', *Eastern European Economy*, 15, 1: 3–23 (Fall 1976).

——, 'The Second Economic Reform and Ownership Relations', *East European Economics*, pp. 33–87 (Spring-Summer 1984).

Belousov, Rem A., 'Vzaimovliyanie obobshchestvleniya proizvodstva i upravleniya', *Voprosy ekonomiki*, 57, 1: 3–14 (January 1985).

Bergson, Abram, 'Income Inequality under Soviet Socialism', *Journal of Economic Literature*, 22, 3: 1052–99 (September 1984).

Bergson, Abram, and Herbert S. Levine (eds), *The Soviet Economy: Toward the Year 2000* (George Allen & Unwin, London and Boston, 1983).

Berliner, Joseph S., *Factory and Manager in the USSR* (Harvard University Press, Cambridge, MA, 1957).

——, 'Planning and Management' in Bergson and Levine (1983) pp. 350–90.

Bim, Aleksandr, and Aleksandr Shokhin, 'Sistema raspredeleniya: na putyakh perestroiki', *Kommunist*, 63, 15: 64–73 (October 1986).

Birman, Igor, *Ekonomika nedostach* (Chalidze, New York, 1983).

Bogomolov, Oleg T., 'Mir sotsializma na puti perestroiki' *Kommunist*, 64, 16: 92–102 (November 1987).

Bornstein, Morris, 'Improving the Soviet Economic Mechanism', *Soviet Studies*, 37, 1: 1–30 (January 1985).

——, 'Soviet Price Policies', *Soviet Economy*, 3, 2: 96–134 (1987).

Borozdin, Yuri, 'Planovoe tsenoobrazovanie v novoi sisteme khozyaist-vovaniya', *Kommunist*, 63, 16: 24–37 (November 1986).

Breslauer, George W., *Khrushchev and Brezhnev as Leaders: Building Authority in Soviet Politics* (George Allen & Unwin, London, 1982).

Brown, Archie, 'Gorbachev: New Man in the Kremlin', *Problems of Communism*, 32, 3: 1–23 (May-June 1985).

Brus, Wlodzimierz, *Ogolne problemy funkcjonowania gospodarki socjalist-ycznej* (Polskie Wydawnictwo Naukowe, Warsaw, 1961; translated into English as: *The Market in a Socialist Economy*, Routledge & Kegan Paul, London and Boston, 1972).

——, *Socialist Ownership and Political Systems* (Routledge & Kegan Paul, London, 1975).

——, 'Wirtschaftsreformen in der Sowjetunion', *Europäische Rundschau*, 1: 15–36 (1985).

Brzezinski, Zbigniew, 'Tragic Dilemmas of Soviet World Power. The Limits of a New-Type Empire', *Encounter*, 61, 4: 10–17 (December 1983).

Bunich, Pavel G., 'Novye usloviya khozyaistvovaniya: dostizheniya, problemy perspektivy', *EKO*, 17, 5: 3–20 (May 1986a).

——, 'Problemy perestroiki mekhanizma upravleniya ekonomikoi', *Ekonomika i matematicheskie metody*, 22, 4: 579–90 (July-August 1986b).

——, 'Mekhanizm samofinansirovaniya', *Voprosy ekonomiki*, 59, 9: 3–13 September 1987).

Bunich, Pavel G., and V. P. Moskalenko, 'Samofinansirovanie: rezultaty i problemy', *Kommunist*, 63, 14: 30–41 (September 1986).

Butenko, Anatoli P., 'O protivorechiyakh sotsializma kak obshchestvennogo stroya', *Voprosy filosofii*, 36, 10: 16–29 (October 1982).

————, 'Otkazatsya ot dogm, izuchat protivorechiya', *EKO*, 18, 4: 127–44 (April 1987).

Cherepakhin, A. M., 'O nekotorykh voprosakh deyatelnosti finansovykh organov po realizatsii Zakona SSSR ob individualnoi trudovoi deyatelnosti', *Sovetskoe gosudarstvo i pravo*, 61, 4: 48–55 (April 1987).

Chernikov, D., 'Intensifikatsiya i proportsionalnost ekonomicheskogo rosta', *Planovoe khozyaistvo*, 63, 6: 63–72 (June 1986).

Chubakov, Genrikh N., 'Napravleniya sovershenstvovaniya roznichnykh tsen', *Voprosy ekonomiki*, 59, 1: 66–76 (January 1987).

CIA, *Handbook of Economic Statistics* (Washington, DC, 1982).

————, *Handbook of Economic Statistics* (Washington, DC, 1986).

Colton, Timothy J., *The Dilemma of Reform in the Soviet Union* (Council of Foreign Relations, New York, 1986).

Danilov, Viktor P., 'Oktyabr i agrarnaya politika partii', *Kommunist*, 64, 16: 28–38 (November 1987).

Deputaty Verkhovnogo Soveta SSSR. Odinnadtsaty sozyv (Izvestiya, Moscow, 1984).

Deryabin, Anatoli A., 'Osnovy perestroiki tsenoobrazovaniya', *Voprosy ekonomiki*, 59, 1: 55–66 (January 1987).

Deryabin, Anatoli A., and Inyatulla K. Salimzhanov, *Tsena – instrument upravleniya ekonomikoi* (Znanie, Moscow, 1985).

Desai, Padma, *The Soviet Economy: Problems and Prospects* (Blackwell, Oxford, 1987).

Ellman, Michael, *Collectivisation, Convergence and Capitalism: Political Economy in a Divided World* (Academic Press, London, 1984).

Ericson, Richard E., 'The New Enterprise Law', *The Harriman Institute Forum*, 1, 2: 1–8 (February 1988).

Fallenbuchl, Zbigniew, 'Present State of the Economic Reform' in Marer and Siwinski (1988) pp. 115–30.

Faltsman, Vladimir K., 'Prioritety tekhnicheskoi rekonstruktsii mashinostroeniya' *Voprosy ekonomiki*, 58, 6: 52–62 (June 1986).

————, *Proizvodstvenny potentsial SSSR: voprosy prognozirovaniya* (Ekonomika, Moscow, 1987).

Fasolyak, Nikolai D., and Zoya I. Barmina, *Materialno-tekhnicheskoe snabzhenie. Slovar-spravochnik* (Ekonomika, Moscow, 1985).

Fedorenko, Nikolai P., 'Planirovanie i upravlenie: kakimi im byt?', *EKO*, 15, 12: 3–20 (December 1984).

Fedorenko, Nikolai P., and Vilen L. Perlamutrov, 'Khozraschetnoe otnosheniya—dinamika i perspektivy', *Voprosy filosofii*, 41, 2: 3–16 (February 1987).

Fuller, Elizabeth, 'Georgia after Shevardnadze: Patiashvili's First Year', *Radio Liberty Research*, RL 271/86 (8 July 1986).

Gaidar, Yegor T., 'Kursom ozdorovleniya', *Kommunist*, 65, 2: 41–50 (January 1988).

Garton Ash, Timothy, 'Reform or Revolution?', *The New York Review of Books*, pp. 47–56 (27 October 1988).

Gelman, Harry, *Gorbachev's Policies Toward Western Europe: A Balance Sheet* (The Rand Corporation, R–3588–AF, Santa Monica, October 1987).

Gendler, Grigori Kh. and Ariadna A. Ovchinnikova, *Leningradski opyt*

(Znanie, Moscow, 1987).

Glushkov, Nikolai T. (ed.), *Spravochnik po tsenoobrazovaniyu* (Ekonomika, Moscow, 1985a).

——, 'Planovoe tsenoobrazovanie: puti sovershenstvovaniya', *Kommunist*, 62, 3: 38–48 (February 1985).

Goldman, Marshall I., *USSR in Crisis. The Failure of an Economic System* (Norton, New York, 1983).

——, *Gorbachev's Challenge. Economic Reform in the Age of High Technology* (Norton, New York and London, 1987).

Gorbachev, Mikhail S., *Korennoi vopros ekonomicheskoi politiki partii. Doklad na soveshchanii v TsK KPSS po voprosam uskoreniya nauchno-tekhnicheskogo progressa 11 iyunya 1985 goda* (Politizdat, Moscow, 1985).

——, *Izbrannye rechi i stati*, Vol. 2 (Politizdat, Moscow, 1987a).

——, *Izbrannye rechi i stati*, Vol. 3 (1987b).

——, *Izbrannye rechi i stati*, Vol. 4 (1987c).

——, *Perestroika: New Thinking for Our Country and the World* (Harper & Row, New York, 1987d).

Gorlin, Alice C., 'The Power of Soviet Industrial Ministries in the 1980s', *Soviet Studies*, 37, 3: 353–70 (July 1985).

Grossman, Gregory, 'The "Second Economy" in the USSR', *Problems of Communism*, 26, 5: 25–40 (September–October 1977).

——, 'Inflationary, Political, and Social Implications of the Current Economic Slowdown' in Höhmann *et al.* (1986) pp. 172–97.

——, 'Roots of Gorbachev's Problems: Private Income and Outlay in the Late 1970s', JEC (1987) pp. 213–29.

Gvishiani, Dzhermen M., and Boris Z. Milner (eds), *Organizatsiya upravleniya. Problemy perestroiki* (Ekonomika, Moscow, 1987).

Hanson, Philip, 'Success Indicators Revisited: The July 1979 Soviet Decree on Planning and Management', *Soviet Studies*, 35, 1: 1–13 (January 1983).

——, 'Superministries: The State of Play', *Radio Liberty Reseach*, RL 167/86 (21 April 1986a).

——, 'USSR — Puzzles in the 1985 Statistics', *Radio Liberty Research*, RL 439/86 (20 November 1986b).

——, 'The Economy' in McCauley (1987) pp. 97–117 (1987a).

——, 'Reforming the Foreign-Trade System' *Radio Liberty Research*, RL 104/87 (19 March 1987b).

——, 'Ownership and Economic Reform', *Radio Liberty Research*, RL 154/88 (6 April 1988).

Hedlund, Stefan, *Crisis in Soviet Agriculture* (Croom Helm, London, 1984).

Hewett, Ed A., *Reforming the Soviet Economy* (Brookings, Washington, DC, 1988).

Höhmann, Hans-Hermann, Alec Nove and Heinrich Vogel, *Economics and Politics in the USSR. Problems of Interdependence* (Westview Press, Boulder and London, 1986).

Hough, Jerry F., 'Gorbachev's Strategy', *Foreign Affairs*, 64, 1: 33–55 (Fall 1985).

——, 'Gorbachev Consolidating Power', *Problems of Communism*, 34, 4: 21–43 (July–August 1987).

Ignatovski, P. A., 'Ekonomicheskaya sila stroya', *Planovoe khozyaistvo*, 65,

3: 42–51 (March 1988).

Ivanter, Viktor V., Yuri R. Leibkind and Vilen L. Perlamutrov, 'Upravlenie khozyaistvom i denezhny oborot', *Kommunist*, 64, 15: 35–44 (October 1987).

Kabalkin, A. Yu., 'Zakon ob individualnoi trudovoi deyatelnosti—vazhny rychag osushchestvleniya sotsialno-ekonomicheskoi politiki', *Sovetskoe gosudarstvo i pravo*, 61, 3: 12–21 (March 1987).

Kamentsev, Vladimir M., 'Problemy vneshnekonomicheskoi deyatelnosti', *Kommunist*, 64, 15: 25–34 (October 1987).

Kaser, Michael, '"One Economy, Two Systems": Parallels between Soviet and Chinese Reform', *International Affairs*, 63, 3: 395–412 (Summer 1987).

Khachaturov, Tigran, 'Sovershenstvovanie upravlenie ekonomikoi', *Voprosy ekonomiki*, 59, 8: 73–85 (August 1987).

———, 'Perestroika v sfere kapitalnykh vlozheni', *Voprosy ekonomiki*, 60, 1: 3–11 (January 1988).

Kirichenko, Vadim, 'Perestroika systemy upravleniya i tsentralizovannoe planirovanie', *Kommunist*, 13: 10–19 (September 1986).

Komarov, Ilya K., *Sovershenstvovanie khozyaistvennogo mekhanizma v stroitelstve* (Mysl, Moscow, 1984).

Komin, Anatoli, 'Perestroika tsenovogo khozyaistva', *Voprosy ekonomiki*, 60, 3: 107–14 (March 1988).

Konstitutsiya (Osnovnoi Zakon) Soyuza Sovetskikh Sotsialisticheskikh Respublik (Yuridicheskaya literatura, Moscow, 1985).

Kontorovich, Vladimir, 'Discipline and Growth in the Soviet Economy', *Problems of Communism*, 34, 6: 18–31 (November-December 1985).

Kornai, Janos, *Economics of Shortage* (North Holland, Amsterdam, 1980).

———, 'The Hungarian Reform Process: Visions, Hopes, and Reality', *Journal of Economic Literature*, 24, 4: 1687–1737 (December 1986).

Kosenko, Vladimir, 'Energiya progressa', *Nash sovremennik*, 54, 2: 115–37 (February, 1986).

Kostakov, Vladimir G., 'Zanyatost: defitsit ili izbytok?', *Kommunist*, 64, 2: 78–89 (January 1987).

Kostin, L., 'Perestroika sistemy oplaty truda', *Voprosy ekonomiki*, 59, 11: 41–15 (November 1987).

Kulagin, G. A., 'Nomenklatura, tsena, pribyl', *EKO*, 16, 11: 89–106 (November 1985).

Kurashvili, Boris P., 'Gosudarstvennoe upravlenie narodnym khozyaistvom: perspektivy razvitiya', *Sovetskoe gosudarstvo i pravo*, 56, 6: 38–48 (June 1982).

———, 'Sudby otraslevogo upravleniya', *EKO*, 14, 10: 34–57 (October 1983a).

———, 'Obyektivnye zakony gosudarstvennogo upravleniya', *Sovetskoe gosudarstvo i pravo*, 57, 10: 36–44 (October 1983b).

———, 'Kontury vozmozhnoi perestroiki', *EKO*, 16, 5: 59–79 (May 1985a).

———, 'Sotsialisticheskie proizvodstvennye otnosheniya: nekotorye aktualnye aspekty', *Izvestiya SO AN SSSR. Seriya ekonomikii prikladnoi sotsiologii*, 2, 7 (July 1985b).

———, *Ocherk teorii gosudarstvennogo upravleniya* (Nauka, Moscow, 1987).

Kushnirsky, Fyodor I., 'Inflation Soviet Style', *Problems of Communism*, 33, 1: 48–53 (January-February 1984).
———, 'The Role of Industrial Modernization in Soviet Economic Planning' in JEC (1987) Vol. 1, pp. 257–73.
Lacis, Otto R., 'Individualny trud v sovremennoi sotsialisticheskoi ekonomike', *Kommunist*, 64, 1: 74–82 (January 1987a).
———, 'Kak shagaet uskorenie?', *Kommunist*, 64, 4: 53–63 (March 1987b).
———, 'Na strezhe revolyutsionnogo sozidaniya', *Kommunist*, 64, 13: 48–58 (September 1987c).
———, 'Zachem zhe pod ruku tolkat?', *Novy mir*, 63, 7: 266–8 (July 1987d).
Legget, Robert E., 'Soviet Investment Policy: The Key to Gorbachev's Program for Revitalizing the Soviet Economy' in JEC (1987) vol. 1, pp. 236–56.
Levchuk, I., 'Problemy perestroiki bankovskogo dela', *Voprosy ekonomiki*, 59, 8: 11–19 (August 1987).
Levikov, Aleksandr I., 'Remeslo', *Novy mir*, 62, 4: 180–98 (April 1986).
Ligachev, Yegor K., 'Gotovyas k partiinomy syezdu', *Kommunist*, 62, 12: 8–22 (August 1985a).
———, 'Sovetuyas s partiei, s narodom', *Kommunist*, 62, 16: 77–92 (November 1985b).
———, 'Nam nuzhna polnaya pravda', *Teatr*, 8: 2–7 (August 1986a).
———, 'Uchit po-novomu myslit i deistvovat', *Kommunist*, 63, 15: 8–23 (October 1986b).
———, 'Chelovecheski faktor khozraschet i perestroika v agropromy-shlennom komplekse', *Kommunist*, 64, 4: 28–42 (March 1987).
Lisichkin, Gennadi, S., *Plan i rynok* (Ekonomika, Moscow, 1966).
———, 'Za vedomstvennym baryerom', *Novy mir*, 61, 10: 167–90 (October 1985).
Malenin, N. S. 'Netrudovye dokhody, spravedlivost, gumanizm i pravo', *Sovetskoe gosudarstvo i pravo*, 61, 10: 57–63 (October 1987).
Malygin, A., 'Obnovlenie osnovnykh fondov', *Planovoe khozyaistvo*, 62, 7: 30–6 (July 1985).
Marer, Paul, and Wlodzimierz Siwinski (eds), *Creditworthiness and Reform in Poland: Western and Polish Perspectives* (Indiana University Press, Bloomington and Indianapolis, 1988).
McCauley, Martin (ed.), *The Soviet Union under Gorbachev* (St. Martin's, New York, 1987).
Medvedev, Vadim A., *Upravlenie sotsialisticheskim proizvodstvom: problemy teorii i praktiki* (Politizdat, Moscow, 1983).
Medvedev, Zhores, *Gorbachev* (Blackwell, Oxford, 1986).
Moskalenko, V. P., 'Khozraschetnaya zainteresovannost v vysokikh konech-nykh rezultatakh', *EKO*, 17, 3: 99–118 (March 1986).
Murphy, Patrick, 'Soviet *Shabashniki*: Material Incentives at Work', *Problems of Communism*, 34, 6: 48–57 (November-December 1985).
Narodnoe khozyaistvo SSSR v 198X g. (Finansy i statistika, Moscow, 198X+1); abbreviated *Narkhoz 198X* for various years.
Narodnoe khoziaistvo SSSR za 70 let (Finansy i statistika, Moscow, 1987); abbreviated *Narkhoz 1986*.
Nemchinov, V., 'Sotsialisticheskoe khozyaistvovanie i planirovanie proizvod-

stva', *Kommunist*, 64, 11: 23–32 (July 1987).

Nikonov, Viktor P., 'Polee zadeistvovat potentsial agropromyshlennogo kompleksa', *Kommunist*, 64, 5: 15–29 (March 1987).

Norr, Henry, 'Shchekino: Another Look', *Soviet Studies*, 38, 2: 141–69 (April 1986).

Nove, Alec, *The Soviet Economic System* (George Allen & Unwin, London, 1977).

———, *An Economic History of the U.S.S.R.* (Penguin, Harmondsworth, 1980).

———, 'Has Soviet Growth Ceased?', *Manchester Statistical Society* (15 November 1983).

Nuikin, Andrei, 'Idealy ili interesy?' *Novy mir*, 64, 1: 193–211 (January 1988a).

———, 'Idealy ili interesy?' *Novy mir*, 64, 2: 205–28 (February 1988b).

Nuti, D. Mario, 'Hidden and Repressed Inflation in Soviet-Type Economies: Definitions, Measurements and Stabilisation', *Contributions to Political Economy*, vol. 5, 37–82 (1986).

O korennoi perestroike upravleniya ekonomikoi. Sbornik dokumentov (Politizdat, Moscow, 1987).

Obolonski, A. V., 'Byurokraticheskaya deformatsiya soznaniya i borba s biurokratizmom', *Sovetskoe gosudarstvo i pravo*, 61, 1: 52–61 (January 1987).

Ochkin, Aleksei, '"Nagulyaet" li tsena pribyl?', *Nash sovremennik*, 55, 12: 154–61 (December 1987).

Ofer, Gur, and Aaron Vinokur, *Private Sources of Income of the Soviet Urban Household*, Rand, R–23590–NA, Santa Monica (August 1980).

Orlov, B. P., 'Tseli srednesrochnykh planov i ikh osushchestvlenie', *EKO*, 18, 11: 34–53 (November 1987).

Otsason, Rein, 'O sovershenstvovanii khozyaistvennogo mekhanizma APK', *Kommunist Estonii*, 6: 52–9 (June 1986).

Palterovich, Delez M., 'Problemy ispolzovaniya strategicheskikh i takticheskikh rezervov mashinostroeniya', *Ekonomika i matematicheskie metody*, 23, 4: 589–601 (July-August 1987).

———, 'Tekhnicheskaya rekonstruktsiya narodnogo khozyaistva', *Voprosy ekonomiki*, 60, 1: 117–26 (January 1988).

Pavlov, Valentin S., 'Vazhnaya sostavnaya chast perestroiki', *Kommunist*, 64, 13: 14–26 (September 1987).

Pavlova, N., and Natalya Rimashevskaya, 'Sistema pensionnogo obespecheniya', *Voprosy ekonomiki*, 59, 10: 21–31 (October 1987).

Petrakov, Nikolai Ya., 'Planovaya tsena v sisteme upravleniya narodnogo khozyaistva', *Voprosy ekonomiki*, 59, 1: 44–55 (January 1987a).

———, 'Zolotoi chervonets vchera i zavtra', *Novy mir*, 63, 8: 205–21 (August 1987b).

———, 'Ukreplenie denezhnogo obrashcheniya i strategiya uskoreniya', *Voprosy ekonomiki*, 59, 8: 3–11 (August 1987c).

Pipes, Richard, 'Can the Soviet Union Reform?', *Foreign Affairs*, 63, 1: 47–61 (Fall 1984).

Popov, Gavriil Kh., *Effektivnoe upravlenie* (Ekonomika, Moscow, 1985a).

———, *Upravleniyu ekonomikoi — ekonomicheskie metody* (Ekonomika,

Moscow, 1985b).

Popkova, L., 'Gde pyshnee pirogi?', *Novy mir*, 63, 5: 239–41 (May 1987).

Poznanski, Kazimierz, 'The Competitiveness of Polish Industry and Indebtedness' in Marer and Siwinski (1988), pp. 45–60.

Protokoly tzw Komisji Grabskiego (Instytut literacki, Paris, 1986).

Rahr, Alexander, 'The Composition of the Politburo and the Secretariat of the Central Committee of the CPSU', *Radio Liberty Research*, RL 89/88 (24 February 1988).

Reddaway, Peter, 'Gorbachev the Bold', *The New York Review of Books*, pp. 21–5 (28 May 1987).

Roucek, Libor, 'Private Enterprise in Soviet Political Debates', *Soviet Studies*, 40, 1: 46–63 (January 1988).

Rumer, Boris, 'Some Investment Patterns Engendered by the Renovation of Soviet Industry', *Soviet Studies*, 36, 2: 257–66 (April 1984).

——, 'Realities of Gorbachev's Economic Program', *Problems of Communism*, 35, 3: 20–31 (May-June 1986).

Rutland, Peter, 'The Shchekino Method and the Struggle to Raise Labour Productivity in Soviet Industry', *Soviet Studies*, 36, 3: 345–65 (July 1984).

Schroeder, Gertrude E., 'Soviet Economic "Reforms": A Study in Contradictions', *Soviet Studies*, 20, 1: 1–21 (July 1988).

——, 'The 1966–67 Soviet Industrial Price Reform: A Study in Complications', *Soviet Studies*, 20, 4: 462–77 (April 1969).

——, 'The "Reform" of the Supply System in Soviet Industry', *Soviet Studies*, 24, 1: 97–119 (July 1972).

——, 'Soviet Economic "Reform" Decrees: More Steps on the Treadmill', *JEC* (1983), Part 1, pp. 65–88.

——, 'Anatomy of Gorbachev's Economic Reform', *Soviet Economy*, 3, 3: 219–41 (July-September 1987).

Selyunin, Vasili, 'Eksperiment', *Novy mir*, 61, 8: 173–94 (August 1985).

——, 'Istoki', *Novy mir*, 64, 5: 162–89 (May 1988).

Selyunin, Vasili, and Khanin, Grigori I., 'Lukavaya tsifra' *Novy mir*, 63, 2: 181–201 (February 1987).

Senchagov, Vyacheslav K., 'Radikalnaya reforma khozyaistvennogo upravleniya', *Voprosy ekonomiki*, 60, 2: 115–27 (February 1988).

Shatalin, Stanislav S., 'Sotsialnoe razvitie i ekonomicheski rost', *Kommunist*, 63, 14: 60–70 (September 1986).

Shenfield, Stephen, 'Making Sense of Prokhanov', *Detente*, 9–10: 28–9 (1987).

Shevchenko, Arkady N., *Breaking with Moscow* (Ballantine, New York, 1985).

Shmelev, Nikolai, 'Avansy i dolgi', *Novy mir*, 63, 6: 142–58 (June 1987).

——, 'Novye trevogi', *Novy mir*, 64, 4: 160–75 (April 1988).

Shramko, Oleg S., *Sumskoe uskorenie* (Politizdat, Moscow, 1986).

Sitaryan, Stepan A., 'Kontseptsiya uskoreniya—politiko-ekonomicheskie aspekty', *Kommunist*, 64, 7: 13–24 (May 1987).

Slider, Darrel, 'Reforming the Workplace: the 1983 Soviet Law on Labour Collectives', *Soviet Studies*, 37, 2: 173–83 (April 1985).

——, 'The Brigade System in Soviet Industry: An Effort to Restructure the Labour Force', *Soviet Studies*, 39, 3: 388–405 (July 1987).

Slyunkov, Nikolai N., 'Rabotat sistemno, s polnym napryazheniem sil', *Kommunist*, 61, 18: 37–48 (December 1984).
———, 'Perestroika i partiinoe rukovodstvo ekonomikoi', *Kommunist*, 65, 1: 11–26 (January 1988).
Solovyev, Yuri F., 'Intensifikatsiya: perestroika na marshe, poisk novykh podkhodov', *Kommunist*, 63, 11: 3–12 (1986).
Sukharev, A., 'Rubl v odnom izmerenii', *Kommunist*, 63, 10: 100–12 (July 1986).
Sutela, Pekka, *Socialism, Planning and Optimality: A Study in Soviet Economic Thought* (Societas Scientiarum Fennica, Helsinki, 1984).
SSSR-GDR: druzhba i sotrudnichestvo (Politizdat, Moscow, 1986).
Tatu, Michel, *Power in the Kremlin* (Viking Press, New York, 1967).
———, *Gorbatchev. L'U.R.S.S. va-t-elle changer?* (Le Centurion, Paris, 1987).
Teague, Elizabeth, 'Ligachev Endorses Hungarian Reforms', *Radio Liberty Research*, RL 163/87 (27 April 1987).
Treml, Vladimir G., 'Income from Private Services Recognized by Official Soviet Statistics', Mimeo. Berkeley-Duke Occasional Papers on the Second Economy in the USSR, Paper No. 11, pp. 4.1–27 (December 1987).
Tur, Viktor A. (ed.), *Nalogi s naseleniya* (Finansy i Statistika, Moscow, 1986).
UN Economic Commission for Europe, *Economic Bulletin for Europe*, 35 (1983).
———, *Economic Bulletin for Europe*, 37 (1985).
US Congress, Joint Economic Committee, *Soviet Economy in the 1980's: Problems and Prospects* (US Government Printing office, Washington, DC, 1983) abbreviated JEC (1983).
———, *Gorbachev's Economic Plans* (US Government Printing Office, Washington, DC, 1987) abbreviated JEC (1987).
Valtukh, K. K., and B. L. Lavrovski, 'Proizvodstvenny apparat strany: ispolzovanie i rekonstruktsiya', *EKO*, 17, 2: 17–32 (February 1986).
Vanous, Jan, 'The Dark Side of "Glasnost": Unbelievable National Income Statistics in the Gorbachev Era', *Planecon*, 3, 6: 1–14 (13 February 1987).
Vneshnyaya torgovlya SSSR v 1986 g. (Finansy i statistika, Moscow, 1987) abbreviated *Vneshtorg 1986*.
Volkova, M. I. *et al.* (ed.), *Politicheskaya ekonomiya: Slovar* (3rd ed., Politizdat, Moscow, 1983).
Voronin, Lev A., 'Ekonomicheski eksperiment—pervye itogi i puti razvitiya', *Planovoe khozyaistvo*, 61, 12: 9–18 (December 1984).
———, 'Sovershenstvovanie khozyaistvennogo mekhanizma—nepremennoe uslovie perevoda ekonomiki na intensivny put razvitiya', *Planovoe khozyaistvo*, 62, 8: 9–17 (August 1985).
Voslensky, Michael S., *Nomenklatura: Die herrschende Klasse der Sowjetunion* (Moewig, Vienna, 1980).
Wädekin, Karl-Eugen, *The Private Sector in Soviet Agriculture* (University of California Press, Berkeley, California, 1973).
Weickhardt, George G., 'Gorbachev's Record on Economic Reform', *Soviet Union*, 12, 3: 251–76 (1985).
Wiles, P. J. D., *Economic Institutions Compared* (Blackwell, Oxford, 1977).
———, 'Economic Policies under Andropov and Chernenko' in Wiles (ed.),

The Soviet Economy on the Brink of Reform (Unwin Hyman, London, 1988).

The World Bank, *World Development Report 1987* (Oxford University Press, Oxford, 1987).

Yakovlev, Aleksandr N., 'Dostizhenie kachestvenno novogo sostoyaniya sovetskogo obshchestva i obshchestvennye nauki', *Vestnik AN SSSR*, 6: 51–80 (1987a).

———, 'Restructuring and the Social Consciousness', *Kommunist Tadzhikistana* translated in FBIS-SOV (7 May 1987b).

Yasin, Yevgeni G., 'Ekonomicheskie normativy v sisteme khozyaistvovaniya: opyt eksperimenta, problemy', *Ekonomika i matematicheskie metody*, 22, 4: 591–608 (July-August 1986).

Yasmann, Viktor, 'Obstacles in the Way of the Cooperative Movement', *Radio Liberty Research*, RL 343/87 (28 August 1987).

Yazev, V. A., 'Novy khozyaistvenny mekhanizm v torgovle', *Sovetskoe gosudarstvo i pravo*, 61, 4: 39–47 (April 1987).

Zaikov, Lev N., 'Nerastorzhima revolyutsionnaya preemstvennost pokoleni', *Kommunist*, 61, 17: 44–56, 1984.

Zalygin, Sergei P., 'Povorot', *Novy mir*, 63, 1: 3–18 (January 1987).

Zaslavskaya, Tatyana I., 'The Novosibirsk Report', *Survey*, 28, 1: 88–108 (1984).

———, 'Ekonomika skvoz prizmu sotsiologii', *EKO*, 16, 7: 3–22 (July 1985).

———, 'Chelovecheski faktor razvitiya ekonomiki i sotsialnaya spravedlivost', *Kommunist*, 63, 13: 61–73 (September 1986).

Index